Teaching Urban Learners

Culturally Responsive Strategies for Developing Academic and Behavioral Competence

Gwendolyn Cartledge
Ya-yu Lo

Research Press
2612 North Mattis Avenue, Champaign, Illinois 61822 (800) 519-2707
www.researchpress.com

Copies of this book may be ordered from Research Press at the address given on the title page.

Composition by Publication Services, Inc.
Cover design by Linda Brown, Positive I.D. Graphic Design, Inc.
Printed by Netpublications, Inc.

ISBN-13: 978-0-87822-554-5
ISBN-10: 0-87822-554-4
Library of Congress Control Number 2005936301

Contents

Figures and Tables

Figures

Tables

Acknowledgments

This handbook reflects the projects and strategies that we implemented on a daily basis in urban schools. We want to acknowledge and thank all of those who contributed directly and indirectly to this effort. Although too numerous to mention all of them by name, we would be remiss not to express appreciation to the Columbus Public School administrators, teachers, and pupils for their generosity and ongoing cooperation in this mission. We thank Mr. Kwesi Kambon, central administrator, who helped us to initiate and maintain the current project. We recognize Drs. Scott Loe and Julie Sentelle for their early work in both of these schools and for setting the tone for the project. We thank Ms. Linda Strong and Florence Allen for welcoming us in their schools. We especially appreciate the positive and extended working relationship with Ms. Theresa Sadek, principal, and her teachers, particularly Francie Medary, Megan Martling, Denise Carskadon, Cheryl Martin, Stacie Santilli, David Brenner, Mary Long, Connie Foster, and Mary Ann Bergman. We appreciate the opportunity not only to try out many of these strategies on these teachers' students, but in many cases their willingness to follow through and continue the strategies on their own. We have immense regard for the terrific students at Hubbard Elementary, who despite their own personal challenges, never stopped trying and were the source of many professional insights and positive moments. We also wish to thank the administrators, teachers, and pupils at Main Street Elementary, particularly Ms. Lyn Fishback, for her unparalleled dedication and responsiveness.

The authors wish to acknowledge and thank the contributors. Their contributions are so valuable because they evolved directly from their own work with teachers and pupils. We are extremely grateful for their work and the beneficial effects of this work on the students as well as the profession. We thank Ms. Lefki Kourea for her contributions of the diagram of urban students' path through schools and her graphics for the social skills lesson. We thank Ms. Carolyn Hainer, school counselor, for her contribution of the scenario with Robert and his football aspirations, and Ms. Eimy Sifuente, for her Spanish translation of the student letter. Special expressions of gratitude are extended to Drs. William Heward and Ralph Gardner, faculty at The Ohio State University and authorities in the field. We appreciate their support of this project and the expertise that they shared with project staff as well as the teachers. We have leaned heavily on their work for the applications used in this project and handbook. Finally, we note that much of the work produced in this book was supported by several funding sources. These include grants from the Ohio Department of Mental Health, Ohio Department of Education, Jennings Foundation Urban Initiative Grant, and the Office of Special Education Programs, U.S. Department of Education (H324T010057-02).

Introduction

This handbook results from several years of consulting in urban schools in several cities throughout the country. Most of our intensive consulting and research occurred in one elementary school (preschool to fifth grade), where the student enrollment ranged from 156 to 202, averaging about 85 percent African American, 13 percent Caucasian, and 2 percent Hispanic/Latino or Asian American. Nearly all the students qualified for free or reduced-price lunches and less than 5 percent of the students lived within walking distance of the school. A principal focus of our most intensive work over the past five years has been to reduce disciplinary and special education (that is, serious emotional disturbances) referrals of urban youth, especially African American males. Our approach centered on reducing the need for such referrals by increasing the academic skills and adaptive behaviors of this most vulnerable population. The strategies and techniques employed were predominantly the research-based practices found in behavioral methodology.

It is common knowledge that poor children typically begin school in a deficit position. Their language and readiness skills are substantially behind those of their more affluent peers. We observed these deficiencies to persist and increase as the students moved through the grades. We also observed corresponding increases in behavior problems for many students. By the time the students reached the intermediate levels—that is, fourth and fifth grades—their classroom teachers often pushed to evaluate and place them in special education. Two-thirds to three-quarters of all the students in this school were performing below grade level, but the pressure for special education placement was greatest for those students who presented a combination of learning (most likely reading) and behavior problems. Although we can long debate the relative impact of reading deficits on behavior problems and vice versa, there can be little question that the growing frustration students experience over their inability to perform at grade level further aggravates problem behaviors. Our approach was to identify those students who evidenced the greatest risk factors (that is, reading and behavior) at the primary grades and to apply academic and behavioral interventions for these students until they reached the intermediate grades. We designed and implemented several interventions for these students both within the classrooms and with pull-out groups. We conducted controlled studies to document the effectiveness of these procedures for this population. We also adopted strategies that are teacher-friendly and easily integrated into regular curricula. This handbook evolved from that work.

Who Should Read This Book?

General and special educators are intended users of this handbook. We especially recommend its use by general educators because we believe the effective use of many of these strategies could potentially ward off the need for specialized interventions or minimize the extent to which these services might be needed.

Perhaps the most critical component of the teaching urban youth equation, possibly even more important than what students bring to the learning environment, is teachers: their backgrounds, experiences, skills, and attitudes. School personnel are extremely powerful, and if appropriately supported and equipped, teachers can empower students and their families to maximize the child's learning, allowing the child to experience greater school and later life success. This handbook is intended primarily for teachers and other school personnel, such as school principals, school psychologists, school counselors, clinicians (for example, reading and behavior specialists), and teacher assistants who are working with urban learners. We believe this handbook would be useful for all those directly or indirectly responsible for increasing the academic and social behaviors of children in the schools. The strategies are not just for remediation; for the most part, they could be applied classwide or schoolwide. Many young, poor children show promise for advanced learning but are not challenged due to low expectations, an inadequate curriculum, or nonstimulating instructional methods.

We also encourage parents to be consumers of this handbook. Parents need to take an active role in the education of their children. This handbook can help parents become more informed about the education process and enable them to collaborate with teachers from an informed position. The more parents learn about teaching their children, the more they will become involved in the schooling of their children and in helping their children to value education, set high expectations for themselves, and appreciate their school experiences.

What Are the Objectives of This Book?

This handbook is organized into four parts: (1) culturally responsive instruction, (2) effective academic instruction, (3) improving social competencies, and (4) parental involvement. Within the parts, each chapter generally contains the following elements in sequence:

- Applied case situation

- Rationale for the strategy

- Definition of the strategy

- Discussion of the importance of the strategy for urban learners

- Benefits of the strategy to teachers (and learners)

- Revisiting the case

- Step-by-step sequence for teachers to implement the strategy

- Strategies to be implemented once a day, once a week, once a grading period, and once a year

- Related readings and Internet resources

Many of the chapters also contain visuals, charts, and figures that help illustrate the concepts.

In Part One, we lay out some of the issues and facts currently prevalent among urban learners and discuss why it is imperative that we single out this population for special attention. We recognize that no group or geographic area is a monolith and that these students will present individual differences as well, but urban environments in the United States create special conditions with enormous impact on the intellectual development and learning of urban children. The culturally responsive section of this handbook is intended to analyze these conditions and specify some critical content that these children must learn; steps that schools might take to empower these youngsters, helping them to become more responsible for their own educational development; and the methods and materials that might be especially effective in engaging the students in the learning process.

The second part, on effective academic instruction, draws heavily on behavioral principles relative to instructional presentations and pupil response. The position taken here is that effective learning needs to be active, and that students need many opportunities to respond to the learning material. Furthermore, teachers need to know when the student has responded correctly and the student needs to be reinforced or corrected immediately so that the student does not practice errors. The strategies described in this section (that is, response cards, peer tutoring, and repeated readings) are those that we and others have validated in the research literature. This list of valid strategies is not exhaustive, but we believe these strategies provide a good basic arsenal that teachers can use to increase pupil response rates for the most critical academic skills. The intent is not to replace the existing classroom curriculum but rather to equip the teacher and other professionals with a set of tools that enable them to deliver the curriculum more effectively and improve the learning environments for impoverished learners.

Part Three, on social competencies, also employs behavioral principles to help teachers become more proactive and effective in bringing about more adaptive classroom behaviors. Exclusionary practices, which are pervasive in our schools—especially for poor and minority learners—tend to be counterproductive, rarely if ever producing desired returns. The procedures detailed in this section are designed to equip school personnel and students with strategies that will help students stay in the classroom and continue responding to academic materials. The objective for this section is that schools achieve positive schoolwide environments, resulting from teachers' acquiring skill in managing well-structured classrooms and in teaching children the requisite social skills to manage themselves throughout the school environment. For students who do not respond well to the preceding strategies, school personnel would collaborate to design individualized behavior plans. Another important objective is that schools improve their overall school climate and disciplinary practice through a comprehensive, system-wide positive behavior and academic support approach.

Parent involvement is important to the educational success of all children. Schools work best when they respect the families of their children and partner with these families in the interest of the students. Thus Part Four focuses on actions schools might take to increase the involvement of urban and culturally diverse families. The objective is for school personnel to be knowledgeable about ways to involve urban families more effectively.

PART ONE
Culturally Responsive Instruction

CHAPTER 1

Urban Learners

Devon

Devon is a five-year-old kindergarten student in an inner-city elementary school. He did not go to preschool, and received no schooling at home. Having had very few literacy-related experiences, Devon knows none of his letters, his letter sounds, his numbers, or how to count beyond five. When he started kindergarten, Devon barely knew what a book was or that the symbols in the book represented words to be read. Devon's academic deficiencies are quite pronounced, and he is one of the lowest-performing students among the twenty-five in his kindergarten class. Nevertheless, Devon enjoys school, looks forward to attending each day, and is eager to learn to read. One-third of the students have had fairly good preschool experiences and are clearly ready to learn in kindergarten. Another third have had some exposure to readiness activities and are trying to keep up with the lessons presented by the teacher. The remaining students present a state of unreadiness similar to Devon's. Their teacher, Ms. Keys, describes them as her "clueless" group, and she is not certain what to do with them.

Devon's low-performing group consists largely of boys and, although they display a desire to learn, they are very active and appear to be in perpetual motion. Ms. Keys constantly reprimands these children, particularly Devon, urging them to sit quietly and to pay attention. Because of this excessive movement, Devon and some of the others in his group are often removed from the learning activity and put in time-out. This means they are missing valuable learning time, causing them to fall even further behind their peers in academic, cognitive, and social development. It is a third of the way through the school year, and Ms. Keys is seriously questioning whether Devon and a few of his group mates will make enough progress to move on to first grade the following year.

This urban kindergarten class is predominantly racial and ethnic minority— that is, 60 percent African American, 20 percent Hispanic/Latino American, 16 percent Caucasian American, and 4 percent Asian American. The students are from a low socioeconomic background, with nearly all of them eligible for free or reduced-price lunch. Many of the students (like Devon) are from single-parent homes where the guardian parent works full time to support the children in the family. Ms. Keys feels that she does not get much support from the families. For example, she has called Devon's mother, Ms. Matthews, many times without much success. Ms. Matthews works long hours and on her days off is not able to get transportation to come to the school. Ms. Keys is extremely frustrated about students such as Devon and some of his peers. She feels there is not much else she can do.

The Needs of Urban Learners

Urban learners are diverse. They include students from every racial, ethnic, linguistic, and socioeconomic background. However, minority groups—that is, African, Hispanic, Asian, or Native American, who are likely to be from lower socioeconomic groups and to present special learning needs in the classroom—disproportionately populate urban schools. Minority learners are the fastest-growing group of school-age students in the United States, and according to the 2004 census, they will make up 24 percent of the school-age population by 2020 and 50 percent by 2050 (U.S. Census Bureau, 2004). Thus the emerging profile of our schools is one of urban schools with poor and minority students, whereas suburban schools are predominantly white and middle income. Poor academic achievement also accompanies the impoverished and diverse image of urban schools. Diane Ravitch (1998) reports data showing that barely half of students in urban areas graduate from high school, and "many of those who do manage to graduate are ill-prepared for higher education or the workplace" (p. 1). The record is even worse in some large cities, where only one-third of the student body and 19 percent of black male students manage to graduate (Hallett, 2004). These data certainly point to school and later-life failure for poor and minority urban learners.

One undesired outcome is the disproportionate placement of these students in special education. As noted in our introductory scenario, many poor children come to school ill prepared for the demands of the classroom. Similarly, the teachers and schools often are not prepared to meet the needs of such large numbers of children who demand more instruction than what is readily available in the classroom. These children fall progressively further and further behind until they are likely to qualify for special education. Although special education ostensibly is intended to help students make progress, it often serves as a one-way ticket out of the general education classroom that results in no greater achievement than if the child had remained in the original placement. The data on disproportionality show that African and Native American children are much more likely than their white counterparts to be referred and placed in special education programs. Furthermore, these students are more likely to be placed in more restrictive settings than those where their counterparts from other races go. That is, minority students are more likely to be placed in self-contained schools or classes rather than in resource rooms or inclusive classrooms. In contrast to their special education fate, African, Native, and Hispanic American students are much less likely to be recommended for gifted programs (Losen & Orfield, 2002).

Another marker of school failure that disproportionately impacts minority learners is disciplinary referrals. These students, particularly African Americans, are at much greater risk for office referrals, suspensions, and expulsions than nonminority students. Within the classroom, teachers are observed to direct more control-oriented behaviors at these students. Students who are not making adequate academic progress, especially as they fall behind and cannot maintain interest in the lessons, will become disruptive in the classroom and increasingly become a target of teacher control. This becomes a vicious cycle, and the pattern escalates until the teacher presses for permanent exclusion from the classroom, either through some alternative placement or through expulsion. Students who are frequently removed from the classroom lose valuable opportunities to learn both academic and social skills. Furthermore, repeated exclusions have a psychological effect, often communicating to students that they are not wanted. These frequent suspensions contribute to the school dropout rate. See Figure 1.1 for a diagram of the impact of these conditions on urban learners.

FIGURE 1.1

Urban Students' Path Throughout Public Urban Schools

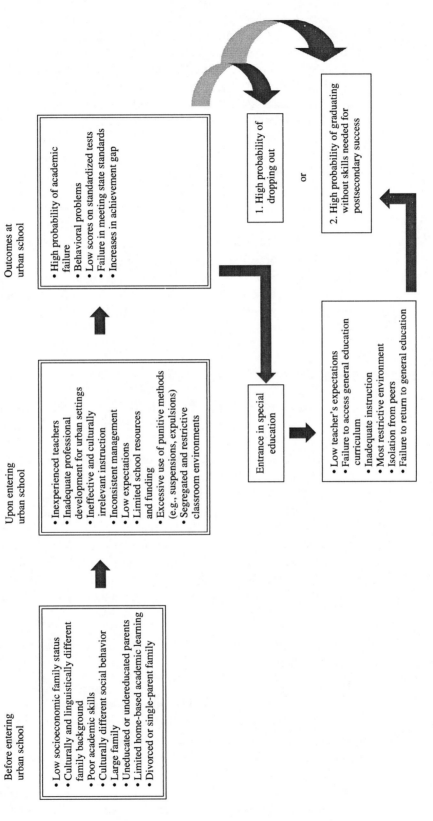

Before entering
urban school

- Low socioeconomic family status
- Culturally and linguistically different family background
- Poor academic skills
- Culturally different social behavior
- Large family
- Uneducated or undereducated parents
- Limited home-based academic learning
- Divorced or single-parent family

Upon entering
urban school

- Inexperienced teachers
- Inadequate professional development for urban settings
- Ineffective and culturally irrelevant instruction
- Inconsistent management
- Low expectations
- Limited school resources and funding
- Excessive use of punitive methods (e.g., suspensions, expulsions)
- Segregated and restrictive classroom environments

Outcomes at
urban school

- High probability of academic failure
- Behavioral problems
- Low scores on standardized tests
- Failure in meeting state standards
- Increases in achievement gap

1. High probability of dropping out

or

2. High probability of graduating without skills needed for postsecondary success

Entrance in special education

- Low teacher's expectations
- Failure to access general education curriculum
- Inadequate instruction
- Most restrictive environment
- Isolation from peers
- Failure to return to general education

Note: From *The Effects of Total Class Peer Tutoring on Sight-word Acquisition, Maintenance, Reading Fluency, and Comprehension for Students at Risk for Reading Failure,* by L. Kourea. Unpublished master's thesis, The Ohio State University. Adapted by permission of the author.

Minority males, particularly African American males, are the most vulnerable segment of our school population for poor school outcomes. These students consistently present the poorest outlook for academic achievement, grade retention, disciplinary referrals, and dropping out of school. The reason for the more deleterious effects on black males is not entirely clear. Some research indicates that compared to black females, black males have lower developmental scores in language and motor skills, but they score at comparable levels on cognitive measures such as the Peabody Picture Vocabulary Test (Davis, 2003). Some speculate that black males do less well because they perceive schooling to be feminine, but Davis notes that young black males begin school exhibiting a genuine desire to learn and an enjoyment of school. Another observation is that from the very beginning of schooling these students are treated differently by teachers. As early as kindergarten, teachers are found to give them lower behavior ratings and have lower expectations of them as potential students. The genesis of this problem may well be a combination of developmental, attitudinal, and instructional factors. What is clear, however, is that too many young people in urban schools fall tremendously short of grade level expectations. Schools and the larger society cannot be indifferent or simply shift the responsibilities to the families. There needs to be joint ownership by all segments of the community, and the schools need to take the lead in moving toward the solution.

What Are Effective Urban Schools?

More than three decades ago, Ronald Edmonds (director of the Center for Urban Studies at Harvard University) began a series of studies nationwide to identify the factors that contributed to academic success within urban schools (Association for Effective Schools, 1996). Edmonds and his fellow researchers found successful schools despite the fact that the children came from homes of poverty and were lacking in many of the conditions typically considered germane to academic performance. The researchers concluded that poor children could learn regardless of family background, and that important factors included the school's mission, expectations, leadership, instructional practices, environment, and family relationships. The professional community has a general consensus with the conclusions of Edmonds and his colleagues. The following listing for school practitioners is consistent with these understandings.

Provide a curriculum and instructional program tailored to the targeted population.

The professional staff at Devon's school has been observing the same pattern for the past ten years. Typically only one-third of the students came to school possessing literacy skills enabling them to readily grasp the lessons as commonly presented by the classroom teacher. The other students struggled academically and failed to achieve grade level performance throughout the grades. Nevertheless, the school persisted in teaching the students in the very same way even though the school was getting the same results, that is, failing to boost the achievement of approximately two-thirds of the students. The staff needed to assess the students, determine strengths and weaknesses, and then identify instructional strategies and allocate resources according to this assessment. For example, the school might train the teacher assistants to conduct lessons with the more able students while the classroom teacher provided intensive instruction with the less skilled students. The staff needed to research and implement instructional programs found to be most beneficial for their struggling learners; instruction prescribed according to the needs of the learner, not according to some abstract theory about learning. Children who fail to make the letter-sound correspondence, for instance, should be taught phonics as needed. It should not be avoided because the classroom teacher dislikes phonics.

Provide a committed and well-trained staff.

Teachers in effective urban schools are committed to the academic and social growth of all their students. They are teaching in this school because they want to teach these students and believe in the inherent worth of their students. The teachers are well trained, confident, and maintain a can-do attitude.

Focus on the students.

Teachers in effective urban schools collaborate and develop a sense of community around the needs of the students. In one school we worked with, for example, the teachers volunteered to supervise Saturday school so that students who received disciplinary referrals would not miss valuable class time through in-school or out-of-school suspensions.

Provide continuous professional development.

This is a critical success factor for effective urban schools. Goals are set for a particular set of skills to be taught. Following an intensive in-service, teachers are coached and closely supervised throughout the year to make sure that they are effective in their teaching. We have found that regular coaching and supervision enhances teachers' repertoires of effective teaching. Ideally, coaches should be full-time members of the school's professional staff; this gives them the best opportunity to produce positive long-term outcomes.

Teach with a sense of urgency.

Too many students in urban schools begin their formal schooling well behind their more affluent age-mates in suburban schools. These children have more knowledge and skills to acquire within the amount of time allocated for all schoolchildren. Furthermore, as they progress through the grades, they are not likely to have the learning advantages of more privileged learners; hence they face an ever-widening achievement gap. Time is of the essence for these students. Instruction needs to be intensified at the earliest grades, and this pace needs to be maintained to make sure that the students are on grade level at the end of each grade. Because of their limited literacy experiences and the rapid passage of time, we cannot afford to wait until the students acquire critical understandings on their own. This is not likely to occur. Students must be taught directly, they must be taught immediately, and they must be taught more, not less, than their affluent peers. For low-performing urban learners, every moment must be consumed with good teaching.

Provide effective academic interventions.

Urban learners not only need to be taught by well-trained teachers, to be taught intensively and urgently, they also need to be taught with effective approaches.

The methods for teaching should be well researched and validated within the research literature. Additionally, school personnel need to make sure that they use practices that work well with their own learners. Teachers need to teach to mastery, not just cover the instructional material. That means that the teacher continues to present a set of sight words or a particular sound, for example, until the students master it. The teacher does not stop presenting it simply because it is the end of the week and time to move on to new material. If most of the other children are ready to move on, provisions still need to be made for more instruction and practice for those who have not yet reached mastery. The way to determine mastery is through progressive monitoring. Daily and weekly assessments will inform teachers of the next steps for teaching these skills.

Set up schoolwide, if not systemwide, programs of instruction and instructional strategies.

Urban learners are highly mobile, often transferring in one school year to two or three different schools within the same district. If all the schools are teaching from the same curriculum, the loss from these changes will be minimized. Uniform programs within schools enable teachers to support and assist one another in their instructional efforts. It also provides for more effective school in-service training and supervision.

Keep students academically engaged in meaningful learning activities with monitored feedback.

The relationship between academic engagement and academic achievement is direct and immediate. Teachers need to become skilled in designing and implementing lessons that keep students responding academically so that they are systematically making desired progress. Effective instruction keeps students and teacher constantly aware of the educational progress being made.

Teach to prevent.

To the extent possible, young urban learners should be enrolled in high-quality preschool programs. There is good evidence that quality preschool programs for urban children of color can lead to reductions in special education enrollments (Smith, 2004). Early learning is extremely important, so every effort needs to be taken to make sure that kindergarten and first-grade classes provide a rigorous instructional program with the most qualified teachers. This is especially the case for young children who may not have had the opportunity to benefit from preschool programs. Prevention efforts need to continue through the grades, making certain that learning and behavior problems do not develop and thus avoiding disciplinary and special education referrals. The prevention efforts made in early years are most likely to pay off later on.

Provide effective schoolwide behavioral interventions.

A pervasive and major concern in urban schools is orderly, socially appropriate behavior. School personnel need to commit to this disciplined environment by planning and implementing schoolwide approaches that teach children how they are to behave and reward them accordingly. The emphasis is not on control but on helping students grow and become socially competent. Rules are clearly stated, posted, taught, and uniformly reinforced.

Behavior management is proactive rather than reactive, catching students' good behavior rather than chasing after inappropriate behaviors. Students feel safe and valued within these schools.

Teach with high expectations.

High expectations are essential for good teaching and learning. Teachers need to be encouraged to set academic and social goals for their classrooms as well as individual students. "The students in my first-grade class will be reading at least sixty words per minute with comprehension by the end of the school year" is an example of a possible academic goal. By specifying this goal, the teacher has a clear sense of what to try to accomplish this year with everyone in the class. Similarly, for behavior the teacher might propose, "Students will use conflict management strategies, and there will be no disciplinary referrals for fighting this school year." These expectations are predicated on effective instruction in reading and social behaviors and the teacher's belief that the students can learn.

Provide adequate materials and resources.

To be effective, urban schools need sufficient instructional materials and supplies. As documented by Jonathan Kozol (1990), there is a pronounced disparity in the supplies and resources found in middle-income schools compared to poverty schools. There is no question that a rich source of available materials contributes to students' learning.

Establish positive, collaborative relationships with families.

Families play a major role in the education of their children, but it must be recognized that impoverished families are at a distinct disadvantage compared to wealthier families. Urban schools will have to bridge that gap. The onus for children's learning must not weigh heavily on poor families. Families with limited skills or resources will not be effective in teaching their children; the classroom teacher must assume this responsibility and serve as the equalizer for poor children (Hale, 2004). Schools will enjoy more respect and responsiveness from urban families as these families see their children making good academic and social progress.

Affirm and nurture students.

All children have strengths and special interests. Teachers need to capitalize on these as a means for affirming and motivating students to remain engaged in school. A low-achieving first grader, for example, might be extremely motivated to tutor a low-achieving kindergarten student. This would be good practice for both as well as enhancing the child's feeling of worth. Creative and committed teachers can find activities or simple praise statements that could help to encourage students.

Reinforce the students' strengths.

Many poor urban students have special gifts and talents. Deliberate efforts should be made to seek out these students early in the grades and nurture their abilities. Since they might not have many enrichment experiences at home or in their communities, it is important that the schools aggressively attempt to nurture these students. Enrichment interventions should not be delayed until the middle grades. Instead, special learning activities need to begin in kindergarten and first grade.

Benefits of Effective Urban Schools

The beneficial effects of effective urban schools are obvious. The neglect that these schools have experienced over the years suggests that a regular accounting of the possible returns would be useful in bringing the requisite assistance and investment in this segment of our pupil population.

- The most obvious desired outcome for more effective urban schools is the increasing academic achievement for their students. Students who perform at expected levels in K–12 schools are then prepared to meet the demands of postsecondary environments.

- Effective schools produce students who are socially competent. These are students who have mastered the interpersonal, intrapersonal, and task-related skills needed to be successful in various undertakings. These are students who possess the self-management skills to achieve socially approved goals and who are sufficiently mature and compassionate to contribute to the well-being of others.

- Effective schools are orderly schools. Students feel safe and valued. Under these conditions, students are at ease and likely to be more productive than under circumstances where order is lacking and a climate of fear and intimidation prevails.

- Effective schools improve the quality of life for urban students. Well-educated students are better able to rise above the conditions of poverty and create for themselves resourceful and more fulfilling lives.

- Effective urban schools provide wholesome working environments for teachers. When schools work well, teacher satisfaction increases and teacher attrition decreases. The teachers become invested in the achievement of their students and enjoy a tremendous sense of accomplishment when their efforts produce the desired results.

- An information-, technology-, and knowledge-based society such as the United States depends heavily on an educated workforce. The need for more highly educated workers increases daily. The challenge for today's students will be not just to find a job but also to create jobs.

- Effective schools contribute to an orderly, stable society. A principal reason for requiring formal education for all of society's members is to ensure the continuation of a culture and its values. Effectively educated urban learners are more likely to embrace this culture, valuing, for example, formal education for themselves and their offspring.

- Effective schools can help lower the rates of crime. Most incarcerated individuals are both poor and uneducated. Some prison officials project the number of prison cells they will need by the number of second-grade students performing below grade level (Hale, 2004). Educated individuals have more options and do not have to rely on criminal activity for survival or social advantage.

- Effective urban schools contribute to an improved quality of life for all members of society. Well-educated urban learners can become contributors to the larger society rather than liabilities, as when they are poorly educated. Resources typically invested in control or social services can then be used to enrich the lives of all.

- Effective urban schools are probably the best vehicle for breaking the cycle of poverty. Effectively educated poor children are likely to avoid the pitfalls of underemployment, dropping out of school, premature parenting, crime, special education, and so forth (Campbell, Pungello, Miller-Johnson, Burchinal, & Ramey, 2001).

Revisiting Devon

Devon was not an isolated case in Ms. Keys's classroom. Although he was among the poorest-performing students in the class, several other students were equally at risk for school failure. Furthermore, based on previous experience, Ms. Keys and the school principal, Mr. Elliot, suspected that most students in the second tier of the class (that is, students who had some advance preparation but not enough to be comfortable) were borderline in their readiness and would gradually fall further behind as they progressed to the upper grades. The intervention team (consisting of Ms. Keys, Mr. Elliot, the school academic and behavioral coach, and the special education specialist) decided that now would be the time to intensify the instruction for all the students in the second and third tiers. Instruction for tier two would have mainly a preventive focus, while instruction for tier three would be both remedial and preventive. The instruction centered largely on prereading and reading skills.

Research in reading indicated that students at this level would benefit from a strong background in phonemic awareness (National Institute of Child Health and Human Development, 2000b). All the students were assessed and the point of intervention was determined for each group. The school coach, Ms. Marvin, taught Ms. Keys, along with Ms. Bryce (the special education specialist) and Ms. Alexander (the kindergarten teaching assistant) how to implement a curriculum on phonemic awareness. The first half hour each morning was allocated to teaching these skills. Ms. Keys taught students in tier two, Ms. Bryce taught students in tier three, and Ms. Alexander practiced related skills with the students in tier one. The students in tier three received an additional half hour of instruction on these skills from Ms. Bryce in the afternoon. At the same time, children in tier one practiced their beginning reading lessons with Ms. Alexander, and tier two received instruction from Ms. Keys on areas of perceived weaknesses. Students were assessed weekly on target skills. This instruction was in addition to and not in lieu of the regularly scheduled reading block Ms. Keys conducted each day with her students.

The afternoon sessions were used as opportunities to strengthen skills that had not been mastered. Students were moved in and out of groups according to their progress on these skills. The intervention team met weekly to assess the individual progress of the students and to make recommendations for changes in the instruction or the placement of students in groups, as needed. The school coach observed the small-group instruction at least once a week to advise the teachers on their instructional strategies. When needed, the school coach would model lessons or prompt teachers to ensure appropriate lesson delivery. Particular attention was given to pupil responses, making certain that each child had many opportunities to respond to the target skills. The instructional team regarded it as equally important that each of the children responded correctly and that they each continued to have opportunities until they were responding correctly without teacher prompting.

The instructional team also wanted to address the behavior issues observed in Devon and several of his young classmates. In addition to being in constant motion, the students often failed to comply immediately after Ms. Keys gave a directive. Observations showed that Ms. Keys frequently repeated her directions to these students and spent considerable time in redirecting them, expending much valuable teaching time. With the instructional team, Ms. Marvin (the school coach) devised a behavior plan designed to increase attending behavior and compliance. It was determined that Ms. Keys needed to be more precise in her directives and to follow her directions immediately with appropriate consequences according to the students' responses. Ms. Keys was taught how to make precision requests (Rhode, Jenson, & Reavis, 1992) and how to respond to student behavior most effectively. Delivering effective consequences meant that students clearly understood the rules; they were praised frequently for following the rules—and they immediately experienced the consequences for any infractions. Ms. Keys was assisted to anticipate student actions and structure her classroom so that many of the current problems could be prevented. The plan was designed so that the overwhelming majority of Ms. Keys's interactions with her students, especially third-tier students, were positive rather than punitive or controlling. Again, Ms. Marvin coached Ms. Keys on these skills, enabling her to increase the attending and compliance behaviors of these students, especially those at greatest risk for school failure.

To increase the success of these students, the intervention team decided it was important to involve the students' parents. The home-school liaison contacted Ms. Matthews, Devon's mother, to schedule an appointment. Because transportation was still a problem for Ms. Matthews, Ms. Keys agreed to meet with Ms. Matthews at her neighborhood library. Ms. Matthews was pleased to meet with Ms. Keys because she had noticed improvement in Devon's academic behavior. She reported that Devon showed real interest in academics. He often picked up reading materials and pointed to letters and made the related sounds. He showed lots of confidence in his ability to read. Ms. Matthews reported that Devon seemed even more excited about going to school each day. She was very pleased about this and hoped that he would continue to make progress and enjoy school.

Ms. Keys reported how pleased she was with Devon's progress. She shared some of the reading and math skills that they were teaching in kindergarten. She also showed Ms. Matthews how she could practice these skills at home with Devon. Ms. Keys modeled this for Ms. Matthews and gave Ms. Matthews a few opportunities to practice how she would use these with Devon. Ms. Keys also shared the progress sheet that she would be sending home to show the progress that Devon was making on these skills. Additionally, she would send on a weekly basis a set of skills that Devon could practice for approximately ten minutes nightly. Ms. Keys and Ms. Matthews would meet monthly to discuss Devon's instructional program and his academic and behavioral progress. Similar meetings were scheduled with other students in Ms. Keys's classroom, especially for students in the third-

and second-tier groups. Ms. Marvin relieved Ms. Keys from some of her late-afternoon teaching responsibilities so she would have time to conduct these meetings.

Devon and his classmates made excellent progress in kindergarten. By the end of the school year they had mastered all their benchmarks for phonemic awareness and had shown definite readiness for reading in first grade. Mr. Elliot, the principal, compared his kindergarten class at the end of the year to the scores from a nearby school with a similar profile and noted that the students in his school performed much better than those in the neighboring school. He also observed that these scores were much better than scores in previous years at his school. This convinced him that these supplementary interventions were worthwhile and he would continue to intensify the instruction for these students as they continued through the elementary grades.

Devon and his classmates also showed substantial improvement in their classroom behavior. Ms. Keys's strategies helped the students to better understand the classroom expectations. Accordingly, instructional activities were more effective and students found school more reinforcing. The intervention team recommended that these procedures be continued in subsequent grades so that students would continue to benefit maximally from their lessons. In fact, these positive outcomes in Devon's kindergarten class convinced Mr. Elliot to start a schoolwide system that will apply effective academic and behavioral approaches across all grade levels.

Effective Strategies for Teachers

Following are steps to be employed by effective teachers for all students. Urban students, even those who are efficient or adequate learners, require continuous and rigorous instruction.

Once a Day

- Implement daily instructional activities with valid, research-based practices such as those discussed later in this handbook.

- Augment instruction with intensive enrichment periods such as those listed here.

- Remind students of their goals for critical basic and social skills. Employ a charting or other record-keeping system that will keep students aware of making their goals and will keep them motivated.

- Provide for needed practice in critical basic skills. When possible, structure this practice through peer-mediated activities such as peer tutoring. Students often enjoy this format, and it enables them to learn while they are teaching.

- Find ways to affirm and encourage students daily. Point out the progress they are making academically and socially. Give individual students some special responsibility (for example, maintaining a neat shelf for the reading books) that makes them feel special.

- Send notes home reporting students' academic and behavioral progress. Although each child gets only one progress note a week, the class might be divided in thirds so that tier one gets the notes on Wednesday (reflecting a period from Wednesday to Wednesday), tier two on Thursday, and tier three on Friday.

Once a Week

- Maintain a progress monitoring system to keep tracking every student's academic and behavior progress. Carefully examine these data to make formal instructional decisions.

- As appropriate, help students set new academic and social goals. These goals should be realistic and should help students make continuous improvement.

- Meet with the school coach weekly to discuss any concerns regarding your teaching and students' learning. Obtain constructive feedback to make instructional plans for the following week.

- Inform parents of their children's progress. Advise parents on how they can intensify their children's learning at home.

Once a Grading Period

- Formally assess each student on critical basic skills. Based on the students' performance, continue with current strategies or revise them in order to increase achievement.

- Assess each student's progress toward meeting annual goals. If the pace of progress seems inadequate, further intensify or alter the instructional program. For example, add an additional fifteen or twenty minutes daily to a student's intervention studies or make sure the student is being taught effectively if the instruction is being delivered by someone other than you.

- Have students prepare "personal progress" notebooks that document their progress throughout the academic year on targeted critical basic skills. Level of performance at the time of the grading period is graphed and entered in the notebook. For example, if a student is reading ninety words per minute at the first grading period, the latest graph of that level of performance is what is entered in the notebook.

Once a Year

- Determine four or five critical basic skills you expect each student in your class to master by the end of the school year—say, reading in connected text 145 words per minute with comprehension; four-digit by two-digit long division by the end of fourth grade.

- At the beginning of the school year, assess all students on the critical basic skills they are expected to achieve by the end of the academic year.

- Identify an instructional program and intervention that might be employed for students failing to meet beginning-of-year benchmarks for critical basic skills. For example, students failing to meet the fluency criterion might be engaged in peer-mediated repeated readings for twenty minutes daily.

- Set up a daily schedule that provides for a thirty- to forty-five–minute period to provide intensive or enrichment studies for all students in the class. That is, those students who are below expected levels in basic skills receive intensified instruction such as noted in the preceding paragraph. Those at or above expected levels would get enrichment studies such as literacy activities that build on and expand their existing skills.

- Identify persons who might be trained to assist in teaching and supervising these intensive and enrichment studies. Teaching assistants and other paraprofessionals in the school could be enlisted to implement and monitor these activities with the students. They could also be instrumental in helping to assess pupil progress and in recording these data for decision-making purposes.

Related Internet Resources

Culturally Responsive Instruction for Urban Learners:
http://education.osu.edu/gcartledge/urbaninitiative/Default.htm

This Web site presents specific academic and behavioral strategies found effective in an elementary urban school. The strategies presented are those validated by research conducted in the schools by the developers or by other nationally recognized researchers. The emphasis is on preventing learning and behavior problems among urban culturally diverse learners.

Institute for Urban Minority Education: http://iume.tc.columbia.edu/

This institute is based at Teacher's College, Columbia University. It conducts research and evaluations; provides information services; and assists schools, community-based organizations, and parent school leaders in program development and evaluation, professional development, and parent education.

National Institute for Urban School Improvement:
http://www.inclusiveschools.org/

This Web site is devoted to issues on urban education. It offers publications and presentations by authorities on instituting effective inclusive urban schools.

CHAPTER 2

Beginning Reading Instruction

Byron

Byron is a seven-year-old African American male in his second year of first grade. He attends an inner-city elementary school. Byron had a very limited kindergarten experience due to frequent moves by his family. He attended several different schools and had many teachers who varied considerably in their curriculum and teaching styles. Byron did poorly in first grade, and his teacher decided to retain him mainly because of his inadequate reading performance. At the end of his first year, the first-grade standardized reading assessments revealed scores of K–5 in letter identification and K–2 in word attack skills. Byron's teacher, Ms. Jones, identified Byron as being at risk for reading failure. He has difficulty identifying the sounds of letters and hence cannot use effective word attack strategies when he comes across an unfamiliar word. Ms. Jones expressed concern about Byron, but she also indicated that she was not sure what she should do with him. Despite small-group instruction three times a week from Ms. Lee, the school reading specialist, Byron continues to flounder severely in reading.

Byron's inability to participate in classroom learning activities due to his reading deficits has resulted in several incidents of disruptive behavior. Classroom observations indicate that he is especially prone to act out when challenged by a difficult reading task. Byron is far behind the other children in his class, so his teacher often leaves him to work on the computer, where he plays games and interacts with other educational programs on multimedia. These activities are of limited academic value, and Byron receives little or no direct instruction on a daily basis from his classroom teacher. Byron's parents are concerned about his poor reading progress, but they are not sure what to do. They try to read to Byron as the teacher advised, but are frustrated in their efforts. Besides, they also have problems in reading and are not much help to their son.

The Scope of the Problem

What is Byron's school outlook if he continues to have reading difficulties? How can Byron's teacher provide him with individualized instruction while attending to twenty other children in the class? What are the essential components of a reading instruction program? This chapter focuses on the "big ideas" of reading, emphasizing the critical and essential elements of beginning reading instruction for primary grades: phonological awareness, alphabetic principle, and fluency. We return to Byron to suggest ways to identify the components that need to be included in his reading program. Later chapters discuss effective instructional strategies for upper elementary and middle school students.

Shobana Musti-Rao and Gwendolyn Cartledge contributed this chapter.

Why Is Reading Important?

Reading as a skill is a common denominator in education and provides opportunities to learn essential skills to become an independent and contributing member of society. Reading at grade level facilitates learning across all subject areas and further translates into meaningful social and economic outcomes for students. Not learning to read is associated with dropping out of school, truancy, juvenile delinquency, and a pervasive feeling of failure. A wealth of research on reading outcomes suggests that reading can be the first line of defense in addressing the academic and behavior problems that students face in schools today. Students who read below grade level at the end of first grade are likelier than their classmates to perform below grade level in reading at the end of fourth grade. The recent report from the National Reading Panel on the status of reading in schools today has provoked a nationwide initiative to establish standards that ensure reading achievement for all students by the end of third or fourth grade. This has led to the resurgence of reading intervention programs that focus on teaching literacy skills as early as preschool and kindergarten. Educators have reached a general consensus that to prevent failure, schools need to make it a top priority that children attain proficiency in reading. Further, it is also agreed that the instruction provided should begin early and include explicit, direct instruction in pre-reading skills.

Reading Instruction for Urban Learners

The report cards of many children in urban schools indicate that they are reading below grade level. The problem is particularly acute in schools with a high proportion of children from minority groups and economically disadvantaged households. Several demographic factors—poverty, racial and ethnic identity, family composition, and the educational level of parents—play an influential role in the learning of these children. They enter school with an inherent disadvantage and find themselves trying to catch up with grade level expectations. This situation places greater demands on teachers to provide instruction to a diverse group of students. Teachers in urban schools often find an especially wide spectrum of reading abilities in their classrooms. In a first-grade classroom of twenty to twenty-five students, for example, some entering students may need to learn the letters of the alphabet while others can already read at or above grade level. Unfortunately, far more will fall on the lower end of the continuum. Teachers thus find themselves in a challenging situation. One teacher told us that she did not have enough time in the day to devote specifically to the poor readers without ignoring other students in the class, and even if she did find the time, she said, she would not know where to begin.

Reading failure is most extensive among children of poverty, especially children of color in our urban schools. Some estimates indicate that 70 percent of fourth-grade students are reading below basic (Lyon, 2003). And few of these children come to school ready to read. Many begin school with approximately half the language skills of their more affluent suburban peers, and the services they receive in school are inadequate to meet their greater need (Hart & Risley, 1995, 1999). At the same time, these children rarely score high enough on standard assessments to achieve the discrepancy needed to be eligible for educational interventions (Hettleman, 2003). Public schools are not providing interventions sufficiently early to avoid failure and permanent special education. These conditions contribute to the ever-widening academic achievement gap between poor urban children and their more economically advantaged peers.

The importance of intervention at the earliest sign of problems in reading cannot be overstated. Some have advised that screenings and interventions begin as early as preschool, and certainly no later than kindergarten. The long-standing policy within special education not to provide services for students with mild disabilities prior to the end of the primary grades means that many students are permitted to experience extensive failure before they become eligible for specialized services, by which point the intervention may be too little too late. "Undiagnosed early reading difficulties rapidly metastasize into academic deficits and disruptive and self-destructive behaviors that special education is powerless to cure" (Hettleman, 2003, p. 7). It may be argued that the stage for poor school performance is set for impoverished children of color at birth, but good evidence suggests that we can ward off later school problems through early identification and academic intervention. There may be a critical period for children to learn to read, probably within the period of four to eight years of age. Children benefit from the frequent presentation of learning materials that enable them to process information quickly and easily. It may be analogous to learning a foreign language in that languages acquired during childhood, before puberty, are typically learned more easily and more thoroughly.

The issue of early intervention in the primary (K–3) grades is particularly contentious. Many general educators insist that early childhood classrooms need only employ "developmentally appropriate" practices, and the reading skills of these children will eventually emerge (Hettleman, 2003). These educators often emphasize "literacy rich" environments where children learn to read as a result of being exposed to and enjoying the written word. The problem for underperforming minority children is that these indirect approaches fail to incorporate the teaching urgency they need to catch up far enough to make the requisite reading progress. As noted previously, specialized services often are not made available until the intermediate grades (or later), when the student is several grade levels behind and reading disabilities are accompanied by behavior problems. Specialized interventions tend to be less beneficial for students beyond the primary grades.

Despite some debate about the most appropriate reading approaches, few question that the process for learning to read begins early in a child's life. From infancy on, young children in literacy-rich homes begin to make associations with sounds, vocabularies, and printed materials that make them ripe for reading at the point of formal school entry. Typically deprived of this critical exposure, impoverished urban learners need preschool, kindergarten, and first-grade experiences to make up for this loss. They need explicit and systematic instruction in the key elements that are universally accepted as being important for reading acquisition. Research indicates that children's exposure to language at home and exposure to reading activities at an early stage affects their ability to understand the phonological distinctions on which the English language is built (Behrmann, 1995). Phonological awareness becomes one of the critical elements.

Phonological Awareness

The term *phonological awareness* refers to the perception that spoken words are made up of a sequence of sound units, or phonological units, that vary in size. The sound units in words can be defined at the syllable, onset and rime, or phoneme level. See Table 2.1 for definition of terms. It involves the ability to hear and manipulate sounds and is concerned with "a broader understanding of the connection between words and sounds" (Chard, Simmons, & Kameenui, 1998, p. 150). The term is often used interchangeably, sometimes erroneously, with *phonemic awareness*, which concerns the phonological unit that is at the phoneme level. (This is discussed further in the next section.)

The importance of phonological awareness in learning to read is well documented in the research literature. These studies not only show a strong positive correlation between phonological awareness and learning to read, they appear to demonstrate that phonological awareness plays a causal role in reading acquisition. In other words, good phonological awareness has a significant influence on learning to read. Smith, Simmons, and Kameenui (1998) report evidence to support the relationship between phonological awareness and reading acquisition and provide the following details:

- The phonological processing ability explains significant differences between good and poor readers.
- Phonological awareness has a causal and a reciprocal relationship with reading acquisition. That is, phonological awareness facilitates reading and is facilitated by reading instruction.
- Deficits and delays in phonological awareness can be reliably identified and measured in young children.
- Phonological awareness is teachable and should be taught explicitly rather than leaving it to develop in the absence of explicit instruction (p. 108).

Phonological awareness is only one area found to play a critical role in reading acquisition. Other areas of reading involve a combination of higher order skills and basic skills. This relationship among the elements of reading led Simmons and colleagues at the Institute for the Development of Educational Achievement (IDEA) in Oregon (IDEA, 2002) to formulate the concept of "big ideas" of reading.

Big Ideas of Reading

The basic premise behind big ideas within the context of a reading program is that certain skills are more important than others and need to be taught more thoroughly. These skills provide the core that allows smaller ideas to be easily understood. Therefore, it is essential that the big ideas are introduced as the basic foundation of reading instruction. These are the five big ideas in beginning reading:

- Phonemic awareness
- Alphabetic principle

TABLE 2.1

Definition of Terms

Term	Definition
Phoneme	The smallest unit of sound in a word; individual sounds. For example, /b/ is the first phoneme in the word *bat*.
Phonological awareness	Conscious ability to detect and manipulate sounds in words; the awareness of sounds in spoken words.
Phonemic awareness	Awareness of phonemes, the discrete individual sounds that correspond to individual letters.
Syllable	The basic phonological unit of speech. It can contain a vowel or an onset and rime.
Onset and rime	Onset is the initial sound or consonant cluster in a word or syllable (e.g., /tr/ in *truck*), and rime is the vowel and any consonant cluster that follows (e.g., /uck/ in *truck*).

- Fluency with text
- Vocabulary
- Comprehension

Phonemic awareness

Phonemic awareness, a component of phonological awareness, is the ability to hear and manipulate sounds in spoken words at the phoneme level. It is the knowledge that words consist of discrete sounds in a particular sequence. Phonemic awareness is a prerequisite to alphabetic understanding (making the connection of print to speech). It is an auditory skill and does not require knowledge of print. These are the critical skills of phonemic awareness:

- Sound isolation: the beginning sound in *man* is /mmm/.
- Blending: /mmm/ /aaa/ /nnn/ is *man*.
- Segmenting: the sounds in *man* are /mmm/ /aaa/ /nnn/.

Alphabetic principle

The ability to associate sounds with letters and use these sounds to form words is referred to as alphabetic principle. In an alphabet-based language such as English, decoding becomes a primary means of recognizing words. Since there are too many words to memorize, children need the skill to read new words they encounter. The ability to read nonsense or pseudo words is reflective of decoding skills. Letter-sound knowledge is a prerequisite skill to word identification.

Fluency with text

One of the ultimate goals of reading, second only to comprehension, is fluency with text. Fluency in reading is characterized by the effortless, automatic ability to read words in text. This skill is developed by translating sounds to letters and letters to words fluently. Fluency not only makes reading effortless but also facilitates comprehension of text.

Vocabulary

Vocabulary refers to the ability to understand and use words to acquire and convey meaning. Children enter school with varied levels of vocabulary knowledge. A rich and functional vocabulary becomes necessary for developing strong readers. Children entering school with limited or poor vocabulary skills soon find themselves falling behind in reading compared to children with a richer vocabulary. Therefore, it is essential that teaching vocabulary become an integral component of the reading instruction that takes place in schools.

Comprehension

Comprehension is the ultimate goal of reading, the ability to extract meaning from text. It is an interaction between the reader and text involving complex cognitive processing. Critical skills such as phonemic awareness, alphabetic principle, fluency with text, and vocabulary all have great impact on reading comprehension.

Prevention and Effective Reading Instruction

One way to reduce the number of students being referred for special education due to reading failure is to adopt a preventive model and start as early as the preschool and kindergarten years. According to Mathes and Torgesen (1998), a preventive approach to reading should encompass early identification of children at risk of reading failure; explicit, intensive, and systematic instruction on core pre-reading and reading skills; and continued support beyond initial instruction. Good reading instruction that is explicit, intensive, and systematic is critical for at-risk learners and needs to be an integral part of their education. Explicit instruction refers to teaching specific reading skills such as phonemic awareness, letter-sound correspondence, and so forth, all of which help students acquire the knowledge to decode print. Explicit instruction requires the integration of modeling, guided practice, scaffolding, and independent practice. It is not merely a combination of various activities. Intensive instruction includes providing a greater number of teaching and learning opportunities with increased repetition of previously learned skills. Systematic instruction is the careful structuring of instruction such that one skill builds on a previously taught skill. While long-term effects of preventive instruction depend largely on the support for reading improvement provided after the commencement of preventive instruction, immediate outcomes for preventive instruction present the possibility of bringing "the word-level reading skills of children at-risk for reading failure within the average range by the end of first or second grade" (Torgesen, 2002, p. 18).

Effective reading interventions should include the following features to increase the likelihood of success:

- Instruction at the phoneme level
- Provision of scaffolding
- Explicit modeling of task prior to student practice

- Strategically integrating phonological awareness and alphabetic understanding
- Using concrete materials to represent sounds

Instruction at the phoneme level

Not all programs that include phonological activities teach skills at the phoneme level. Some may provide instruction at the syllable and onset/rime levels. While several activities can start out with larger units, it is important that instruction for preschool and kindergarten students include the phoneme levels. For example, the student is taught that the sounds in *cat* are /c/ /a/ /t/. The sounds in *truck* are /t/ /r/ /u/ /ck/. The student learns to discriminate smaller units of sounds in words presented orally.

Provision of scaffolding

Mediated scaffolding is one of the instructional principles that "refers to the personal guidance, assistance, and support that teachers, materials, or tasks provide a learner during the initial stages of beginning reading instruction" (Coyne, Kameenui, & Simmons, 2001, p. 67). In the context of a reading program, scaffolding requires providing students with "orchestrated instructional examples" (Good, Simmons, & Smith, 1998) to facilitate learning. The examples provided will not only demonstrate or illustrate the concept but also provide repeated practice for that concept. For example, in identifying the initial phoneme in the word *sit* (that is, /sss/), the student will be given multiple words with the same phoneme such as *see*, *sun*, *say*, and *sam* until the initial sound of /sss/ is established. The teacher holds up a picture card of *mat*, for example, and says, "This is *mat*; /mmm/ is the first sound in *mat*. What is the first sound in /mmmat/? (Teacher places emphasis on the initial sound; student responds.) This is *mouse*; /mmm/ is the first sound in *mouse*. What is the first sound in /mmmouse/? (Teacher places emphasis on the initial sound; student responds.) The use of multiple examples during the phoneme instruction will allow students to transfer the taught concept across words.

Explicit modeling of task prior to student practice

This feature is in line with an instructional principle called *conspicuous strategies*. Conspicuous instruction has been found to produce greater effects in beginning reading than implicit or embedded instruction. The three characteristics designed to teach the phonological strategies of blending and segmenting are when (1) teachers model the skills by overtly drawing attention to sounds within words, (2) teachers provide students with multiple opportunities to respond once the skills are modeled, and (3) students are allowed to practice and manipulate sounds with concrete representations such as moving tiles into boxes that represent the sounds in words. The following example illustrates the explicit instruction model:

> Teacher holds up the letter "m" and says, "The name of this letter is 'm.' Say the name of the letter with me." [Students say "m."] "Good, what is the name of this letter?" [Students say "m."]

In this example, the teacher models the correct response, provides the student with the opportunity to practice with the teacher, and then allows for independent response from the student. This example illustrates the instructional components of *model*, *lead*, and *test* that are most important to effective instruction. In contrast, instruction that is not explicit may involve the teacher's asking, "What is the name of this letter?" without any prior modeling.

Strategically integrating phonological awareness and alphabetic understanding

A reading program is considered effective only if instruction in phonological awareness is integrated with instruction in letter-sound correspondence (Good, Simmons, & Smith, 1998). Research has clearly indicated the combined effect of these two components for successful reading. Strategic integration requires planning and sequencing of interrelated tasks to promote skillful word reading. Building on the preceding example of explicit instruction, here is an example of integrating phonemic awareness with letter-sound correspondence:

> *"The first sound in apple is /aaa/. Say the first sound with me"* [Students say /aaa/.] *"Good, what is the first sound in apple?"* [Students say /aaa/.] *"The letter 'a' makes the /aaa/ sound."*

Adding a writing component to this example—having the student trace or write the letter "a"—is also an example of strategically integrating phonologic and alphabetic skills.

Using concrete materials to represent sounds

The reading programs should include materials that provide common visual stimuli. The materials need to be consistent across activities and letters to keep the attention between the teacher and student constant. Concrete materials facilitate the learning of difficult phonological tasks by attending to the transitory nature of sound, the abstract characteristics of isolated sounds, and the need to memorize phonological information. Concrete representation involves using a neutral object to represent a sound instead of asking the student to mentally isolate the first sound away from the rest of the word and then say the first sound aloud. A common example of a segmenting activity using concrete materials is to move letter tiles or objects into boxes as sounds in a word are pronounced. Other examples include individual letters printed on cards for students to trace over with their fingers, or letter tiles or magnetic letters for the students to move around, and so on.

In addition to these five features, an intervention program that has been shown to be effective with target children and has empirically validated evidence is most desirable. Time allocated for instruction, the level of teacher-directed instruction involved, and the cost of the program are some factors that also need to be considered when selecting a beginning reading program. The "Teacher Resources" at the end of this chapter give suggestions for possible programs.

Dynamic Indicators of Basic Early Literacy Skills

Instruction is not complete without evidence that clearly shows its effectiveness. The link between intervention and assessment is also a critical one in teaching children to read.

Preventing reading failure requires more than just teaching the skill. It requires dynamic, prevention-oriented, school-based systems to constantly monitor the progress of children in the school, especially in the elementary grades. The Dynamic Indicators of Basic Early Literacy Skills (DIBELS), developed by Roland Good and Ruth Kaminski at the University of Oregon, is an assessment system to monitor growth in the acquisition of critical early literacy skills. More information on the DIBELS can be obtained from their official Web site. The address is provided at the end of this chapter.

The Importance of Literature

The emphasis on early intervention and phonemic awareness does not rule out the importance of literature and literacy-rich environments; quite the contrary. We strongly advocate that parents and teachers provide many, many opportunities for young children to experience and enjoy books. From infancy on caretakers and teachers should read to children, should encourage children to make sense from pictures and various symbols, and should model the value of reading to children. Reading to children and bombarding them with lots of literacy experiences helps them to develop language and critical readiness concepts. Unfortunately, many of our urban learners have few such experiences before they come to school. The problem is worsened by the fact that they often attend schools where resources are limited—books are often scarce, and many urban schools do not have a certified librarian who can make available for these students the kinds of books that they will find most beneficial. It is hoped that school personnel will do all that is possible to secure these materials for their students.

We recommend that teachers read to children daily. As children mature, they should be encouraged to read along with teachers, to talk about what they read, and to write about what they read. It is also good to get children to write their own stories and to read them to others. These are all activities that children will enjoy and that will enable them to become more literate. We especially recommend that children have the opportunity to read stories that are diverse in terms of culture and gender. All children should be exposed to a diversity of books. At the end of this chapter is a listing of some books with culturally diverse content that would be of interest to young readers.

Revisiting Byron

At the beginning of the school year, Ms. Jones, the first-grade teacher, administered the DIBELS assessment to all the students in her class. Results of the assessment showed that besides Byron, five other students in her class needed intensive instruction in letter-naming and phoneme-segmentation tasks. Every morning, the teacher engaged small groups of children in reading activities during center time. Ms. Jones decided that she would group the children according to their assessment scores so that she could provide instruction focusing on their specific areas of need. Byron was grouped with two other children to receive daily twenty minutes of instruction in phonemic awareness, letter-names, and letter-sounds.

To make sure that the instruction was explicit and systematic, the teacher used a commercial reading curriculum that complemented the DIBELS assessment system. The reading program also included features that represent effective instruction (e.g., instruction at the phoneme level, explicit modeling of skills). Since Byron and his five classmates were receiving instruction from Ms. Lee, the reading specialist, they decided that Ms. Lee would come into Ms. Jones's classroom and provide the small-group phonemic instruction for both groups. This instruction supplemented and complemented the other reading instruction Ms. Jones provided. Additionally, Ms. Lee developed practice activities reflecting these skills so that Byron could practice them at home and during center time in the classroom. As his parents noted Byron's progress, they began to take more interest in his home practice activities. They began to help Byron read simple books.

In the classroom, Byron and his five peers progressed through their daily lessons and started to read CVC (consonant-vowel-consonant) words. Ms. Jones also observed that the students were able to generalize the skills to other classroom activities. Byron started to volunteer in class to answer questions about beginning and ending sounds in words and was observed to be more confident in picking up a book to read. Clearly, Byron continues to need more intensive instruction to gain fluency with connected text. However, he is off to a much better start this year. Byron's classroom behavior has also changed—he isn't disrupting reading lessons nearly so often as last year.

Effective Strategies for Teachers

Prevention needs to begin before the first grade—certainly before the child fails. If possible, these strategies should be initiated in preschool or kindergarten and continued through first grade. It is most important that teachers not wait until students have learned to expect to fail before employing these strategies. Preventive reading instruction should start on the first day of school and continue throughout the school year. Following are some strategies that teachers can employ in their classrooms. At the beginning of the school year, select a good assessment system that will not only serve as a screening device but also can be used as a progress monitoring system. Assess all the students in your class on their early literacy skills—phonemic awareness, alphabetic principle, and reading fluency. Determine the level and intensity of instruction that your students need and group them accordingly. Assess the students at the middle and again at the end of the school year.

Once a Day

- Allot fifteen to twenty minutes of small-group instruction, possibly during center time, for phonemic awareness and alphabetic principle training. The type of instruction you provide will depend on the ability levels of students in each group. One group may have already established the early reading skills and may need instruction in high-frequency sight words, while another group may need instruction in letter-names and letter-sounds.

- Provide explicit and systematic reading instruction to students based on their instructional needs. Be sure to incorporate the critical features of effective instruction such as introducing the task, modeling the task, and providing guided practice before providing independent practice.

- Maintain a log or make notes of the lesson that was covered and any observations or information about the students in your reading groups to assist you in modifying your lessons. For example, if Jack was particularly distracted for the last two days and you think it may be because he was sitting next to Jill, then you can move Jack away from Jill and observe his behavior.

- As part of the morning drills, engage all students in your class to chorally respond to the letter-names and letter-sounds introduced the previous day. This will serve as a warm-up or review activity before you start a new lesson.

- Read a story to the children.

Once a Week

- Conduct a quick assessment of students in early literacy skills. An assessment system like the DIBELS involves one-minute timed assessments that are not time-consuming.

- Record the scores of each student. Entering the scores in a computer spreadsheet might be an efficient way to keep track of data and generate graphs and figures for later review.

- For students who are able to read words in connected text, send home a book every Friday and encourage them to read aloud to their parents or siblings. Provide a token reward on Monday for returning the book and bringing back a note saying that they read the book at home.

Once a Month

- Analyze the data obtained from your weekly assessment and make important instructional decisions. You can look at the students' individual data and decide if anyone has made progress and can be moved to a higher group, needs to remain in the same group, or should be grouped with students receiving more basic instruction.

- Review individual data with the school reading specialist. Discuss what has worked well and what strategies need to be revised or intensified for specific students.

- Send home a note informing the parents of the letter-names and letter-sounds that their child has learned and encouraging them to practice or test the students with those letters at home.

Once a Year

- Attend a professional development workshop or seminar on teaching beginning readers effectively.

- Read a set of research-based articles on effective strategies for teaching beginning at-risk readers.

- Evaluate the intervention program for at-risk beginning readers with the school reading specialist and other school personnel. Discuss what worked best and what needs to be revised. Identify other resources as needed.

Related Internet Resources

A Tale of Two Schools: http://www.readingrockets.org/tv/order.php

> Narrated by Morgan Freeman, this documentary tells the story of two schools and their reading programs. It is a tale of hope, faith, and power commitment among adults to see their students succeed in school. Video or DVD can be ordered from this Web site.

Big Ideas in Beginning Reading: http://reading.uoregon.edu/

> Big Ideas in Beginning Reading (BIBR) gives educators and administrators a valuable new educational resource. The BIBR Web site elucidates the five big ideas (phonemic awareness, alphabetic principle, fluency with text, vocabulary, and comprehension) that the DIBELS measures were designed to assess. The BIBR Web site includes sections on the big ideas, assessment, instruction, and the schoolwide reading model.

Great Leaps Reading: http://www.greatleaps.com/

> The official Web site of the Great Leaps Reading Program provides information on this empirically validated reading program. The program focuses on areas of phonics, sight phrases, and reading fluency.

Headsprout: http://www.headsprout.com/

> Headsprout is a research-based supplemental reading program for children from K to 2+. This Web site offers the program for use in both home and school. A free trial enables parents and teachers to test the program before purchasing it.

Jamestown Education: http://www.glencoe.com/gln/jamestown/

> Jamestown Online provides supplemental reading materials for middle school, high school, and adult learners. The Web site provides a search for reading materials according to the readability levels and includes an online catalog.

National Reading Panel: http://www.nationalreadingpanel.org/

> The National Reading Panel (NRP) was formatted by the National Institute of Child Health and Human Development (NICHD, 2000a, 2000b) in 1997 to provide research assessment of reading instruction approaches. Since then, the NRP has published a number of reports on the effectiveness of different approaches used to teach children to read. These reports have had great impact on both research and practice in reading.

Official Web site of Dynamic Indicators of Basic Literacy Skills: http://dibels.uoregon.edu/

> The DIBELS Web site contains complete information on the assessment measures, benchmark goals, and downloadable materials needed to assess the different skills in reading acquisition. The Web site also offers an optional additional service, the DIBELS Data System, that allows schools to enter students' data online and generate automated reports.

Scott Foresman Early Reading Intervention:
http://www.scottforesman.com/eri/

> This is a research-based reading program that identifies at-risk students in kindergarten and first grade and provides intervention to improve on early reading skills. The program complements the DIBELS assessment system. Teachers can make decisions regarding student placement and monitor progress periodically.

U.S. Department of Education—Improve Student Performance:
http://www.ed.gov/teachers/how/read/edpicks.jhtml?src=In

> This Web site provides a rich list of research-based resources related to improving student performance. Resources include assessment reports, presentations, workshops, centers, and other official and useful Web sites, education reforms, and so forth.

Sample Multicultural Books for Urban Early Learners

Preschool

Bryan, A. (1991). *All night, all day: A child's first book of African-American spirituals.* New York: Atheneum.

Demi. (1990). *The empty pot.* New York: Henry Holt. [Asian]

De Paola, T. (1981). *The comic adventures of old Mother Hubbard and her dog.* San Diego: Harcourt Brace Jovanovich.

Dorros, A. (1991). *Abuela.* New York: Dutton. [Hispanic]

Greenfield, E. (1978). *Honey, I love you: And other love poems.* Illustrated by Leo & Diane Dillon. New York: HarperCollins. Includes a poem about Harriet Tubman. [African American]

Hendershot, J. (1987). *In coal country.* Illustrated by Thomas B. Allen. New York: Knopf.

Hoffman, M. (1991). *Amazing Grace.* New York: Dial Books for Young Readers. [Black]

Jakes, J. (1986). *Susanna of the Alamo: A true story.* San Diego: Harcourt Brace Jovanovich.

Keats, E. J. (1976). *The snowy day.* New York: Puffin.

Longfellow, H. W. (1983). *Hiawatha.* Illustrated by Susan Jeffers. New York: Dial Books for Young Readers. [Native American]

McKissack, P. C. (1986). *Flossie and the fox.* Illustrated by Rachel Isadora. New York: Dial Books for Young Readers [African American]

Ringgold, F. (1991). *Tar beach.* New York: Crown. [African American]

Rylant, C. (1985). *When I was young in the mountains.* Illustrated by Diane Goode. New York: Dutton.

San Souci, R. D. (1989). *The talking eggs.* Illustrated by Jerry Pinkney. New York: Dial Books for Young Readers. [Black]

Steptoe, J. (1987). *Mufaro's beautiful daughters: An African tale.* New York: Lothrop. [African]

Young, E. (1989). *Lon Po Po: A Red Riding Hood story from China.* Translated & illustrated by Ed Young. New York: Putnam. [Asian]

Primary to Grade 3

Adler, D. A. (1989). *Jackie Robinson: He was the first.* New York: Holiday House. [African American]

Adoff, A. (1970). *Malcolm X.* New York: HarperCollins. [African American]

Bond, C. T. (1989). *A book of famous black Americans.* Illustrated by Joyce Beecher King. With bibliography and activities. Livonia, MI: Partner Press.

Bruchac, J. (1993). *The first strawberries: A Cherokee story.* New York: Dial Books for Young Readers. [Native American]

Carter, P. (1990). *Harriet Tubman and Black History Month.* Silver Burdett. (African American). Englewood Cliffs, NJ: Scholastic.

Conrad, P. (1991). *Pedro's journal: A voyage with Christopher Columbus.* Philadelphia: Boyds Mills Press.

Curtis, J. (2002). *I'm gonna like me: Letting off a little self-esteem.* New York: Joanna Cotler Books.

Fritz, J. (1983). *The double life of Pocahontas.* New York: Putnam. [Native American]

Garcia, M. (1987). *The adventures of Connie and Diego/Las aventuras de Connie y Diego.* San Francisco: Children's Book Press. [Hispanic]

Goss, L., & Barnes, M. E. (1989). *Talk that talk: An anthology of African-American storytelling.* New York: Simon & Schuster.

Greenfield, E. (1989). *Nathaniel talking.* Black Butterfly. [African American]

Hoffman, M., & Binch, C. (1995). *Boundless grace.* New York: Dial Books for Young Readers. [Black]

LL Cool, J. (2002). *And the winner is . . . .* New York: Scholastic Books.

McGovern, A. (1977). *Wanted dead or alive: The story of Harriet Tubman.* New York: Scholastic. [African American]

McKissack, P. (1987). *Mary McLeod Bethune: A great teacher.* Berkeley Heights, NJ: Enslow. [African American]

Myers, W. D. (1993). *Brown angels: An album of pictures and verse.* New York: HarperCollins. [photographs, poetry, affirming]

Myers, W. D. (1995). *Glorious angels: A celebration of children.* New York: HarperCollins. [photographs, poetry, affirming]

Surat, M. M. (1983). *Angel child, dragon child.* Milwaukee: Raintree. [Asian]

Taylor, M. D. (1976). *Roll of thunder, hear my cry.* New York: Dial Books for Young Readers. [African American]

Taylor, M. D. (1991). *Let the circle be unbroken.* New York: Puffin. [African American]

Vo-Dinh. (1970). *Toad is the emperor's uncle: Animal folktales from Viet-Nam.* New York: Doubleday. [Asian]

Yarbrough, C. (1979). *Cornrows.* New York: Coward-McCann. [African American]

Zolotow, C. (1963). *The quarreling book.* New York: Harper & Row.

Teacher Resources

American Library Association. (1992). *Best of the best for children.* New York: Random House. Gives titles with descriptions of books, magazines, videos, and computer software. Available in many libraries.

Database of Award Winning Children's Literature. http://www.dawcl.com/.

Hearne, B. (1990). *Choosing books for children: A commonsense guide.* New York: Delacorte.

Lewis, V. V., & Mayes, W. M. (1998). *Valerie and Walter's best books for children: A lively, opinionated guide.* New York: Avon Books. This book gives "opinions" about children's books for children from birth to age fourteen. It also categorizes books according to subject matter including issues relative to social development.

Library of Congress. (n.d.) *Books for Children.* List of more than one hundred of the best children's books recently published. Available from the Consumer Information Center, Pueblo, Colorado 81009. Item 101Z.

PART TWO

Effective Academic Instruction

CHAPTER 3

Principles of Effective Instruction

Angela

Angela is a fifth-grade student in her urban neighborhood school. During her primary grades, her teachers regarded Angela as a good student. She paid attention in class and always did her homework. Although she was slightly below grade level in reading, she was not of major concern to her teachers because she performed better than about 50 percent of her classmates. Things changed for her in the intermediate grades. Angela found it harder and harder to pay attention in class. She attended all her classes, but her mind often drifted as her teacher lectured.

Social studies was the worst class for Angela. She knew she should be listening to the teacher but the material was not very interesting. In Angela's class, the teacher, Mr. Donaldson, required very little response from his students. It was the teacher's job to talk, the students' job to sit quietly, take notes, and pay attention. When Angela's teacher did recruit student comments, he asked the questions and called on one of the students who had raised a hand. Weeks could go by without Mr. Donaldson recruiting an answer from every student in class.

In Angela's class, the lack of individual student participation incorporated in the lessons was rather common. Angela complained that they did the same thing every day and she did not like trying to remember names of places or people. She especially did not like trying to remember dates. She has not done well on her tests or assignments. Mr. Donaldson sent notes home to her parents to advise them to get Angela to study harder.

Importance of Effective Instruction

Every child (and especially every urban child) needs an effective educational program designed and implemented by a teacher who can maximize the time that the student is learning in the classroom. When provided with effective instruction, all students can make robust academic improvements.

Angela is a typical example of the underachieving students commonly seen in urban classrooms. Teachers expect every student in the classroom to sit quietly, listen, stay on task, pay attention to the teacher's instruction, and learn. Although legitimate, this assumption misses the mark for many students, especially those in urban settings, who either do not have the requisite skills to attend to and perform the tasks independently or do not benefit from passive learning without a well-designed instructional structure. In addition, this expectation places more weight on students to self-regulate their behavior than on teachers to provide structured and engaging instruction. Most educators

Michael "Chuck" Lambert, Ya-yu Lo, and Gwendolyn Cartledge contributed this chapter.

would agree that good instruction is the most important factor in determining students' academic achievement and success. Almost all successful learning results from good teaching. This is even more true for urban, impoverished learners who are not enriched with resources to self-discover or self-learn. It is therefore imperative for classroom teachers to be equipped with instructional strategies that can efficiently and effectively address the academic needs of urban learners.

What Is Effective Academic Instruction?

Supported by research, educators have identified several factors that make up effective instruction. The principles that follow pull heavily from the tenets of Direct Instruction (Engelmann, 1999) as well as the views of several noted education authorities.

Have a clear academic focus and clearly specify learning goals.

To bring about the desired academic effects, classroom teachers need to avoid classroom activities that are only indirectly related to academic instruction. For example, for several decades beginning in the 1960s, children in special education classrooms spent many hours with perceptual motor activities considered likely to promote learning abilities that would foster academic achievement. These activities did not lead to academic improvements, and they cost valuable instructional time. Along with having an academic focus for academic achievement, teachers need to have a clear understanding of their learning goals. These are often called *pinpoints*. Pinpoints define what we expect students to have mastered within a specified time period. For instance, *at the end of the second grading period all the first-grade students will read a passage at sixty words a minute with comprehension, or the third-grade students will compute ten two-digit by two-digit multiplication problems within a specified time period.* Clearly defined goals provide instructional direction, help dictate instructional strategies, and let you know whether and when your instruction has been successful.

Provide for high rates of overt responding.

Researchers have found that academic achievement is not highly correlated with passive on-task behavior (Stallings, 1980). In other words, staying on task and paying attention to the instruction does not necessarily guarantee improved academic performance. In fact, John Dewey, one of the founding fathers of the American educational system, contended that learning is an active process and that students learn by doing (Dewey, 1916). Therefore, students need to be more active in what they are being taught so that they actually learn it. When planning instruction to promote active learning, teachers may find it useful to distinguish the differences among *on task, opportunity to respond,* and *active student response.*

On task is probably the most common term used to describe a student who is paying attention to a teacher's lesson or an assigned activity in the classrooms. Staying on task is also most likely a required skill for every student. Although it is important that a student stay on task in order to participate in class activities or to master the curriculum, staying on task is not equivalent to learning and should not be a stopping point for achievement expectation.

Opportunity to respond (OTR) is the interaction between a teacher-presented question or prompt (that is, an instructional antecedent) and a student response to the instructional prompt (Greenwood, Delquadri, & Bulgren, 1993). Researchers have suggested that increased OTR resulted in positive student learning and students' academic success. Simply said, when students are given ample opportunities to respond to the presented tasks, they are more likely to be engaged in the instructional materials and to receive practice opportunities that ultimately lead to better learning and higher academic achievement. However, OTR is again not equivalent to the amount of responses students actually produce. In many cases, students may still not actively respond to the instructional materials even when the classroom teachers provide a high level of OTR. This is even more likely to be the case for low-performing students, who are apt to be resistant to academic responses without careful planning.

Different from OTR, *active student response (ASR)* refers to a measurable and observable response a student makes to instructional prompts (Heward, 2000). The definition of ASR requires that a student not only pay attention to the instructional antecedent but also produce an observable response. Examples of ASR are acts such as sentences read, problems solved, words spelled, words written, steps completed, items explained, and so forth. Higher levels of ASR have been related to improved student achievement and are evidence of active student engagement. Several specific strategies reliably produce higher levels of ASR as well as higher levels of student achievement when compared to more traditional, lecture-type teaching approaches. Examples of these classroom strategies include choral responding, response cards, guided notes, peer tutoring, and repeated readings.

Choral responding refers to students' responding in unison to teacher-presented prompts or questions; response cards are cards or signs students hold up to display their response to the teacher's questions (Heward, 1994). *Guided notes* are structured worksheets or handouts that allow students to follow through on the materials presented by their classroom teacher. *Peer tutoring* engages members of the class to help their fellow students learn the academic content, and *repeated readings* provide students with repeated opportunities to read and reread assigned reading passages. Common features of these strategies are that they all provide (1) fast pace with high levels of ASR, where students actively respond to the instructional materials, (2) monitored student practice with frequent and immediate performance feedback, and (3) immediate feedback to the teachers to determine whether or not more practice is necessary. It is these features that characterize effective academic strategies. Our own research gives us a basis to discuss the application of response cards, peer tutoring, and repeated readings later in this handbook. Readers are referred to Heward (1994) for a more detailed discussion of choral responding and guided notes.

Teach for fluency or automaticity.

Related to pupil responding and instructional pacing is the importance of fluency. Lessons presented at a brisk pace will enable students to respond at high rates to the teacher's instruction, resulting in higher academic achievement (Gunter, Reffel, Barnett, Lee, & Patrick, 2004). Research findings indicate that students should have at least four to six responses with 80 percent accuracy when being presented with new material and at least eight to twelve responses with 90 percent accuracy when being presented with review material. However, Gunter and his colleagues report that their direct observations in many elementary classrooms failed to find response rates that approached the levels designated as optimal for academic achievement.

High response rates are important to help students become automatic in their responses. Through repeated high-rate practice, students develop the desired level of fluency, which forms the basis for learning new material. The acquisition of new material is easier when prerequisite skills are mastered. Students will have much difficulty reading a second- or third-grade text, for example, if they are still struggling with the recognition of words that were to be mastered in first grade. When students are able to read those words rapidly and immediately, they are then able to learn more difficult words and to read them with comprehension. A case can be made for overlearning the subject matter: This is particularly true for critical skills, which serve as the building blocks for higher level skills.

Teach for accuracy and constantly monitor student performance.

Student practice through high response rates is beneficial only if students are responding accurately. The advantage of the strategies presented in this handbook is that monitoring the students' overt responses allows teachers to immediately identify and correct errors. Students are then directed to make the correct response and to make the correct response repeatedly until they are responding errorlessly without teacher prompting. At that point, students are considered to be able to practice a skill independently. To illustrate, suppose a student named Randy practices his reading daily through twenty minutes of silent reading but does not seem to be making much progress in his overall reading achievement. His teacher then pairs Randy with another student to read orally in repeated readings and discovers that Randy is miscalling many of the words and thus failing to fully comprehend the passage. During repeated readings, Randy is immediately corrected for his errors and is required to repeat the corrected words several times. Randy then rereads the passage several times until he reads it errorlessly and with total comprehension.

It is also important to constantly monitor student performance, especially in the critical skill areas, to make sure that students are making the desired progress in a timely fashion. Constant monitoring can be daily, weekly, or even every two weeks, but it needs to be frequent enough so that adjustments can be made before too much time has elapsed. Struggling learners cannot afford weeks or months of repeatedly practicing the same errors while the instruction fails to meet their needs. Unfortunately, it is not uncommon for an entire academic year to pass before the teacher realizes with the end-of-year assessments that a student has missed all the desired benchmarks. With a goal of 120 words per minute, for example, the teacher may find that Randy is not making much progress beyond the 80 words per minute he displayed during an initial assessment. It may be necessary to change the instructional materials, assign a different partner, or reduce the level of the materials in order to get Randy to respond more consistently and accurately to the task. Once Randy has reached the desired level of performance, he can then more ably move on to the next higher level.

Another important consideration is that evaluations need to be fair and cred-ible (Resnick, 1999). Students need to be evaluated in ways that they view as fair, but most important, evaluations need to be aligned with the curriculum being presented. Student ratings may vary considerably if the assessment measures do not reflect the material that has been taught. On the other hand, assessments should be constructed according to absolute standards so that students and teachers can be confident in student learning.

Establish high minimum standards.

At-risk learners will not reach desired levels of performance unless we set high expectations for them. Resnick (1999) points out that achievement is based on more than innate ability—direct and sustained effort is a major factor. Setting a minimum standard that every first-grade student will read sixty words per minute with comprehension by the end of the school year may be higher than any level achieved in previous years, but it is the minimum goal if urban learners are to achieve and maintain grade-level performance. Implied in this standard is that tremendous effort will be expended by both pupils and teachers. As Resnick points out, the school will have to organize for this type of effort. Since many, if not most, urban learners come to school with readiness levels behind those of their affluent peers, the effort needs to be maximized in the earliest school years.

Engelmann (1999) advises that we need to accelerate the learning of children who are at risk "so that they leave kindergarten academically *ahead* of affluent children—reading and performing in math at around the 2nd grade level" (p. 77). Engelmann argues that the early grades (preschool, kindergarten, and first grade) are the best times to push for this acceleration, since during this period family members are most likely to be able to assist learning. If they have to wait until after kindergarten, students will continue to fall behind, and the gap between them and their affluent peers will steadily widen.

Build on student successes.

Students are an extremely important part of the achievement equation. They not only need to put forth good effort, they also need to believe that they are able to achieve the specified goals. Otherwise, they will not keep trying. Perhaps the best way to accomplish this is to use strategies such as the ones recommended in this handbook, which are predicated on student success and provide for explicit displays of success through goal setting, charting, and graphing. A most rewarding observation in our work with urban learners was in the heightened levels of confidence they displayed in their ability to per-form. After several weeks of practice through repeated readings, for example, students readily undertook their reading assignments, took pride in reaching their reading goals, and began to seek out other materials to read. We got re-ports of increased confidence both from parents and from other teachers. Many students asked to continue the repeated reading activities because they felt they helped them become better readers. When students experience a sense of accomplishment, they are likely to take on even greater challenges.

Promote higher order thinking.

An important goal of formal education is to help young people engage in higher order thinking and effective problem solving. Teaching students to think with-out a knowledge base is not realistic, nor should one attempt to get learners to acquire knowledge without emphasizing thinking (Resnick, 1999). Thinking and problem solving can be promoted by asking students challenging questions. We should present many questions, and present them within the context of the subject matter. Higher order thinking and problem solving might be presented most effectively in certain formats. For example, there is evidence that reasoning strategies have been used to improve the subject matter thinking for students with learning disabilities (Grossen, 1991). By encouraging students to think and to think logically, we can improve their academic performance as well as their ability to think and act wisely within social situations.

Emphasize reading.

Reading really is fundamental; the point cannot be cited too frequently. Students who fail to become efficient readers are doomed to failure in school and in later life. This is particularly the case for urban learners from low socioeconomic backgrounds, who often have limited options if they do not master the school's curriculum. Although schools often specify ample time periods for reading blocks, classroom observations show that students are not actively engaged in meaningful reading activities for extensive periods during these reading blocks. We recommend that teachers make sure students know how important reading is, find ways to reward students for reading books and independently completing them, and structure classroom activities so that students can support each other's reading (Bell, 2002/2003). Possible examples for peer-supported activities include peer tutoring, cross-age tutoring, peer-mediated repeated readings, and small-group student-directed readings. The last example simply involves teaching the students how to engage in a small-group (two or three other students) reading activity such as round-robin reading. One student is assigned to be the "teacher" and makes sure that each student gets a chance to read and correct errors. Students have to be trained how to do this, but following initial training, this can be a useful and meaningful way to provide reading practice. The other examples are described in this handbook.

Importance of Effective Academic Instruction for Urban Learners

The importance of increased academic instructional time with high levels of student response is especially relevant to urban classrooms where instructional shortages are more evident. Research in urban classrooms reveals the following:

- Teachers spend less than 6 percent of class time in directing reading (teaching reading) and less than 1 percent of their time with student questions (asking students questions or discussing a question with a student) (Sindelar, Espin, Smith, & Harriman, 1990).

- Only 2 percent of class time is spent in engaging students in repeated practice (review) activities and only 2 percent of the day in having students read aloud (Stallings & Freiberg, 1991).

- On average the urban teachers allocated 75 percent of the school day to academics, and yet only 1 percent of the day was actually spent in instruction. Some students averaged no more than twenty seconds in directed reading instruction each day, while other students spent only five seconds per day practicing basic math facts (Hall, Delquadri, Greenwood, & Thurston, 1982).

Unfortunately, students spend very little time in the school day learning, and teachers spend very little time in the school day actively teaching. Considering that urban students already lag behind their nonurban peers, the lack of active engagement in academic learning severely aggravates their underachievement.

Based on our many years of working in urban schools, we have found that academic time is disproportionately devoted to student seatwork, where students are engaged in independently completing written worksheets or reading silently. Although these activities provide students with practice necessary to build proficiency for newly learned skills, to be effective, such practice also requires intensive and careful monitoring of students' performance. This independent seatwork typically is given with good intentions but with inadequate planning that overlooks the need for continuous monitoring and immediate feedback. As a result, students often practice their mistakes extensively before corrective feedback is provided. Considering how long it takes for students to get their graded worksheets back from their teachers and how many times they may have practiced making the same mistakes in the interim, it is not surprising that many of our students continue to experience academic difficulty. In addition, students who have difficulty following teacher requests and managing their time independently (the students who exhibit problem behaviors) are even more prone to failing academically.

Learning academic skills is the historical purpose of schooling, and it seems clear that our students need to learn more and learn better. The fundamental problem lies in the fact that learning cannot be directly observed or measured. What we can observe are behaviors that are the result of learning (that is, having the students do what they were taught). This leads to the importance of developing instruction that can produce high levels of student response so that teachers can ensure that students are not only engaged in the instruction but also are progressing to better learning.

Benefits of Effective Academic Instruction

Effective academic instruction offers many benefits for classroom teachers as well as students. For classroom teachers, the adoption of effective academic strategies allows them to

- Fulfill their responsibility to provide instruction that can result in high student achievement.
- Frequently monitor students' progress and provide immediate feedback to students' responses.
- More efficiently deliver content learning in well-structured lessons.
- Structure a variety of instructional presentations to increase students' motivation for learning.
- Highly engage students in the academic instructional materials they have to master.
- Focus on academic teaching rather than managing behavior (since the students are more likely to pay attention and stay on task when they are actively responding).

- Determine whether or not the students understand or learn the contents (that is, only when students respond actively so that teachers can see and observe can they be assured that the students get it).

For students, effective academic strategies are beneficial for the following reasons:

- Effective academic strategies result in higher student academic achievement and better learning.

- Students are more engaged in instructional materials and find it easy to maintain high levels of on-task behavior.

- As students become more proficient in academics, their motivation to learn and their self-confidence increase.

- Students' positive academic achievement is strongly correlated with their positive social behaviors.

- Students enjoy effective academic strategies.

Revisiting Angela

Instead of focusing solely on getting Angela to study harder, Mr. Donaldson decided to try to restructure his social studies class. In addition to Angela, this might also help at least the other 50 percent of the students who were not doing well in his class. He noticed that most of his students were having trouble taking notes during his lectures. He decided to reduce his lectures to about fifteen minutes of the class time, and to provide guided notes so that the students would only have to write in the missing words as he talked. He presented his lectures on an overhead projector so that students could follow along and find the words they needed to fill in the blanks. After his lecture, he checked the students' understanding by getting them to explain each concept using choral responding. About two weeks later, when the students became skilled with guided notes, he then trained them in using response cards. He gave the students white dry erase boards so that when he asked a question about each concept, the students could write the answer on the board and hold it up when directed by Mr. Donaldson.

A few weeks later, to increase student interest and vary his instruction further, Mr. Donaldson had students play games to practice these concepts. For example, students might be divided into teams during the response cards activity, and the team with the most correct initial responses would be the winner. Other examples included devising games in the form of various card games or board games such as Monopoly, where students would play in small groups. To foster higher level thinking and problem solving, Mr. Donaldson began to take a social studies concept, divide the students into groups, and give them directions for some small project. For example, when studying productivity and entrepreneurship, students would be encouraged to make some small product in class, such as paper puppets, give their product some unique design, and then try to sell it to their classmates, using classroom tokens for currency. The students would compete to see which group could make the most sales or design the most entertaining and creative sales pitch.

Angela began to respond positively to Mr. Donaldson's revised classroom structure. She and her classmates were so busy responding to his lessons, they did not have time for their personal discussions. Besides, they enjoyed the activities where they helped each other practice the social studies concepts. Angela especially enjoyed the special projects in the small groups where they worked hard to come up with clever and different ways to sell their products to others. These activities made it much easier to learn and remember the social studies materials. She was making much better grades in social studies. Angela began to think about herself as a good student who could do well in all her classes.

Incorporating Effective Academic Instruction in Your Classroom

When initially incorporating academic strategies into your teaching, it is important not to change too much about your instruction at one time. A key to successful adoption of any of the effective academic strategies is careful planning and thorough preparation. It may be frustrating and overwhelming to implement several new strategies at one time. They should be introduced gradually as students evidence comfort and skill with a strategy.

The strategies outlined in this handbook do not have to be included in every lesson in every subject, nor should they be. Instead, we advise that you start with one strategy and identify one class or subject (for example, vocabulary development, phonics, reading comprehension, spelling, math, or science) where you think this strategy might be helpful. Considering the critical importance of reading and math, these basic skills might receive priority. You may want to first incorporate one strategy for a partial class period (for example, a five-minute review period or a ten-minute student practice period), and then gradually increase the amount of time to use the strategy. It is also helpful to assess your current teaching and determine the extent to which you give students opportunities to respond or make sure they actively respond to academic tasks. This information will help you identify the time and subject areas where you would like to improve students' engagement and learning outcomes.

Second, once you have decided the strategy and picked the class period in which you will implement it, you will then prepare your students for the new activity. Although students are generally attracted to any of the effective academic strategies, it is imperative to explain clearly to your students what the rules are and what they will be doing during the lesson before you start implementing the new approach. Third, you will implement the strategy and evaluate its impact on the performance of your students. After both you and your students are comfortable with the new strategy, see how you may be able to incorporate this strategy into another subject or class. And finally see and decide how you could incorporate another strategy that may benefit your teaching and your students' learning. Systematically implementing these new strategies over a period of time may prove to be more effective than completely reworking your teaching style and strategies all at once.

Effective Strategies for Teachers

Effective academic strategies are shown to be beneficial to both teacher and students. The most apparent outcome is the improvement of student achievement. Following are strategies teachers will find useful in achieving this goal.

Once a Day

- Implement one or multiple effective academic strategies that produce high levels of active student response.

- Closely monitor students' performance (that is, overt, observable responses) during the instruction when using the academic strategies.

- During the lesson, use the information you are gathering from your students' responses to make changes in your lesson (that is, make assessment-based instructional decisions). If students are making mistakes or appear to have some confusion, seize this teachable moment to provide additional examples or explanation so as to ensure students' understanding. Catching students' errors early saves instructional time. It takes much more time to have to go back and reteach after students have had the opportunity to practice errors.

- Arrange all the needed instructional materials to be used during the lesson before you start. Good preparation is a key for successful implementation of effective instruction.

- Keep your lesson consistent daily, using only one strategy initially to avoid confusion. Once you and your students become fluent and familiar with the activities, you may decide to adopt additional strategies. It is important to keep the routine at first so that students can follow it easily.

- Briefly remind students of their roles prior to the instruction to increase the flow of the lesson. For example, if you are using guided notes during science lessons, remind students to follow along and fill words in the blanks. If students are engaged in a response cards activity, you may wish to remind them to hold up the cards on your signal.

Once a Week

- At the beginning of each week, remind students of the rules, expectations, or directives that they should attend to when engaging in the academic strategies during the lessons.

- Reflect on your own teaching. You may wish to ask yourself the following questions: Is there any way I could have made the lesson more active for the students? Did any of the examples appear to be confusing rather than helpful for the class? What could I change next time to maximize the effects of the lesson? How are my students responding to my lesson? What progress do my students make as a result of my lesson?

- Implement progress monitoring on students' academic performance and use the evaluation results to modify your instruction. Use a simple record-keeping sheet for this purpose. Specific strategies are provided in other chapters of this handbook.

- Provide a reward system to reinforce students' academic improvements. This is the best tool to motivate students' learning.

Once a Grading Period

- Send a report to parents communicating your implementation of the teaching strategies, how your students improve academically, and how parents may be involved in using some of these strategies at home.

- Consult with more experienced teachers in implementing the active student responding strategies and ensure the quality of the implementation. Invite them to visit your classroom when these strategies are in place and obtain suggestions for improvements when applicable.

- Investigate other active student responding strategies that might be helpful to incorporate in your lessons. For which specific lessons would these strategies prove to be most effective? How would these strategies best meet your needs and those of your students?

Once a Year

- Review methods and procedures of effective academic strategies and determine which ones you may introduce into your teaching.

- Plan your lessons and prepare materials that you will need for the effective academic strategies. Students can be of great help in preparing some of the instructional materials, such as response cards, sight word index cards, and tutoring folders.

- Train your students in using the planned strategies. Ensure that students are instructed about the routines and the expectations when engaging in the academic strategies (for example, watch for cues, use the response cards appropriately).

- Share your experience in effective academic strategies with other teachers so that they may also benefit from implementing them.

Related Readings

Heward, W. L., Gardner, R., III, Cavanaugh, R. A., Courson, F. H., Grossi, T. A., & Barbetta, P. M. (1996). Everyone participates in this class: Using response cards to increase active student response. *Teaching Exceptional Children, 28*(2), 4–10.

Hirsch, E. D. (1999). *The schools we need and why we don't have them.* New York: Anchor Books.

Related Internet Resources

Good Classroom Teaching for All Kinds of Learners:
http://www.hellofriend.org/teaching/good_classroom.html

This Web site specifies ten things that teachers can do to help students learn. It also provides tips on teaching for understanding and how to use multisensory teaching techniques and active learning strategies in instruction.

Guided Notes: A System of Learning with Lecture:
http://www.studygs.net/guidednotes.htm.

Includes description of guided notes and strategies for completing and using guided notes. This Web site provides tips on content of guided notes, what to do before and after the lecture, and how to evaluate the usefulness of the guided notes.

Intervention Central: http://www.interventioncentral.org/

This Web site offers fruitful tools and resources for teachers and parents to promote positive learning environments for all students. Various practical strategies and specific activities for academic learning (as well as social behavior) are provided, including effective ways to improve reading fluency, reading comprehension, writing, and math. Assessment tools and teaching manuals are available for teachers to download as well.

CHAPTER 4

Academic Proficiency Through Response Cards

Mr. Clark

In a fourth-grade urban classroom, Mr. Clark was explaining to twenty-two of his students the concepts of fraction, numerator, and denominator. He asked the class what the denominator is in 4/5.

Tara, sitting at the back of the classroom, raised her hand and hoped that Mr. Clark would call on her. She raised her hand for every single question Mr. Clark presented, but he never called on her. Again, Mr. Clark called on another student to answer the question. Tara got angry with Mr. Clark and decided to bury her head in her arms. Mr. Clark didn't notice.

Brad, the student Mr. Clark called upon, was sitting toward the front of the room. He had a learning disability and little confidence in his ability to do the math work. He received remedial reading instruction in the special education classroom. He also frequently raised his hand and wanted to participate in the lesson. However, when—as now—he got called on and gave an incorrect answer, he told himself that he was stupid and would then refuse to continue to raise his hand and participate in the lesson.

Jimmy was a high-achieving student in the class. As Mr. Clark was delivering the instruction, Jimmy was reading the library book placed in his drawer. Jimmy rarely raised his hand to answer a question, but Mr. Clark sometimes called on him anyway—and Jimmy often answered correctly when he was called on. Jimmy felt that the class was boring and that he had better things to do than listen to Mr. Clark, so he paid no attention to the exchange with Brad.

This was Mr. Clark's fifth consecutive session on fractions; however, half the class still did not do well on the quiz. Five minutes into the lesson, he noticed that more and more students were either off task or disruptive. Mr. Clark did not understand why his method of whole-class lecture did not work for this class. With his previous students (in a suburban school), he spent only one session of lecture on basic fractions and the students acquired the concept very well, with no need for further explanation.

This chapter discusses *response cards*, an effective instructional strategy for group instruction. It is based on the work of William Heward (for example, see Heward, 1994, 2003; Heward et al., 1996).

Why Use Response Cards?

Like Mr. Clark, many classroom teachers are challenged to structure a group lesson where every student in the class is attentive and actively engaged. A common practice by many classroom teachers is to present a question to the entire class and call on a student to answer the question. Besides its simplicity and ease of implementation, this approach appeals to teachers because they assume that it is useful for all students, who will attend to the question, raise their hand to participate, and learn the concept either by answering the question when called on or by listening to other students' responses.

Although posing general questions is a common and pervasive practice in our schools, however, few if any low-achieving students benefit from it. Close observations in these classrooms frequently reveal that only a limited number of students (typically the same students) raise a hand, are called on, and actively participate in the instruction.

Response cards offer classroom teachers an alternative to this one-student-participates-at-a-time instructional method, allowing them to deliver a group lesson where every student can actively respond to, participate in, and learn the instructional materials. Response cards are appropriate for all students, but especially beneficial for passive learners who often sit and wait for others to respond, for low-achieving students who find it embarrassing to answer a question in public, and for students who frequently exhibit off-task behavior during a lesson. In addition, with response cards, teachers can easily detect each student's response and subsequently provide immediate and specific feedback on students' performance.

What Are Response Cards?

According to Heward (2003), response cards are items—cards, signs, boards, or anything else—that can be held up by all students in the class to display their responses and answers to teacher-presented questions or problems. The classroom teacher can easily adapt response cards for all subjects to increase students' participation and learning. In general, response cards can take two forms: preprinted cards and write-on blanks. We provide a brief summary of the two forms of response cards here. Readers are encouraged to consult the article by Heward and his colleagues (1996) for a more detailed description.

Preprinted response cards

Preprinted response cards either come in sets like flash cards, with one response preprinted on each card, or as single preprinted cards with multiple answers on them. When using preprinted response cards, students select the response they wish to display with their fingers or use clothespins or some other movable device. Some examples of preprinted response cards include True/False cards, colors, shapes, punctuation marks, parts of speech, math operation signs, phonemes, solar system components, and concepts such as facts versus opinions and before versus after. See Figure 4.1 for examples.

Preprinted response cards are easy for students to manipulate and can be displayed rapidly, therefore providing higher rates of student response than available with write-on response cards. In addition, preprinted cards make it easier for the teacher to grasp the students' responses and can allow the teacher to ensure initial student success with few errors by introducing a small number of cards. As students master the skills, additional cards can be added. However, preprinted response cards can have some disadvantages; students are limited to the responses printed on the cards, and the cards are limited to recognition materials only and thus inappropriate for concepts that require long or multiple answers.

FIGURE 4.1

Examples of Preprinted Response Cards

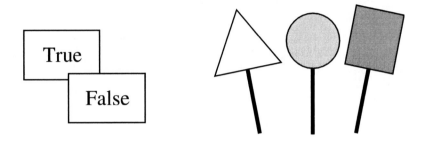

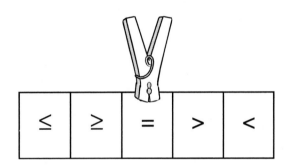

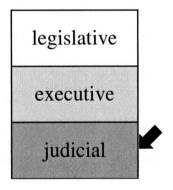

Write-on response cards

Write-on response cards are blank cards or boards students use to mark or write their answer, which can then be erased for the next question item. Teachers can purchase white laminated shower board, found in many builders' supply stores, and cut it up for write-on response cards. Some teachers may decide to simply laminate an office file folder for students to write on. Unlike preprinted response cards, write-on response cards can easily be used for curriculum contents that have many potential correct answers as well as for tasks that require the students to provide a longer answer (for example, two to three words). They have potential disadvantages of their own, however, including the potential for lower rates of student response when compared to preprinted response cards, difficulty in detecting students' responses quickly, and a relatively higher rate of response errors for the students.

Why Response Cards for Urban Learners?

As discussed in Chapter Three, professionals and researchers uniformly find that poor urban children tend to lag behind in basic skills and experience higher rates of school failure when compared to their middle-class or suburban peers (Hart & Risley, 1999). Unfortunately, urban children are also likely to be the recipients of inadequate instruction, characterized as lacking structured lessons, providing indirect questioning, offering few academic opportunities to respond, and delivering little or no feedback. When compared to their suburban peers, urban minority students were given significantly fewer opportunities to respond—and in order to receive comparable opportunities they would have to remain in school for the entire summer (Arreaga-Mayer & Greenwood, 1986). However, urban children do not need to spend more time in school; what is needed is that their school time be used more effectively. It is disconcerting to note that in many urban settings, only a fraction of the day (as little as 1 percent) is spent in direct instruction, only twenty seconds a day spent actually reading, only five seconds a day in practicing math facts (Hall, Delquadri, Greenwood, & Thurston, 1982).

Limited instruction is especially damaging for students in urban schools since, as noted, many of these children start out behind and receive far too little supplementary academic instruction outside the classroom to catch up and keep up with their nonurban peers. A better use of academic time through effective instruction is therefore an important task for urban teachers. Effective use of instructional time means that students are provided with high rates of instructional prompts or questions from the teacher, students actively engage in the instruction by making frequent academic responses, and students receive immediate and specific feedback on their performance (Heward, 1994). Response cards have been demonstrated to be an effective strategy for increasing student participation and the academic performance of urban learners across various subject areas (for example, see Gardner, Heward, & Grossi, 1994; Lambert, Cartledge, Lo, & Heward, in press). Effective education requires everyone to respond and to remain actively engaged in the learning process. Response cards provide students with an effective and enjoyable tool for learning concepts thoroughly through their own engagement in the instruction. In addition, it has been demonstrated that active student responding through response cards reduces disruptive behavior of students during lessons (Lambert et al., in press). Having to attend to instruction means less time for students to become distracted by other stimuli in the room or to disrupt others. Thus delivering effective instruction not only increases students' academic performance, it also reduces classroom problem behaviors.

Benefits of Using Response Cards

Teachers and students can derive many benefits from using response cards during instruction:

- The cards give all students constant opportunities to respond to the instructional materials.

- The practice maximizes student engagement and participation during the lessons.

- The practice produces high levels of learning trials per minute for all students.

- The practice increases student academic performance and produces more learning than the traditional one-student-at-a-time question-and-answer lecture.

- All students in the class can participate without having to wait to be called on.

- Teachers can deliver whole-class instruction effectively by keeping the lesson at a fast pace and interactive with all students.

- Teachers can evaluate individual students' responses and provide immediate and corrective feedback.

- Students can learn from watching others.

- As students engage with the instruction, they are less likely to stray off task or be disruptive and more likely to be on task.

- Low-achieving students are less likely to be intimidated or embarrassed for making an incorrect response in front of peers.

- Students are rewarded by their own success and therefore are encouraged to participate in the instruction more actively.

- Response cards are appropriate for any subject matter and curriculum concept.

- Response cards are cost effective and can easily be made or purchased at a low price.

- Most response card materials are durable and can easily be used across lessons (for example, write-on response cards, True/False cards, Yes/No cards), thereby increasing the utility of response cards.

- Students find response cards more enjoyable than raising their hands to respond.

Revisiting Mr. Clark

Tara, Brad, and Jimmy were just some examples of students who were inattentive during Mr. Clark's math lesson. Many other students in the class seriously needed to learn the concept of fractions. Feeling frustrated about his students' low math performance and high levels of off-task behavior, Mr. Clark knew that he had to try something different in his lesson. Then he remembered the in-service he'd attended about a month before on effective teaching, where the speaker talked about the use of response cards to increase students' academic performance and on-task behavior during group instruction. Mr. Clark was eager to give it a try.

Mr. Clark first created twenty-two sets of preprinted response cards, with one card printed with the word *numerator* in big letters (against a green background) and the other *denominator* (against a red background). He also wrote down twenty-five questions about fractions on a transparency for his first response cards lesson. Mr. Clark then explained to his students that they were going to do a "response card learning game" during each math lesson. After he read a question to the class, he wanted everyone to hold up their selection of the cards (that is, either "numerator" or "denominator") to display their answer. Mr. Clark modeled several learning trials and had his class practice a few. Everyone in the class did well during the training and it was time to start the lesson using response cards.

Mr. Clark was amazed by how well his students attended to the instruction and how well they participated in learning fractions, numerators, and denominators. For the entire ten minutes of the first math lesson when the response cards were used, Mr. Clark did not observe any off-task behavior from his students. Tara, Brad, and Jimmy—as well as the rest of the students (even those sitting in the back corner of the room)—were holding up their response cards with the correct answer. More important, the next weekly quiz showed that his students were getting the concept of fractions correct.

After a few sessions of adapting the preprinted response cards, Mr. Clark decided to extend the activity by having the students use write-on response cards. He passed out twenty-two laminated office file folders along with dry erase markers and paper towels. This time, he increased the difficulty of the questions so they required a bit more thinking time (for example, "What fraction of the rectangle is printed red in this picture?") than the earlier questions that had preprinted response cards (for example, "Is number 5 in the fraction 4/5 a numerator or denominator?"). All students continued to do well during the lesson as well as on the quizzes. Mr. Clark was pleased that he learned the teaching method of using response cards from the in-service workshop.

Incorporating Response Cards in Your Classroom

As mentioned earlier, response cards can easily be adapted for any subject matter and curriculum content. In addition, they can be incorporated into many parts of the lessons, from learning a new concept to practicing a newly taught skill or reviewing a previously learned task. The flexibility of response cards enables classroom teachers to adopt them with ease. The following are useful steps for incorporating response cards in your classroom.

Preparation

Developing response cards can be fairly simple and easy once you decide which skills you want your students to practice with response cards. Preparing preprinted response cards may take a bit more time than write-on response cards, as you have to choose and print out the tasks. However, creating a set of response cards such as those shown in Figure 4.1 for a class of twenty students may take only an hour, or even less. These cards can easily be created in most word processing programs, printed on color-coded paper, and then laminated. When creating response cards, you want to make sure that the cards are clear enough for you to see and easy for students to display. You may want to consider the print font and size, color, shape, and so on. When creating preprinted response cards, it is also good to consider printing the same answer (for example, "YES/TRUE") on both sides of the card to avoid confusing students. Once durable response cards are created, you can use them for several school years. So the time and effort are well spent.

Another preparation for the use of response cards is to have a list of questions on hand to help you move through the lesson at a fast pace. Most classroom teachers have already done this as they prepare for the traditional question-and-answer lecture (that is, calling on one student at a time to answer a question). Listing questions to be presented prior to the lesson is especially important and useful if preprinted response cards are used. This is because the questions will need to be phrased in such a way that the correct answer is among the responses students are given to select. For example, for TRUE or FALSE response cards, all the questions should be constructed in a true-or-false format. For write-on response cards, you may limit the responses to two or three words in order to keep a lively, fast pace. See Figure 4.2 for a list of sample questions on fractions to be presented during a five-minute write-on response cards lesson.

Student training

Student training on how to use response cards can be minimal. From our experience, students often can master the skill after a fifteen-minute training session. Two of the most important aspects of training are "when to use it" and "how to use it." Teachers need to identify cueing words to prompt students when exactly to hold up and put down their cards. Cues such as "Cards up" and "Cards down" are perfect for this purpose. Students should be instructed to hold their selected card over their head and directed toward the teacher when the cue "Cards up" is given, so that their answers can be seen, and then put down their card when they hear "Cards down." Cues are especially important for an orderly lesson and to help you maintain the pace. During the training, demonstrate how to manipulate the cards based on the cues for several trials while the students watch. Then students should be given several opportunities to practice how to use the cards. You may consider using simple questions that you believe all the students will answer correctly for the initial trials to ensure student success. More difficult questions can be added gradually. It is also important to let students know that it is OK to look at other classmates' response cards if they need to because students can benefit from watching others.

As one part of the student training, it is important to specify a few simple, brief rules for using response cards. For example: (1) listen to directions carefully, (2) use cards only when instructed, and (3) respond when asked. Each of the rules should be stated positively, taught directly through modeling and practice, and reviewed periodically where needed. Teachers may wish to take a minute to review the rules by instructing students to repeat the rules in unison prior to each response card session.

FIGURE 4.2

Sample Questions for a Write-On Response Cards Lesson

Lesson: Math (fraction)　　　　　　　　Date: 5/11/05　　　　　　　Time: 1:20–1:25 P.M.
Activity: 5-min write-on response cards (review session)

Questions to be presented:　　　　　　　　　　　　　　　　　　　　　　Answer:

1. What is the numerator in the fraction $\frac{3}{4}$?　　　　　　　　　　　　　　　　(3)

2. In a fraction, what is the number that says how many equal parts there are in the
   whole object? _____　　　　　　(denominator)

3. What fraction of the rectangle is shaded?　　　　　　　　　　　　　　　($\frac{2}{6}$)

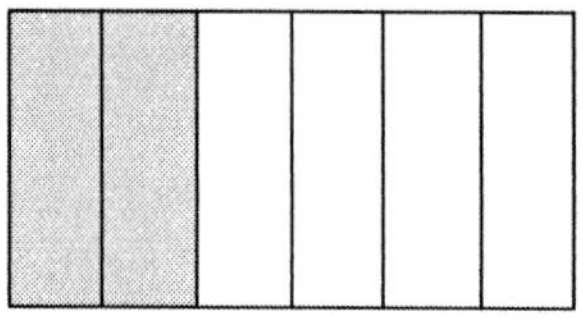

4. What fraction of the crayons is green color?　　　　　　　　　　　　　　($\frac{1}{3}$)

5. In a fraction, what is the number that says how many parts there are
   in the fraction? _____　　　　　　(numerator)

6. Which one is larger: $\frac{2}{5}$ or $\frac{1}{5}$?　　　　　　　　　　　　　　　　　　($\frac{2}{5}$)

7. Which is the numerator in the fraction $\frac{6}{9}$?　　　　　　　　　　　　　　　(6)

8. What fraction of the square is shaded?　　　　　　　　　　　　　　　　($\frac{6}{7}$)

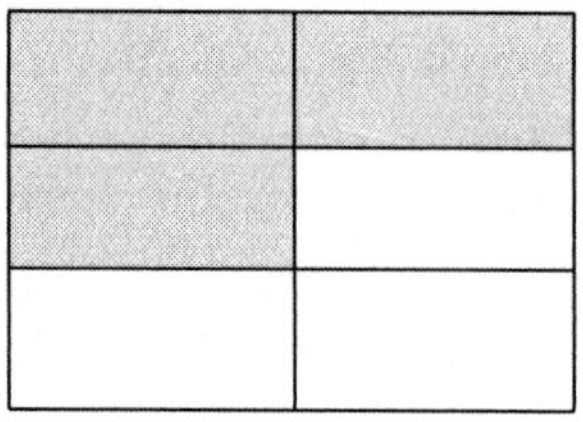

9. Which one is larger: $\frac{4}{7}$ or $\frac{6}{7}$ or $\frac{2}{7}$?　　　　　　　　　　　　　　($\frac{6}{7}$)

10. In the fraction $\frac{9}{16}$, the number 16 is called the _____.　　(denominator)

Delivering lessons with response cards

Once students are trained to use response cards, a real lesson can start. After you present a question to the entire class, allocate a moment (for example, five seconds or sufficient time for answering the problem) for the students to choose or write their answers and then cue students to hold up their cards. At this point, scan the students' answers. If all of your students provide the correct answer, deliver quick and positive feedback (for example, "Very good!" "You are all correct") and then move on to the next question. If only a few students respond incorrectly, point out the correct answer specifically (for example, "Yes, five is the denominator in four-fifths") and then move on to the next question. If more than half the class fails to provide the correct answer, explain the problem to the entire class with the correct answer (for example, "Only couple of you got this right. Let's look at it together . . . .") and then immediately repeat the same item again. It is always good to have the class practice a question that caused this kind of difficulty again after a few learning trials to make sure that students still can answer the question correctly.

Keep in mind that response cards are more effective when used to provide many chances for students to respond within a short period of time (say, five to ten minutes) than when used for few responses sporadically during the entire lesson (Heward et al., 1996). Teachers are well advised to keep the response cards lesson short yet truly interactive, with high student response rates.

Combining response cards with other effective instruction methods

Response cards can easily be combined with other instructional methods that also provide high rates of student response throughout a lesson period or a school day to maximize students' learning. For example, a fourth-grade teacher may implement total class peer tutoring (see Chapter Five) for the beginning ten minutes of a language arts class for students to practice ten frequently used sight words selected from their daily reading passages. Students then participate in paired repeated reading (see Chapter Six) to practice the reading passages for fluency building. Finally, the teacher may incorporate response cards for students to practice recall or comprehension skills based on the passages they just read or spellings of the sight words they practiced during peer tutoring. Combining various effective instructional methods not only can increase students' active participation and responses to the ongoing instruction but can also sustain student interest in learning during the lessons.

Evaluating student performance

It is important to evaluate student performance regularly. Many teachers use weekly quizzes for this purpose. While response cards allow teachers to detect each individual student's response easily during the response cards sessions, the regular test scores provide permanent records of students' performance and can be used to determine what specific skills should be strengthened through additional instruction. It is critical to keep in mind that the test scores should be carefully reviewed to identify students' skill deficits rather than solely for administrative requirements.

Effective Strategies for Teachers

Teachers who wish to incorporate response cards in their classroom may find the following tips useful:

Once a Day

- Schedule and conduct daily response cards sessions.

- Remind students of the rules for using response cards prior to each session. Provide brief modeling and practice where necessary.

- Be prepared with all the necessary materials (for example, response cards, dry erase markers, paper towels, transparencies) prior to each response cards session.

- List all the planned questions on transparencies prior to each lesson to ensure that the lesson is presented at a smooth and fast pace and that students are provided with visual prompts when working on the questions. This will also help to ensure the quality and quantity of the questions within the lessons.

- Try to present at least two questions per minute when using write-on response cards, and four questions per minute when using preprinted response cards to ensure high rates of student opportunities to respond.

- Shorten the "transition time" between questions (what researchers call the *intertrial intervals*) to maintain a lively, fast pace during each lesson.

- Establish a clear and consistent cue (for example, "Cards up"; "Cards down") for students to hold up and put down their response cards.

- Provide specific and immediate feedback on students' performance ("Yes, *walk* is a verb." "Excellent, when all of its sides are equal, it is an *equilateral* triangle.").

- Repeat the same item again if the majority of students provided an incorrect answer to that question.

- Allow students to offer additional questions for the entire class to practice using response cards.

- Reward students by providing them with a few minutes of free drawing or doodling time on the write-on response cards after a good lesson.

Once a Week

- Adopt and incorporate both preprinted and write-on response cards as appropriate to better meet students' level of performance and the lesson objectives. For example, use preprinted response cards for recognition skills during the first three lessons of the week and write-on response cards for recall questions during the last two lessons.

- Devise a simple data-keeping method to evaluate how well students learn concepts and skills through response cards. Providing weekly quizzes is a good option for this purpose.

- Evaluate students' performance to see what additional modifications (for example, types and difficulties of questions, types of response cards) are needed so that students' learning can be maximized.

- Consider whether more individualized and intense small-group instruction may be needed for certain students who constantly have difficulty with the presented concepts.

Once a Grading Period

- Send home a report regarding students' good performance during response cards at least every grading period. Both the students and parents enjoy receiving such a report.

- Check each of the response cards to make sure they are all in good shape. Replace old or damaged cards with new cards.

- Occasionally, you may select students to lead a response cards session as a reward. However, close monitoring is necessary.

Once a Year

- Plan for response cards lessons and determine the content areas or skills for which you would like to adopt response cards.

- Prepare and develop response cards materials. Make sure the cards are durable and are easy for students to manipulate.

- Train students how to use response cards during the first few lessons through modeling several learning trials and providing student practice.

- Engage students in creating response cards when appropriate.

- Plan a midyear or year-end open house for parents and other teachers to see a brief demonstration of a response cards session. Students enjoy being recognized how well they can do! Other teachers may find response cards beneficial and would also like to adopt them.

Related Internet Resources

Intervention Central Group—Response Techniques:
http://www.interventioncentral.org/htmdocs/interventions/groupresp.shtml

The Intervention Central, created by Jim Wright, is a user-friendly Web site containing many intervention ideas. It offers two group-response techniques: choral responding and response cards based on the work of William Heward.

Strategies for Effective Group Instruction:
http://education.osu.edu/wheward/PAES831.htm

This Web site contains lecture notes created by professor William Heward at The Ohio State University for a graduate course entitled "Strategies for Effective Group Instruction." This course provides many research-based, practical strategies for designing group instruction, including choral responding, response cards, guided notes, and peer tutoring. Many related articles are also provided in a list of professor Heward's publications.

CHAPTER 5

Academic Proficiency Through Peer Tutoring

Ted

Mrs. Smith just finished introducing this week's new high-frequency sight words to her second-grade students. Although she spends about thirty minutes reviewing the words each day, she is concerned that at least half to two-thirds of her twenty students will not learn to read these words fluently. These students are currently below grade level in reading and Mrs. Smith knows they will not become efficient readers until they are able to read these sight words effortlessly. She has a comprehensive reading program that includes sight words, phonics, and comprehension. She wants to concentrate her practice activities on learning high-frequency sight words as well as encouraging students to read connected text.

Mrs. Smith knows that her students need individual attention and more practice to become proficient. The size of her class and the other teaching demands prohibit her from providing the one-on-one practice needed by all her students. She also knows that her students are unlikely to learn these words on their own or to receive additional practice at home. The urgency of the situation weighs heavily on her. If these students do not make substantial progress in second grade, they may never become adequate readers. She has also begun to notice increases in behavior problems among several of her poorer readers. She suspects that these problems will steadily increase as the students continue to lose ground academically. Take Ted as an example. At midyear, Mrs. Smith administered the Slosson Reading Achievement, a sight word test, and the results indicated that Ted's sight word skills were at the first-grade level. Ted was known for his behavior problems as well. He was uncooperative, easily frustrated, and aggressive. His off-task behavior was problematic, not only affecting his academic achievement but also disrupting other students in the class.

Mrs. Smith has the same concern with learning math facts. She decided to research strategies that she could easily and efficiently incorporate into her classroom that would provide sorely needed practice in these critical skill areas. Mrs. Smith decided to use reciprocal peer tutoring for her entire class.

Why Use Peer Tutoring?

Peer tutoring is one strategy that promotes high rates of correct student response, which is critical for academic achievement, as described in Chapter Three. Peer tutoring is a proven practice that is uniformly and enthusiastically endorsed by educators, teachers, and researchers. It is clear that peer tutoring helps children learn, and it has been used successfully with various student

Suha Al-Hassan contributed this chapter.

populations across several content and academic skill areas including math, spelling, reading fluency and comprehension, sight words, social studies, and health and safety (see related reading list at the end of the chapter for these research studies).

Here are some reasons why teachers are encouraged to use peer tutoring as an instructional strategy:

- As the old saying goes, "Those who teach learn twice."

- The more students are in contact with and respond to academic materials at their instructional level, the greater the academic gains.

- Students progress best when they are working at their own pace and level.

- Peer relationships often have less rigid characteristics than teacher-student interactions in a school setting, making peer tutoring an especially effective instructional method.

- Students learn better with greater academic improvement. They also tend to enjoy school when they are learning.

What Is Peer Tutoring?

Peer tutoring is the delivery of instruction by one student to another student. Peer tutoring may occur in an informal manner, as when one student volunteers or is assigned to tutor another student. However, the strategy we are referring to in this chapter and in the research literature is an organized and systematic procedure. Peer tutoring is highly structured; it provides multiple opportunities for students to respond, and it provides praise for correct responses and immediate corrective feedback for incorrect responses. Students are trained in their roles as both tutor and tutee.

Peer tutoring may be used to teach novel skills, to practice newly taught concepts, or to practice previously taught skills that the student failed to master. In addition to basic skills, peer tutoring has been used successfully to teach concepts from content areas such as social studies or health (for example, Utley et al., 2001).

Several formats of peer tutoring can be used in the classroom. Depending on the instructional purposes, students' academic levels, or schedule availability, teachers can determine the most appropriate format to be implemented in their classrooms. The most widely used formats of peer tutoring include total class, cross-age, small-group, one-to-one, home-based, and reverse-role tutoring. Definitions, advantages, and limitations of each tutoring format have been identified by Miller, Barbetta, and Heron (1994) and are briefly described in the following sections.

Total-Class Peer Tutoring

Total-class peer tutoring involves the entire class simultaneously participating in tutoring dyads. In other words, each student in the class is paired with another student to engage in academic instruction. During each tutoring session, students alternate between tutor and tutee roles. Teachers might pair students on a random basis, according to ability levels, or by compatibility. Teachers would be wise to avoid pairing students who are likely to engage in conflicts.

Advantages

An advantage of total-class peer tutoring is that the whole class can participate in peer tutoring at the same time, each of the students getting practice on the skills that they particularly need. In practicing high-frequency sight words, for example, each child's folder contains the words that the child needs to learn, and those are the words being taught by the tutor during the activity. Since the whole class is engaged in peer tutoring simultaneously, teachers and students tend to like this format.

Disadvantages

A disadvantage of total-class peer tutoring is the amount of preparation needed to set up the program, train the students, and coordinate the materials. Once the program is put in place, however, the time invested is minimal. The resulting student progress greatly justifies the time spent.

Cross-Age Peer Tutoring

Cross-age tutoring occurs when an older or more skilled student is paired with a younger or less skilled student to deliver instruction. The role in this type is fixed. For example, a fifth-grade student tutors a second-grade student on high-frequency sight words. An age difference of two or more years usually delineates the roles. Sometimes, however, roles may be delineated more by ability than by age. A third-grade student may be assigned to tutor another third-grade student with a disability. The differences in skill levels between the tutor and tutee need not be large because both members of the dyad benefit from the experience. Cross-age tutoring can also be carried out in the form of total-class peer tutoring. For example, for a twenty-minute afternoon period three times a week, all the students in a fourth-grade class participate in delivering instruction to the students in a first-grade class.

Advantages

Cross-age tutoring has special advantages in that it often requires less training of the tutors due to their higher skill levels. It is not necessary to teach fourth-grade tutors who are at grade level, for example, the sight words for second-grade low-achieving students. Additionally, cross-age tutors often avoid the potential conflict issues that might occur among classmates.

Disadvantages

A typical problem with cross-age tutoring is scheduling. Teachers in different classes often find it difficult to arrange their respective schedules to accommodate these interactions. Although cross-age tutors may find it personally rewarding to help the less skilled students, they might not benefit academically if the material is substantially below their own academic level.

Small-Group Peer Tutoring

Within small-group tutoring, two procedural variations are possible: The sessions can be conducted with selected students who need additional practice with skills, or the whole class can participate in the small-group tutoring on a rotating basis. While the teacher works with one group, a second group participates in peer tutoring, and the remainder of the class engages in independent seatwork or other cooperative groups. Groups rotate daily (or weekly) so each group engages in each activity.

Advantages

Small-group peer tutoring is an option the teacher can use in lieu of independent seatwork. It could be scheduled during periods when the teacher is providing instruction to other small groups in the class. The advantage is that no additional class time is necessarily allocated to peer tutoring.

Disadvantages

An obvious disadvantage of this type of scheduling is that the teacher is not available to constantly monitor and provide feedback during peer tutoring. Students need to be well trained in the tutoring and behavioral expectations.

One-to-One Tutoring

One-to-one tutoring differs procedurally from other tutoring programs in the identification of participating tutors and tutees. Only selected tutees, typically students needing remedial support, participate in the one-to-one tutoring format. These students are paired with selected tutors (perhaps highly skilled peers, peers also in need of remedial work, or cross-age tutors). Members of the dyad may receive and provide tutoring in the same content area, or they can each tutor in an area where they are highly skilled.

Advantages

One-to-one tutoring can be scheduled more easily and can be limited to those with the greatest need. It also allows the teacher to provide for tutoring in a variety of subject areas.

Disadvantages

A difficulty with this system is that tutors will have to be trained individually, which may take up quite a bit of valuable teacher time.

Home-Based Tutoring

Home-based tutoring programs use parents or siblings as tutors. Many parents want to help their children's academic skill development, and research consistently shows that families can successfully instruct their child at home. This can be quite effective when the school provides guidance, sufficient training, and feedback. However, some parents may need more school-based support than others to carry out the tutoring sessions appropriately. Other parents may be too anxious or have limited time or skills.

Advantages

Home-based tutoring is an excellent way for families to become involved in the schooling of their children and to promote their children's progress. Families can tutor not only during the school year but also during vacation periods, when students are likely to lose ground.

Disadvantages

Parents or other family members need to be trained in appropriate tutoring procedures. This requires an investment of time and materials from the teacher.

Reverse-Role Tutoring

Reverse-role tutoring is where a student with disabilities acts as a tutor to a nondisabled student. This provides a unique and self-enhancing role for the student with a disability. The student with the disability is typically older than the tutee but relatively unfamiliar with interacting with others from a position of strength. Tutoring gives the student the opportunity to assist a younger student while simultaneously improving on interpersonal and academic skills. The younger student, who is not disabled, is provided with the opportunity to practice and obtain mastery with the academic material. Reverse-role tutoring is often organized outside the general classroom environment.

Advantages

In addition to building needed academic skills, an important feature of this type of tutoring is the potential boost to the student's self-image, particularly for the student with a disability. Another advantage relates to social relationships. Both members of the dyad may acquire more positive attitudes toward each other, therefore benefiting interpersonally from the one-to-one interaction in the tutoring situation.

Disadvantages

A disadvantage of this tutoring format is the demand on teacher time. Under these circumstances the teacher would have to closely monitor the activities of each tutoring pair.

Why Peer Tutoring for Urban Learners?

In poor urban classrooms, children are typically reading below grade level, often at the 20th or 30th percentile. These children begin their formal schooling with literacy skills behind those of their more affluent peers and continue to fall further behind as they move through the grades. In a class of twenty-five to thirty first graders, it would not be uncommon for two-thirds or three-fourths of those students to be reading below grade level. Considering the limited resources of urban schools, one-to-one (adult-to-student) tutoring for seventeen to twenty students in each class is not a realistic option. The issue remains, however, how to intensify the instruction and help the students make the necessary gains to become proficient learners.

Reciprocal peer tutoring appears to be one viable alternative. Since the 1980s, numerous studies have demonstrated that peer tutoring is effective in bringing about increases in basic skills such as reading, math, and spelling (for example, Greenwood, 1991). Many of these studies have been conducted in urban schools with culturally and linguistically diverse students, particularly African Americans. In addition to improvements in academic performance, some of these studies also showed that students were more likely to remain on task and engage in fewer disruptive behaviors when they participated in peer tutoring. At the end of this chapter are references for some of these studies.

Many urban children, particularly those from culturally diverse groups, come from collectivistic backgrounds, where the emphasis is on the group rather than the individual. Through their extended families and other community networks, these youngsters often have been socialized to work with and care for group members. These youngsters often enjoy working in groups or in pairs, especially if they believe that they are working toward some common goal. The peer group often is quite important to these young people, especially the males. Peer tutoring helps create a community of learning that is endorsed and supported by the peer group. Students welcome the chance to participate in this peer-based, rewarding environment that is teacher approved and leads to greater school success.

Peer tutoring activities can be extremely affirming for students, especially students who have been struggling with the learning process. Peer tutoring not only gives the students the opportunity to act as tutors, but through the charting procedures enables students to view on a daily basis the progress they are making in learning the subject matter. Students who previously saw themselves as failures, who were preoccupied with what they could not do, who had begun to explore other sources of self-esteem—perhaps antisocial ones— now begin to see themselves capable of learning and of helping others to learn. These students can begin to value the culture of the school and learn to direct their behavior accordingly.

For these and many other reasons, peer tutoring is most appropriate for and appealing to urban learners. Teachers would be well advised to structure their classrooms to allow for peer tutoring as an ongoing learning strategy.

Benefits of Peer Tutoring

Peer tutoring is not only beneficial to tutors and tutees, it also offers several benefits to teachers.

Benefits to Tutees

- Students receive immediate reinforcement and corrective feedback.
- Students receive intensive one-on-one instruction with lots of chances to respond to the material.
- Students can gain more self-confidence in their ability to learn.
- Students are more engaged and less disruptive or off task.
- Students can improve their academic performance.
- Instructional content can be individualized to meet each student's needs.
- Students with disabilities can be included with their nondisabled peers.
- Students can learn appropriate interaction skills and increase positive social interactions with peers.
- Students become excited about teaching and learning as well as the progress they are making.

Benefits to Tutors

- In many cases, tutors make even greater academic gains than tutees from teaching skills to their peers. (Again: "Those who teach learn twice.")

- Peer tutoring fosters more positive attitudes toward self and school.

- Students take ownership and leadership of learning and become more responsible for completing assignments and controlling their behavior.

- Students enjoy being tutors and therefore are motivated to help their peers.

Benefits to Teachers

- Teachers can offer individualized instruction without imposing constant demands on their own time or their financial or technological resources.

- Teachers can include students with disabilities in general education settings.

- Class learning rates improve without increased instruction time.

- Teachers can simultaneously implement lessons at different skill levels to address a greater range of learning needs in one classroom.

- Teachers can modify the materials to accommodate changes in the academic needs of students and the physical environment in the classroom.

- Class environments improve as students increase on-task behavior and decrease disruptive behaviors.

Revisiting Ted

As noted at the beginning of the chapter, Ted had poor reading skills and significant behavioral problems. Mrs. Smith's decision to incorporate peer tutoring in her classroom had a significant impact on her students. Ted was one of the students who benefited greatly from the reciprocal peer tutoring. His academic achievement and his behavior improved dramatically. Ted enjoyed the peer tutoring activity. He especially enjoyed being the tutor. During periods of peer tutoring, his off-task behavior decreased noticeably and he displayed more considerate and respectful behaviors to his peers and teachers. Ted was also observed on many occasions to make a comment such as "Come on, J. Let's go fast with the words" or "J., sit up and look at the word" to encourage and keep his partner on task. In addition, Ted was able to deliver a variety of social praise to his tutee and felt proud when he and his partner were able to read all the words correctly. When Mrs. Smith administered the Slosson Reading Achievement test at the end of the school year, after only four months of peer tutoring, Ted's reading skills registered at the second-grade level, documenting a full year's gain.

Incorporating Peer Tutoring in Your Classroom

Using an example of teaching sight words, this section provides step-by-step instructions on incorporating a total-class peer tutoring program in your classroom. The procedures and figures we describe pull from the work of Cooke, Heron, and Heward (1983) and Al-Hassan (2003). You will need to modify this format according to your needs (for example, adjusting for level of students, subject areas, and tutoring formats).

Materials

Assemble the following supplies for the tutoring project:

Folders: Manila office file folders (8.5" × 11") are appropriate for tutoring. Put the name of each tutor on the tab of a folder, and put a progress row chart resembling a path with fifty to a hundred boxes on the inside left of the folder and three envelope pockets on the inside right of the folder. Label one pocket with the word "GO" in a green circle, one pocket with the word "STOP" in a red hexagon, and the third pocket with the word "STAR."

For each tutee, make up a "star card"—a 3" × 5" colored index card with the tutee's name and two 10 × 10 square grids—and put it in the STAR pocket.

Throughout each peer tutoring session, the teacher marks the grids on the students' star cards with marker stamps to reward students for correctly carrying out the procedures and for staying on task. On the back panel of the folder there is a "smiley face" and an "X" upon which the tutor places correct (smile) and incorrect (X) responses during the testing phase. See Figure 5.1 for a sample tutoring folder. Figure 5.2 is an example of an attractive progress row chart.

Word cards: Plain 3" × 5" index cards can serve as word cards. Each index card should be printed with a word in large font on one side and the same word in small font along with a 1" × 2.5" ten-square grid for recording the testing results on the other side. See Figure 5.3 for a sample word card.

Timer: A standard digital timer or a kitchen timer is appropriate to time sections of each peer tutoring session.

Crayons: Color Splash crayons are needed for students to color in the squares on the progress charts.

Self-inking stamps or stickers: The self-inking stamps or stickers are used to mark students' star cards to reward students for staying on task and correctly carrying out the tutoring procedures.

Pretest

It is recommended that teachers administer a pretest before teaching any academic skill. In our example of teaching sight words using peer tutoring, it is essential for the teachers to use the list of sight words that they are planning to teach throughout the year and pretest the students on these words. This should take place to determine the number of high-frequency sight words in each student's repertoire and to identify the words that the students need to learn and practice. Pretest data can also be used to pair students for peer tutoring according to their ability to identify sight words.

Tutor Training

The tutor training should be conducted prior to the first day of the peer tutoring session. This phase consists of one orientation session and three training sessions, which last approximately thirty minutes each. During the

FIGURE 5.1

Sample Tutoring Folder

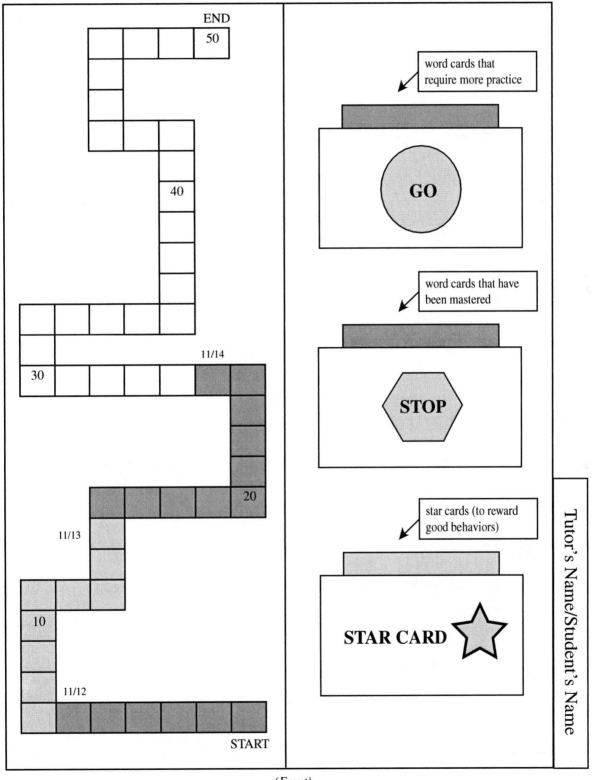

(Front)

Figure 5.1 (continued)

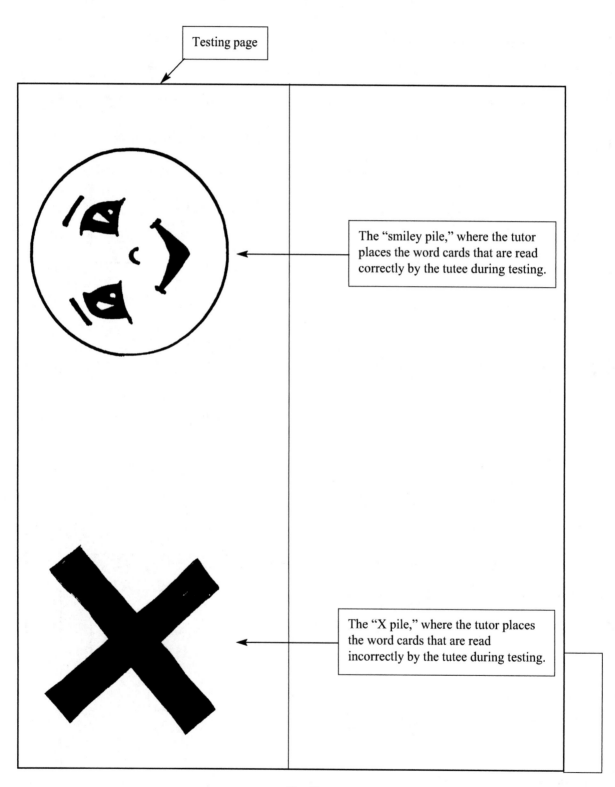

Testing page

The "smiley pile," where the tutor places the word cards that are read correctly by the tutee during testing.

The "X pile," where the tutor places the word cards that are read incorrectly by the tutee during testing.

(Back)

FIGURE 5.2

Sample Progress Row Chart

FIGURE 5.3

Sample Word Card

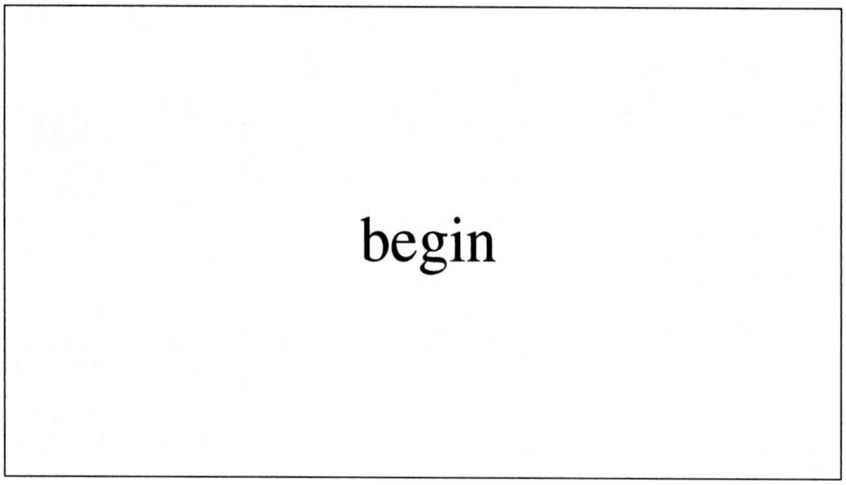

begin

(Front)

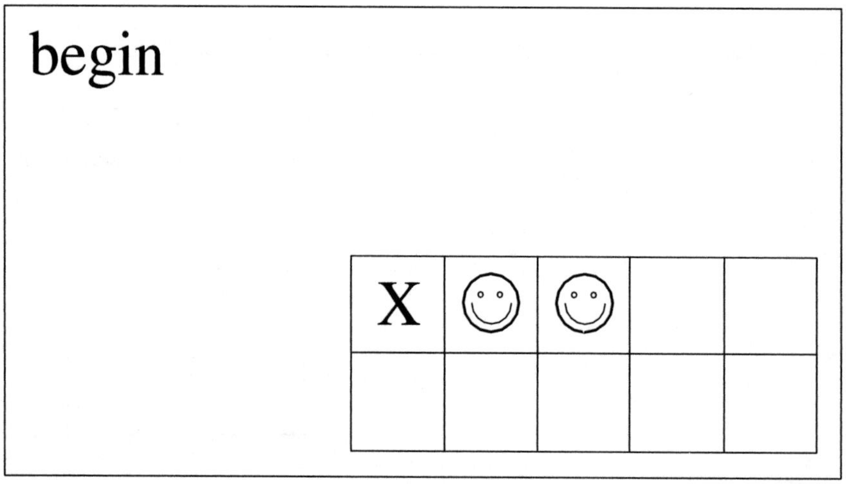

begin

X	☺	☺		

(Back)

orientation session, students should be presented with an overview of peer tutoring and be familiarized with the parts of their peer tutoring folders. Subsequent tutor training sessions should address the following topics: tutor huddle, practice, and prompting and testing. Each training session should consist of explanation, modeling, role plays, and independent practice with feedback until all the students can demonstrate the steps correctly.

Steps of Peer Tutoring

A typical peer tutoring session often takes approximately thirty to forty minutes, including tutor huddle, practice, testing, and charting.

Tutor huddle

The tutor huddle takes place at the beginning of peer tutoring sessions. Students usually engage in this activity for four to six minutes. The purpose of tutor huddle is to make sure that all the tutors have the ability to distinguish the correct responses from the incorrect responses emitted by their tutees. Tutor huddle, therefore, may not be needed for certain skills (such as math facts) in which an answer to the question is provided to the tutor on the flash card.

During a sight word peer tutoring session, students meet in small groups to practice the words that they will be teaching to their partners. (Note: Make sure that members of tutoring pairs are in different tutor huddles.) Prior to attending the tutor huddle, tutoring partners exchange their folders and each group goes to its designated area. During tutor huddle, the students display all their partners' cards to the other members of the huddle group and read the words out loud to the group. When the word is read correctly, the other group members reinforce the correct responses by saying yes. The reader then moves on to the next word card. When the response is read incorrectly, the other huddle members read the word correctly together out loud. The tutor then repeats the word correctly before moving on to the next card. This process allows the tutors to practice reading the words they will teach their partners. Students are instructed to raise their hands to ask the teacher for help only when no one in the tutor huddle knows how to read the word. Similarly, during tutoring sessions themselves, tutors raise their hands for teacher assistance if they find themselves unable to read the word.

Practice

After tutor huddle, the students move to a preassigned spot to meet their partners and begin the tutoring practice session. Practice consists of two six-minute sessions in which the actual teaching of the high-frequency words takes place. The students sit at their assigned seats, facing each other. The teacher should give each student the chance to begin tutoring. During the first six-minute practice session, the peer tutoring folder belonging to the first tutee is opened between the tutor and the tutee. The tutor removes the tutee's word cards from the "GO" pocket and presents the cards to the student one at a time with the word facing the tutee. When the tutee reads the word correctly, the tutor praises the student for correct responses by saying, "Good" or "Great," and then proceeds to the next card. When the word is read incorrectly or when three seconds elapse with no response, the tutor says, "Try again" or "Try it." When the word is read incorrectly again or takes longer than three seconds, the tutor says the correct word to the tutee. The tutee then repeats the correct response. After all the cards are presented, the tutor shuffles the cards and presents them to the tutee again. The procedure continues as many times as possible until the first six-minute period elapses. At the end of the six-minute practice, the tutoring partners reverse roles and engage in a second six-minute practice session.

Testing

After the completion of both practice sessions, the students begin the testing phase. Testing is the portion of the tutoring session where the tutees demonstrate what they have learned from the practice by reading the words correctly. After the teacher announces the first testing session, the first tutor in each pair conducts the testing with the first tutee. The tutor removes the partner's word cards from the "GO" pocket and then turns over the folder so that the assessment page (the one with a smiling face and a large "X") is displayed. Each word is presented only once to the tutee. Words are presented one at a time. The tutor does not provide any praise or corrective feedback during the testing phase. When the word is read correctly, the tutor places the card onto the smiling face on the folder. When the word is read incorrectly or when the three-second time limit elapses, the tutor then places the card onto the "X." After all the words are tested, the tutor draws a circle in the box of the grid on the back side of the cards that are on the "smiling face" pile (indicating correct), and cards that are on the "X" pile are marked with an "X" (indicating incorrect) in the grid. Once all the cards are marked, the cards and folder are set aside for the second testing session to commence. Then the tutor and tutee switch roles and follow the same procedures to conduct the second testing.

Charting

After completing both testing sessions, the tutor counts how many correct words the tutee had in that particular session and places all the cards back in the "GO" pocket to be practiced in the next session. All the cards are placed in the "STOP" pocket by the end of the week, indicating the end of practice for this particular set of words. The two students then switch their folders. Each student colors one box on the left panel charting area of the folder for each word read correctly.

Step-by-step procedures for a peer tutoring session are listed in Table 5.1.

Effective Strategies for Teachers

The following offers useful, practical strategies for planning and implementing an effective peer tutoring program in your classroom.

Once a Day

- Establish a daily peer tutoring schedule and conduct the session daily.
- Praise the students for their good behavior during tutoring sessions.
- Make sure that students are charting their daily progress.
- Set a daily reward system.

TABLE 5.1

Step-by-Step Peer Tutoring Session

Step 1. Preparation

- Teacher distributes tutoring folders to the students.
- Teacher prompts students to switch folders with partners (say, "Switch").

Step 2. Tutor Huddle (4–6 minutes)

- Teacher announces "Tutor Huddle" and sets the timer.
- Students sit with their tutor huddle members at assigned area.
- Students take out the word cards from "GO" pocket and take turns reading the words.
- Teacher circulates around the huddle groups to provide assistance and monitoring.

Step 3. Practice (12 minutes)

- Teacher prompts students to go to their tutoring area and assigns the student who will be the tutor first.
- Teacher announces "First Practice" and sets the timer for 6 minutes.
- First tutor presents the word cards, provides praise when the tutee responds correctly ("Good job"), and provides prompts when the tutee responds incorrectly ("Try again" "Say . . .").
- Teacher announces "Second Practice" and sets the timer for another 6 minutes.
- Students exchange roles for tutoring.
- Teacher circulates around the room, monitors students' behavior, and provides reinforcement or corrective feedback.

Step 4. Testing

- Teacher announces "Testing."
- First tutor conducts first testing with no prompts; places correct responses on the "smiley pile" and incorrect responses on "X"; provides praise at the end of testing.
- Second tutor conducts second testing.
- Students mark "O" for correct responses and "X" for incorrect responses on the back of the word cards.

Step 5. Charting

- Students color the number of correct responses on the charting sheet.

Step 6. Conclusion

- Teacher announces that peer tutoring has ended.
- Teacher collects students' tutoring folders.

- Monitor the students' folders before and after each peer tutoring session.
- Randomly select a few students for testing. Praise the students when they respond correctly and provide corrective feedback for incorrect responses. Encourage students to work hard and do better the following day.

Once a Week

- Pair students according to the academic level.
- Conduct a weekly pretest for the words that the students are to practice.
- Prepare a set of five to ten index cards with sight words written in black ink for each student.
- Talk to the students about the peer tutoring activity and discuss any concerns or observations.
- Invite other teachers and parents to your classroom to share with them the peer tutoring activity.

Once a Grading Period

- Evaluate the peer tutoring activity and modify the procedures as appropriate. You can do this, for example, by observing how certain students work together, the seating arrangement, the appropriateness of the peer tutoring schedule, and the adequacy of the selected skills.
- Discuss with other teachers the possibility of incorporating peer tutoring in teaching a variety of academic skills.
- Posttest the students to evaluate the words learned and the word retention skills. Include the unretained words in the future tutoring sessions for further practice.
- Identify students who may not respond favorably to peer tutoring and provide additional assistance or instruction.
- Provide tangible rewards, either to individual students or to the whole class.
- Celebrate students' success in learning the skills through peer tutoring.
- Send home a "peer tutoring report" along with the word cards so that parents are aware of the skills their child has been practicing and therefore can offer reinforcement or additional practice with their child.

Once a Year

- Choose the academic skill that you want to teach using peer tutoring, along with the tutoring format you wish to implement.
- Conduct a pretest of the chosen skill.
- Prepare the tutoring materials (including folders, index cards, progress sheets, and additional testing worksheets). Teachers can make good use of assistance from parents and students in this effort.
- Train the students to carry out a peer tutoring activity.

- Communicate with parents and discuss the students' progress. Involve parents or siblings in home-based tutoring during summers either on novel skills or the skills students have been practicing over the school year.

Related Internet Resources

Classwide Peer Tutoring-Learning Management System (CWPT-LMS):
http://www.lsi.ku.edu/jgprojects/cwptlms/html2002/index.htm

> CWPT-LMS, developed by Charles Greenwood and Mary Abbott, is a system of classwide peer tutoring programs with computer software supports to help teachers and practitioners implement the program effectively. This Web site provides the CWPT-LMS online training module as well as many materials for developing a CWPT.

Juniper Gardens Children's Project: http://www.jgcp.ku.edu/Site_Map.htm

> The Classwide Peer Tutoring program (CWPT) was first developed by researchers at the Juniper Gardens Children's Project to improve academic achievements of children from urban, low-income families. Their long-standing research studies show that classwide peer tutoring is effective for a wide range of student populations including impoverished children.

Peer-Assisted Learning Strategies (PALS):
http://kc.vanderbilt.edu/kennedy/pals/index.html

> PALS is a peer-mediated program developed to help teachers accommodate diverse learners in learning reading and math. PALS is a version of classwide peer tutoring in which children help each other in learning specific skills. This Web site provides information regarding the rationale, procedures, and outcomes of the PALS. It also includes demonstration videos.

CHAPTER 6

Oral Reading Fluency Through Repeated Reading

Nelson

Mrs. Anderson begins the history lesson by requesting that the class open their books to page sixty-two, and she asks Nelson to begin reading at the top of the page. "Ch- . . . Ch- . . . Chap- . . . Chap—ter Four: Th- . . . The . . . Az- . . . Azte . . . Aztec . . . Emper . . . Empi . . . Empire," Nelson stammers his way through the opening line. Other students squirm impatiently as Nelson struggles to complete a paragraph of text. Even Mrs. Anderson (who is quite patient with her students) can hardly maintain attention through the long, disconnected oral reading. Mrs. Anderson wonders how any of her students, Nelson included, could possibly retain any meaning from the passage when it takes nearly five minutes to complete just one paragraph. She also notices the embarrassment on Nelson's face when the other students sigh loudly and supply words when their impatience gets the better of them.

Mrs. Anderson recognizes that requests for students to read aloud in class are usually met with frustration, resistance, and even anger. She has raised this concern with other teachers, who attribute her fifth-grade students' reluctance to growing pains or shyness. However, Mrs. Anderson knows that this reading problem goes deeper than that. Even in one-on-one reading situations, at least half of her students read so slowly that it is nearly impossible to make sense of the passage. Mrs. Anderson dutifully checked her class's reading achievement scores for potential clues to figure out why her students have such difficulty. She found them generally below grade level in reading and she suspected that spending long periods on word attack skills would not appreciably increase reading fluency.

Mrs. Anderson accessed the National Reading Panel's Web site, looking for information regarding the component skills involved in reading. There she found information on oral reading fluency, the missing ingredient in her comprehensive reading program. Mrs. Anderson and other teachers at her school have emphasized mainly sight words and comprehension in their reading programs. Somehow oral reading fluency has been forgotten. Many teachers assumed that with the prerequisite skills in place, most students would simply become more fluent with time and practice. However, Mrs. Anderson now realizes that it is time to address this deficiency directly. She decides to build a repeated reading program into her existing curriculum.

Why Use Repeated Reading?

Oral reading fluency is developed on two levels: speed and accuracy. The rationale behind repeated readings is based on the automatic information processing

Amanda Yurick contributed this chapter.

theory first described by LaBerge and Samuels in 1974. The concept is simple. When students can read fluently (with speed and accuracy), that is, with automatic decoding of text, their attention can become more focused on extracting meaning from the passage. Teachers can do two things to help students develop automatic reading skills. First, students should be instructed in strategies that will help them decode unfamiliar words. Second, the teacher can make fluency-building practice a part of daily classroom activities. Practicing repeated reading can be a fun, motivating activity for students. It is also a great way to engage stubborn readers and help them progress relatively quickly.

Here are some other reasons to use repeated reading:

- Students get lots of engaged reading practice, which may be necessary to increase oral reading fluency.

- Students can work in pairs, which promotes social skills and cooperation. This model also allows the teacher more freedom to monitor and manage many students at once.

- "Nothing succeeds like success." Students monitor their own performance and create visual depictions of their daily progress.

- Students—even those who are usually the most reluctant readers—report enjoying repeated reading practice.

- Student graphs enable the teacher to make instructional decisions at a glance and can be motivating to the learner.

- Repeated reading is a low-cost, low-tech, easily implemented strategy that does not take a lot of class time to produce results.

What Is Repeated Reading?

Repeated reading is a fluency-building strategy that consists of rereading a short, meaningful passage several times (Samuels, 1979). The students all read and reread the selected passage until they can achieve a preset fluency criterion, which is based in part on number of words read per minute. Then the process is repeated with a new passage.

The fluency criterion can be framed in different ways. Depending on the needs of the students and the type of repeated reading activity chosen, the teacher may decide to set the criterion as an oral reading rate standard, a rate plus accuracy standard, or a requisite number of repetitions standard. For example, after selecting a passage of text, one teacher may determine that a given class of fifth-grade students needs to read the passage at least 145 correct words per minute (CWPM). However, another teacher may select a passage and set the fluency requirement at five whole reading repetitions before moving on. According to the criteria for the Dynamic Indicators of Basic Early Literacy (DIBELS; Good & Kaminski, 2002), the following fluency goals are recommended:

First grade: 40 CWPM

Second grade: 90 CWPM

Third grade: 110 CWPM

These goals (or benchmarks) are minimum standards a student should achieve by the end of a certain grade level for not falling behind the following year. Based on our work, we have found that even students who were two to three years behind their grade level on reading could reach the suggested criterion shortly after they began regularly participating in repeated readings.

Repeated reading is an adaptable strategy for many types of classrooms, different ages of readers, and many types of texts. It can be used in a second-grade classroom with students reading about Martin Luther King Jr., or in a fifth-grade special education classroom with students reading fiction. The repeated reading procedures are also appropriate for high school or even post–high school readers to increase oral reading fluency. In addition, students of all ages find this activity highly engaging and motivating. The possibilities are limitless because reading practice is beneficial in any subject matter at any age!

According to classroom needs, repeated reading can be built into an existing reading program, or it can even be built into lessons for other subject matter. The following list, although not exhaustive, serves as an orientation to the flexibility of the technique. With a little creativity, any teacher can set up fluency instruction in any type of classroom!

Assisted and unassisted

The *assisted* repeated reading uses a tape recording or oral guide (teacher reads aloud) for students to follow. For example, the teacher reads a selected passage aloud and then asks for students to read the passage. One advantage is that this approach allows the teacher to control the pace of reading and also to monitor for appropriate tone and inflection. Careful monitoring of students' reading behavior is especially critical when a tape recording is used so that students do not practice errors that go undetected by the teacher. The *unassisted* format promotes independent reading by assigning a passage for repeated reading to be done silently. In this case, students are simply assigned a passage of text to be read silently several times. This activity should conclude with an oral reading for evaluation. Since the unassisted format is carried out independently by the students, we suggest that it be used only for advanced students who have demonstrated good reading behavior. Furthermore, this format is most appropriate for practicing fairly familiar passages to prevent students from practicing errors if monitoring from the teacher is unavailable.

Direct instruction

This format employs a recitation approach with basal literature. The teacher reads the story aloud to the class, and the group engages in a group comprehension activity. Echo or choral reading is also used in the direct instruction approach. A typical direct instruction repeated reading activity generally includes the recitation of a basal series text by the teacher, followed by students reading orally after the teacher when directed to do so. Finally, the teacher would ask students to chorally respond to comprehension prompts outlined in the basal series.

Centers

Many elementary classrooms already have reading centers established. In this case, the teacher can provide books and tape recorders and tapes of the stories at the center if the assisted strategy is preferred. If unassisted reading is preferred, students may practice reading and tape-record themselves for immediate feedback. The centers can be structured to provide for a timing center if the fluency criterion includes a speed and accuracy component. Thus reading centers can incorporate repeated readings, a recording and timing center, followed by a graphing or public posting center.

Small-group instruction

This approach permits for more individualized attention. Teachers can group students either with a variety of ability levels or similar ability levels in reading and practice activities such as those described in the direct instruction approach.

Paired and peer-mediated repeated reading

Students are paired together and alternate reading to one another. The alternations can be divided by number of repetitions or by paragraphs in the story. This approach also lends itself to a tutor/tutee relationship and provides maximum practice and feedback for readers. In this format, the teacher first decides to evaluate fluency, either by number of reading repetitions or by speed and accuracy. Next, the teacher pairs two students as reading partners. Pairing can be done by similar reading abilities or by cross-age or differing ability formats. Finally, students are given a period of time (for speed and accuracy work) or a requisite number of total repetitions (for repetition work) and begin reading to one another, alternating turns by paragraphs. Detailed steps for a peer-mediated repeated reading program are provided later in this chapter.

Using this format in repeated reading work offers several advantages. First, the teacher is not instrumental in the delivery of content and can therefore attend to students' needs more immediately and individually. Also, this format promotes positive student interactions. Students become allies in reading strategies and work together to achieve more fluent reading. Additionally, this format provides the most active reading engagement for each student. Students are not required to sit for long periods waiting for their turn. During paragraphs in which one partner is listening while the other reads, the listening student can be responsible for evaluating the speaker's reading and providing corrective feedback where needed.

Building Oral Reading Fluency in Urban Learners

According to the National Assessment of Educational Progress Nation's Report Card for the year 2002, 45 percent of fourth-grade students living in an urban setting read at the "Below Basic" level (Grigg, Daane, Jin, & Campbell, 2003). Additionally, 54 percent of students who are eligible for the free and reduced-price lunch program and 60 percent of African American fourth-grade children read at the "Below Basic" level. Though many reading scores are improving (for example, 70 percent of African American fourth graders in 1994 scored at "Below Basic" compared to 60 percent in 2002), the implications for these findings are especially relevant to inner-city populations. Struggling urban learners disproportionately are children of color and inner-city residents from low socioeconomic backgrounds. These factors need to be taken into consideration when designing a comprehensive reading program for urban learners.

To combat the reading failure of urban youth, it is important to provide instruction that will address the needs of the students and be most effective for their learning styles. In their review of the existing scientific literature, the National Reading Panel (2000) found instruction that used repeated readings consistently showed gains in word recognition, fluency, and comprehension for students included in these studies. Similarly, Yurick, Robinson, Cartledge, Lo, and Evans, (2004) conducted peer-mediated repeated readings with eight fifth-grade urban students for a five-month period and obtained an average of four months' gain in word knowledge and nine months' gain in comprehension as measured on standardized reading tests. Robinson (2004) and Staubitz, Cartledge, Yurick, and Lo (2004) replicated Yurick et al.'s findings with fourth-grade general education students and intermediate-aged students with emotional and behavioral disorders. These studies provide convincing evidence of the beneficial effects of repeated readings on the reading performance of urban learners.

These findings also support the position taken by Williams and Newcombe (1994), who advise, "Urban students will benefit from school environments in which they can learn from their mistakes, are effortful in their learning, and fully engage themselves" (p. 76). Effortful and engaged learning needs to be an aim when choosing instructional methods for critical academic skills, especially those needing remediation. To master these skills, students need good instruction and plenty of practice. The type of repetitive practice accepted by athletes and musicians can be successfully applied to reading. Practice can facilitate mastery in reading just as it does in other areas and can be the foundation for promoting generalization of the skill to other passages (O'Shea & O'Shea, 1988).

The benefits of high rates of practice and the correlation between practice and mastery would hardly be argued by well-intentioned educators. However, fluency training is a neglected aspect of reading instruction in too many classrooms and is still often referred to as the "forgotten goal." Many classroom teachers tend to overly emphasize building reading comprehension without incorporating the fluency piece into the reading curriculum. In these classrooms, teachers hope that fluency will develop as a natural result of lessons. Unfortunately, this is rarely happening in urban classrooms. Research has suggested that fluency is not simply an end result, it is an important gateway to reading comprehension (National Institute of Child Health and Human Development, 2000a). It is becoming apparent that fluency is something that needs to be trained for and not something that will happen automatically.

Benefits of Repeated Reading

Both teachers and students derive a number of benefits from a repeated reading program:

- It promotes mastery learning, which is more likely to sustain itself over time.

- It allows students to monitor, graph, record, and evaluate their own performances. This lets them see their own progress, and it can alert the teacher if the trend turns downward.

- It provides intensive fluency instruction and maximizes student engagement.

- It sets up the students for success, thereby increasing the likelihood that they will become more confident in their reading ability.

- It lets students work at their own pace. Some students will reach the criterion in three readings, others will take more repetitions, but every student will progress.

- It promotes eagerness to achieve and positive reading attitudes in even the most reluctant readers.

- It promotes student independence in reading.

- It can be structured to fit most any classroom.

- It is low-tech and inexpensive in terms of teacher time and money.

- It maximizes student on-task time. There is no downtime during the procedure.

- It is an efficient instructional tool that produces noticeable results in a short period of time.

In addition, easy-to-implement reinforcement procedures can be added. Small rewards can be a large incentive for students to improve reading. Once students learn the procedure, they can practice on the school bus or at home with friends or family. They often find that they enjoy taking responsibility for their own reading achievement and may demonstrate that leadership behavior in other academic areas. Problem behaviors are rare among students engaged in repeated reading, and it can thus be an effective strategy for chronically disruptive students.

The school has no required series of books to buy. Repeated reading can be used with any type of text, fiction, nonfiction, content material, or enjoyment material. Levels of reading materials can be adjusted according to student needs, thereby accommodating even the most level-diverse classroom.

Best of all, students improve academically, and they love it!

Besides all these benefits, peer-mediated repeated readings have many other advantages unique to that approach:

- Students can be taught to tutor each other, reducing the need for teacher-directed instruction.

- Students receive immediate and precise feedback from their trained partners.

- Students have many opportunities to practice and improve social skills and peer interactions.

- Students are taught critical analysis skills in order to correct their partners. This attention to detail can foster more accurate reading and improve self-correction rates when they are reading for themselves.

- Students learn good listening behavior, which is a useful skill in other academic areas.

- Teachers have more freedom to monitor students and direct more focused attention to individual students.

Revisiting Nelson

Nelson's slow, laborious oral reading prompted Mrs. Anderson to think about how to increase her students' oral reading fluency. Since she had so many slow readers, she decided to do total-class peer-mediated repeated reading. After three twenty-minute sessions of material preparation and student training, her class was off and running. The students eagerly anticipated their reading time and even complained that it was too brief! Mrs. Anderson had built a reward system into the procedure to reinforce students who met the fluency criterion, yet she found that the daily graphing was actually rewarding enough for many students. Mrs. Anderson observed some very positive changes in her fifth graders. Students took their responsibilities as peer reading tutors very seriously and worked hard to correct, praise, and push each other on to success. Though skeptical at first, she found that her students graphed their scores honestly and handled the material and tape recorder very responsibly. Mrs. Anderson checked her students' graphs and tapes each week and could easily and efficiently direct her attention to those who needed it. Since almost all her readers were quite slow, she started the pairs on reading material well below their reading level. This ensured immediate and quick success to build student confidence. After three months of using this strategy three times per week, Nelson had moved through grade levels three, four, and five. He finished the year working on fluency in a sixth-grade text. Nelson's parents, school administrators, and Mrs. Anderson all observed Nelson's oral reading with pride because Nelson was now a more confident, accurate, and fluent oral reader.

Incorporating Repeated Reading in Your Classroom

Repeated reading is an adaptable fluency-building strategy. There are many ways to modify the procedures to fit a variety of models (assisted and unassisted, direct instruction, centers, small-group, and paired repeated reading). The following sections of this chapter will serve as a guide for setting up total-class peer-mediated repeated reading. The examples given will be based on a class of fifth graders reading one to two levels below grade. However, this strategy can be modified and applied to any class from first grade to post–high school readers.

Materials

The class will need the following simple supplies:

Folders: Manila file folders work well for repeated reading. However, any type of 9″ × 12″ folder could be used. Folders could be marked with a red or blue sticker to help students determine who will begin reading first each day. Several items (which can be created using a word processing program) should be inside the student folder at all times:

1. *Graphing sheet.* A simple graphing sheet on which students can record daily performance should be included in the folder. The scale of the X-axis should reflect the anticipated number of sessions. The Y-axis should reflect the criterion number of words per minute. The intervals should be large enough to plot between but small enough to detect

changes. Intervals of 20 should be sufficient if the criterion is set between 120 and 160 correct words per minute. See Figure 6.1 for an example of a graph.

2. *Listener log.* This basic table is a place for students to record their partner's reading errors during the repeated reading practice. Students are responsible for stopping and correcting their partner when a mistake is made. The words that were read incorrectly by the partner are then recorded on the listener log. This log provides teachers with information on the words each student misread and could be used for additional instruction where appropriate. For example, the teacher may include the misread words in the students' word bank for a peer tutoring sight word program. If a photocopy of the passage (rather than the actual book) is used, teachers may instruct the listener to underline the misread words on the photocopy while the partner is reading. The listener log can then be filled out after the ten-minute repeated reading ends. This will increase the time each student actually reads during the repeated reading without taking time for the partner to write down the misread words. See Figure 6.2 for a sample listener log.

3. *Good listener card.* Part of the reinforcement component of repeated reading involves observing students for good *listening* behavior. Since active listening and error correction are important parts of the strategy, students are expected to be attentive and engaged even when they are not the reader. This card can be made out of a regular index card and is meant to display an accumulation of stickers rewarded when the student is observed demonstrating good listening behavior (following along in the text and accurately carrying out the error-correction procedures). Teachers may choose to provide small tangible rewards when a student achieves a requisite number of stickers.

4. *Reading correction procedure.* A specified correction procedure of three basic steps should be pasted to the inside of the folder. This procedure needs to be visible to the student during the repeated reading practice. When the reader makes a mistake, the listener applies the correction procedure and records the misread word on the listener log. This written list of error correction procedures is especially important for students' initial repeated reading practice as a visual prompt. As students gain proficiency in following the correction procedure, the prompting steps will become less necessary. Figure 6.3 shows an example of a repeated reading folder containing a graphing sheet, a good listener card, and a prompt for error correction procedures.

5. *Brief instructional prompts.* This is optional, but it may be useful to slip some basic reminders into the student folders, especially in the beginning, when students are not yet totally comfortable with the procedure. Reading instructions might include a list of numbered steps such as these: (1) fill out name, date, and book title on the listener log, (2) display correction procedure and good listener card, (3) open book to assigned passage and count paragraphs, (4) set the timer for ten minutes, and (5) start the timer and get reading! If students are tape-recording themselves at the conclusion of the practice period, operating instructions for the tape recorder and graphing prompts may be helpful. An example of repeated reading instructional prompts is provided in Figure 6.4.

FIGURE 6.1

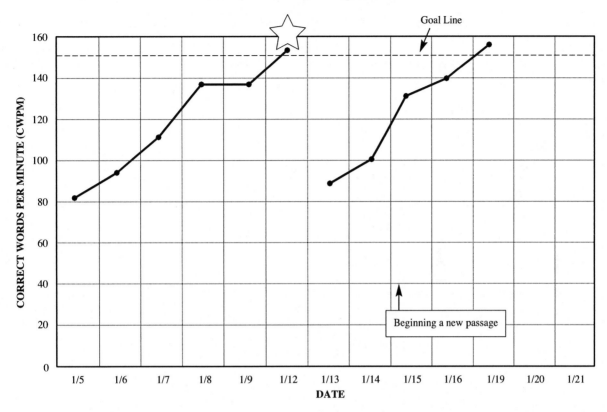

Sample Graphing Sheet

Pencils: Students will need pencils to record partner errors in the listener log and also to graph their own daily score. They should not use a pen for either of these items.

Timer: A simple kitchen countdown timer can be purchased at minimal cost ($5–$10). If possible, provide each student pair with their own timer to operate so they can briefly pause the timer when necessary. This will allow the remaining students to continue the exercise without interruption when an unpredictable event occurs (for example, a student comes in late, needs to use the restroom, or stops to ask the teacher a question). If cost does not permit, one timer can be used for the entire classroom.

Books: As mentioned previously, almost any type of book can be used with repeated reading. Here are some considerations when choosing books:

- It is most advantageous in terms of progress evaluation to use a series of books at a consistent level, such as Sunshine books, Scholastic books, or pair-it books.

- Begin with material at least one level below the student's current reading level, which is not always the same as the student's grade level. Make sure students can achieve a minimum of 95 percent accuracy on this reading level (that is, the student makes fewer than five errors for each 100 words read). Improvements in oral reading fluency are greatest when students are not struggling with decoding skill.

- Choose books that are of high interest to students.

FIGURE 6.2

Sample Listener Log

Listener Log

Reader: __Mary__   Listener: __Nelson__

Book title: __Helen Keller__

Date	Page #	Misread word	Did I correct it?
1/7/06	32	delicious	✓
	32	sausage	✓
	32	familiar	✓
	32	horror	✓
	33	stumbling	✓
	33	grabbing	✓
1/8/06	33	institute	✓

- Select passages from within those books that have an appropriate number of words, depending on the fluency criterion. For example, if the CWPM criterion is 140, the passage should be between 150 and 200 words. Do not choose passages any more than 75 words over the criterion because that will reduce the number of possible repetitions in a practice session and increase the number of sessions necessary to reach the goal. Also avoid using passages shorter than the designated criterion because oral reading fluency may not show up precisely when timed for one minute (that is, during evaluation) if the student has to reread from the beginning of the passage.

- Whenever possible, reduce the amount of picture content on the pages. Students should be as focused on text as much as possible during fluency training, and picture cues can be distracting. Also, pictures reduce the amount of text that can appear on a page, necessitating more page turns, which is a fluency blocker.

Student Training

Total-class training for repeated reading should be conducted over four sessions. The duration of the training sessions will vary from approximately twenty-five to

FIGURE 6.3

Sample Repeated Reading Folder

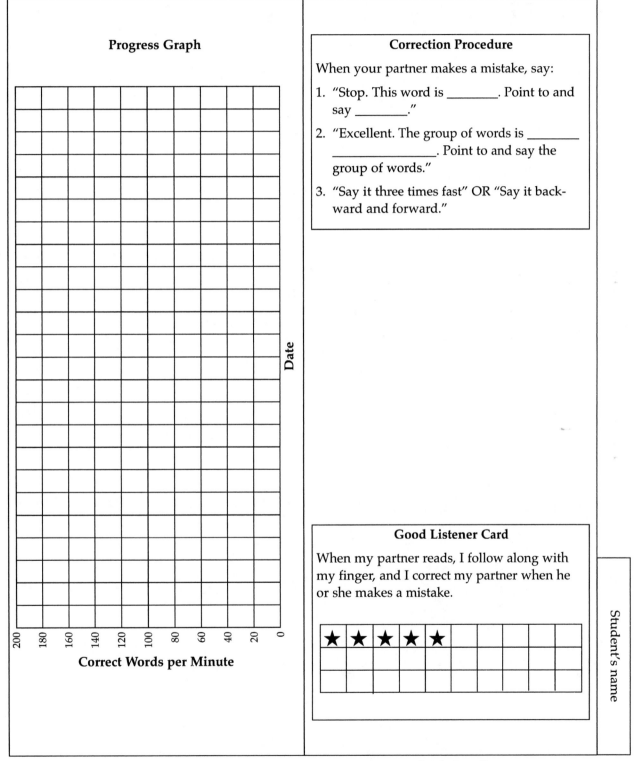

Progress Graph

Date

Correct Words per Minute

200 180 160 140 120 100 80 60 40 20 0

Correction Procedure

When your partner makes a mistake, say:

1. "Stop. This word is _____. Point to and say _____."

2. "Excellent. The group of words is _____ _____. Point to and say the group of words."

3. "Say it three times fast" OR "Say it backward and forward."

Good Listener Card

When my partner reads, I follow along with my finger, and I correct my partner when he or she makes a mistake.

★ ★ ★ ★ ★

Student's name

(Left Panel)   *(Right Panel)*

FIGURE 6.4

Sample Instructional Prompts

TIME FOR REPEATED READING

1. Fill out name, date, and book title on the listener log.

2. Display correction procedure and good listener card.

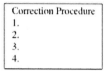

3. Open book to assigned passage and count paragraphs (if odd number, take consecutive turns; if even number, take turns starting each repetition).

4. Set the timer for ten minutes.

5. Start the timer and get reading!

6. Complete one-minute timing and graphing.

forty minutes. First, pair comparable readers together. Next, give the students reading folders, familiarize them with the contents, and pass out books. Finally, tell the class that over the next couple of days, they will be learning how to do a new reading activity. Briefly explain the concept and then begin training. The general framework for training is as follows: good listener training, good reader training, student demonstration, and timing and graphing training. Since all students will be acting as both reader and listener during repeated reading, the entire group can be trained at the same time. Tables 6.1 through 6.4 provide information on the four-day training, which will serve as a guide for teachers to conduct the training activities.

Steps of Repeated Reading

Here are the main points to consider for this activity.

Before you begin: Prior to the first repeated reading session, all student materials should be compiled and ready to use (see "Materials" section for more information). If students will be using their own timers and tape recorders, these items should be tested for low batteries or other problems. It is recommended to decide in advance what goal you will set for students and make them aware of the goal. Set a reasonable goal for students according to their grade level and reading ability (refer to the discussion at the beginning of this chapter). Some students may reach fluency rather quickly, so it is important for the teacher to have the next passage selected. Texts should increase in difficulty each time fluency is reached. Beginning at least one grade level below the students' actual reading levels and then moving to the next grade level text is recommended. For example, the fifth-grade readers begin with a text on a fourth-grade level. Once fluency is reached (for example, 145 CWPM), the students then practice on a fifth-grade text. Once fluency is again reached, the students then begin practice on a sixth-grade text, and so forth. If desired, the student may read more than one passage at each grade level before moving to the next grade level. It is important, however, that the student move to increasingly difficult material as rapidly as possible. This challenges the student and promotes reading skill.

The teacher should have several levels of passages selected and ready for students to begin reading. Finally, in the preparation stage, the teacher should have a clear plan regarding how and when rewards will be delivered to students. The teacher can determine the days of good listener card drawings ahead of time. However, these days should be a surprise to students, to encourage them to work hard every day.

Student pairings: When pairing the students for total-class repeated reading, it is most common to pair students according to their reading level. Teachers can use the pretest information on the student's reading fluency (CWPM) for this decision. Frequent regrouping may be necessary as students progress over time. It is not unusual that a student's partner is absent or one student in a pair reaches fluency while the other does not. When a student absence occurs, the teacher may try to find another student in the class (on the same level) and pair them together. When students in a pair reach fluency at different times, it is usually possible to find another pair that has also reached fluency at different times. In this case, student pairs can be swapped. It is perfectly OK to change student pairs frequently, as long as the pairs are reading at the same level. If rematching

TABLE 6.1

Activities for Day 1 Training: Good Listening Behavior

Minutes	Activity	Teacher behavior	Student behavior
5	Modeling	Teacher and assistant model the procedure briefly. Select a short passage to demonstrate all aspects of repeated reading (reader alternation, following along, corrections, filling in listener log).	Observe
5	Discussion	Ask students what behaviors they see when it's the teacher's turn to be a good listener. Model the procedure again. Write student observations on the chalkboard.	Expected responses: taking turns, following the text with finger, helping partner correct mistakes, and writing mistakes down on the listener log.
5	Clarification	Expand good listener behaviors on the chalkboard; discuss each of the three good listener behaviors individually.	Respond to questions, follow along in text with oral reading, locate the correction procedure in the student folder.
		(1) *Alternating turns at the beginning of each paragraph:* Explain that a paragraph begins with the indentation of a sentence. Ask each student to provide the first word of a new paragraph in a text to ensure understanding.	
		(2) *Following along with finger:* Tell the students that this is a way to know where their partner is reading so that they can correct their partners. Practice by reading orally to the students and asking them to follow with their fingers. Alter reading speed to check for accurate following.	
		(3) *Following correction procedures when the partner makes a mistake and writing mistakes down in the listener log:* Direct students to the correction procedure pasted inside the folders. Model the use of the correction procedure and write the incorrect word on the listener log sheet.	
10	Student practice	Direct this activity by selecting a student in each pair to begin reading. Provide opportunity for students to practice each of the good listener behaviors. For example, tell students that you are looking for the good listening behavior of taking turns. Tell students to begin reading, and when students are observed to take turns correctly, place a sticker on the good listener card. Allow enough turns to provide an opportunity for each student to receive a sticker.	Listen to teacher instructions, practice specific good listening behaviors.

Minutes	Activity	Teacher behavior	Student behavior
5	Reward procedure and questions	Explain the reward system: tell students that the stickers you have been placing on their cards will help them work toward earning prizes for being good listeners. The reinforcement procedure can vary according to specific classroom needs. For example, the group-oriented contingency described in Chapter Nine may fit into the repeated reading reward system. Take student questions regarding any confusion with good listener behaviors. Always include in your response (and end with) a demonstration of the desired behavior.	Listen, ask specific questions.
10	Student practice	Direct students to practice reading a passage together. Observe each pair. Deliver specific praise and corrective feedback ("Yes! You followed the correction procedure exactly! I like the way you remembered to write the mistake in the listener log." Or, "You are not following along in the text. Show me how you follow along.")	Practice reading with partners, demonstrate all components of good listening behavior.

TABLE 6.2

Activities for Day 2 Training: Good Reading Behavior

Minutes	Activity	Teacher behavior	Student behavior
5	Review	Ask students to recall the component behaviors of good listening (taking turns, following text with finger, correcting partner's mistakes, writing mistakes in the listener log). Write the responses on the board. Ask students to demonstrate each behavior.	Recall good listening behavior, demonstrate good listening behaviors.
5	Modeling	Teacher and assistant model the procedure briefly. Select a short passage to demonstrate all aspects of repeated reading (reader alternation, following along, corrections, filling in listener log).	Observe.
5	Discussion	Ask students what behaviors they see when it's the teacher's turn to be a good reader. Model the procedure again. Write student observations on the chalkboard.	Expected responses: taking turns, reading loud enough for partner to hear, attempting to sound out unknown words.
5	Clarification	Expand good reading behaviors on the chalkboard; discuss each of the three good reading behaviors individually.	Respond to questions, observe.

Table 6.2 (continued)

Activities for Day 2 Training: Good Reading Behavior

Minutes	Activity	Teacher behavior	Student behavior
		(1) *Alternating turns at the beginning of each paragraph:* Have each student provide the first word of a new paragraph in a text to make sure they understand how to recognize paragraphs.	
		(2) *Reading loudly and clearly enough:* Tell the students that they have to read loudly and clearly enough for their partner to hear with no whispering or yelling. Allow each student to read a short sentence for practice.	
		(3) *Sounding out unknown words:* Tell students that they should always try to sound out unknown words, and not wait for their partner to tell them the word.	
10	Student practice	Select a student in each pair to begin reading. Allow students to practice each of the good reading behaviors. For example, tell the readers that you are looking for the good reading behavior of reading loudly and clearly enough. When students are observed reading audibly, place a sticker on the good listener cards.	Listen to teacher instructions, practice specific good reading behaviors.

TABLE 6.3

Activities for Day 3 Training: Demonstration of Repeated Reading Activity

Minutes	Activity	Teacher behavior	Student behavior
5	Review	Ask students to recall the component behaviors of good listening (taking turns, following text with finger, correcting partner's mistakes, writing mistakes in the listener log) and good reading (taking turns, reading audibly, attempting unknown words). Write the responses on the board. Ask students to demonstrate each of these behaviors.	Recall and demonstrate good listening and reading behaviors.
5	Modeling	Teacher and assistant model the procedure briefly. Select a short passage in order to demonstrate all aspects of repeated reading (alternating readers, following along, making corrections, filling in listener log)	Observe.

Minutes	Activity	Teacher behavior	Student behavior
5	Modeling examples and counterexamples	Tell the students that you will be playing a short game. Tell them that when you and your partner model repeated reading, there may be some aspects of the procedure that are right and some that are wrong. Tell them to raise their hands when they see something that is being done incorrectly. Provide a sticker for each correct answer. Vary the demonstrations to include examples and counterexamples of both good reading and good listening behavior.	Observe and recognize correct and incorrect reading and listening behaviors.
10	Student practice	Direct students to practice reading a passage together. Observe each pair. Deliver specific praise and corrective feedback ("Yes! You followed the correction procedure exactly! I like the way you remembered to write the mistake in the listener log." Or, "You are not following along in the text. Show me how you follow along.")	Practice reading with partners, demonstrate all components of good reading and good listening behavior.

TABLE 6.4

Activities for Day 4 Training: Timing and Graphing

Minutes	Activity	Teacher behavior	Student behavior
10	Student practice	Direct students to practice reading a passage together. Observe each pair. Deliver specific praise and corrective feedback. This activity may be preceded by a brief review, if necessary.	Practice reading with partners, demonstrating all components of good reading and good listening behavior.
10	Timing and graphing	1. Demonstrate setting a timer for one minute. 2. Display a transparency of text. Start timer. 3. Begin reading rapidly. When timer stops, note which word was the last word read. 4. Ask students to help you count how many words you read. 5. Present a transparency of a graph and plot the number. 6. Tell students that the final step is to ask your partner how many errors were made during the practice session. Note errors on the same graph by plotting them with an "x."	Listen, count.
5	Timing and graphing practice	Tell students you will play a graphing game. Ask each student to come to the overhead projector and plot the information you give. Orally give a variety of examples such as: 135 words	Plot information on transparency.

Table 6.4 (continued)

Activities for Day 4 Training: Timing and Graphing

Minutes	Activity	Teacher behavior	Student behavior
		on day 16; 13 errors on day 2; 167 words and 7 errors on day 5, and so on. Give praise and corrective feedback, as necessary. Provide a sticker for each correct response.	
15	Modeling	Conduct an entire repeated reading session. 1. Set timer for ten minutes. 2. Monitor reading and listening behavior during practice session. 3. Ask students to set timers for one minute (tape-record if desired). 4. Direct students to graph words read per minute and errors. 5. Monitor graphing and provide stickers during both practice and timing sessions.	Independent demonstration of repeated reading procedures.

pairs is not possible, the teacher or an aide should serve as the student's partner that day.

When possible, it is preferable to pair students who will progress together and get along well together. However, it is possible that a teacher may find that some pairs are a good match academically but not a good match in terms of behavior. If students are disruptive, they are not following one or more of the good reading and good listening behavior expectations outlined in the training and therefore will not receive stickers for good behavior. We have found that the good listener cards are very motivating to intermediate-age elementary students and that the reward incentives have allayed most behavior problems.

Setup: When it is time for students to begin repeated reading practice, it helps to have a clear sequence of instructions. This avoids chaos and confusion in the classroom. The following is a list of instructions to give to the entire class. Do not give the next direction until each student has complied.

1. Take out repeated reading folders, books, and timers.
2. Raise your hand if your partner is not here or you are starting a new book (regrouping partners may be necessary at this time).
3. Take your materials to your assigned reading station.
4. Display your good listener cards.
5. Set timers for ten minutes.
6. Begin reading.

Practice: Immediately prior to the practice section, the teacher should remind students that a fluent reader reads with expression and inflection, not word-by-word or rushing through the passages. A modeling from you will be very beneficial for students' fluency building. If student pairs are practicing different passages, modeling each of these passages may not be possible, so another common passage may be modeled for a large group prior to student practice. During repeated reading practice, the teacher should walk around the classroom observing each student pair. Stickers should be provided or withheld according to behaviors observed. Students should be reading aloud, alternating by paragraph. The listener should use a finger to follow each word of text the partner is reading. When the reader makes a mistake, the listener should recite the correction procedure exactly from the prompts pasted into the folder. The students should also make note of the errors on the listener log. Failure to adhere to these procedures should result in corrective feedback from the teacher. When reading, students should read loudly enough so that the listener can clearly understand the reader. When the pair reaches the end of the passage, they then go to the beginning of the passage and begin again, making sure they are consistently alternating paragraphs. For example, if the number of paragraphs in the passage is even, upon beginning the next repetition, students will find that they are reading the same paragraphs they read the first time, thus never having an opportunity to read all of the text in the passage. If the number of paragraphs is odd, this will not be a problem, and students can simply continue taking turns at the start of each repetition. Students should continue repeated readings until the timer goes off.

Timing and graphing: The pair decides which student will read first. They set the timer for one minute. The listener says, "Ready, set, go," and starts the timer. When the timer sounds, the pair counts the total number of words read and plots that number on the graph. The number of errors (determined by the number of underlines placed in the text by the listener) is counted and plotted as well. The same timing instructions apply to the other student in the pair.

After the repeated reading practice session, students should return to their seats and resume class work. A drawing of good listener cards or recognition of students who have reached fluency can be done at the conclusion of the session. It is preferable to give rewards right after the practice session to build a relationship between good reading behavior and rewards. Using the graphing information, it is also important for the teacher to carefully review students' progress periodically, especially to detect any stagnation (flat line) or drop (decreasing trend). When a student fails to progress in a desired direction, this is a red flag for the teacher to change something about the procedure. By no means should a student embark on a downward trend. If this occurs, consider letting students redo a daily timing to increase the score, if it is very close to the previous day's. Otherwise, consider dropping a level, changing partners, or increasing the worth of the tangible rewards. Also consider the possibility that boredom is a factor. After a while in the repeated reading practice, students may become bored. A new twist, a game, or a good listener card drawing might do the trick to pull students out of the doldrums. Remember, motivation and momentum are the keys to fluency work.

Effective Strategies for Teachers

Teachers are encouraged to employ the following strategies to increase the effectiveness of a repeated reading program.

Once a Day

- Allot a regular academic period (for example, 10:00–10:20 a.m.) and conduct a repeated reading session.
- Model fluent reading for all students before they are required to practice in pairs. The modeling allows students to visualize how a fluent reader reads.
- Praise students and give corrective feedback as necessary.
- Monitor student graphs; make sure the students are plotting the data correctly.
- Encourage students to surpass their best scores.
- Randomly select a few students to read for you. This is the time you can test how well the students can read and whether the program helps them become more fluent in oral reading.

Once a Week

- Conduct an informal discussion about how well the students like the repeated reading program, and consider suggestions students make.
- Collect and review all student graphs, noting students' data that is stagnant or trending downward (for those students, consider moving to a lower level book or modifying the instruction).
- Review data in terms of students who are close to fluency; plan possible alternative pairings.
- Change student pairs as necessary (disruptive, dissimilar levels, and so on).
- Keep current on passage selections; have many different levels ready.
- Invite parents to the Friday session; encourage them to participate.
- Update materials in student folders (for example, insert new listener logs, good listener cards, or graphs).
- Conduct a good listener card drawing and provide rewards to encourage students' progress.

Once a Grading Period

- Review all student data; modify pairings or materials as necessary.
- Create a student questionnaire regarding the aspects of repeated reading that they like or may not like. Consider this valuable information when modifying procedures.
- Send a progress report home to parents indicating CWPM at the beginning of the grading period, middle of the grading period, and end of the grading period.
- Evaluate each student on an unknown passage of the same level he or she is currently working. For example, if Nelson is now working on a fifth-grade level passage, select another fifth-grade level passage that he has never seen and ask him to read orally. Evaluate for CWPM and number of errors. This evaluation may provide useful in-

formation as to whether the student transfers the learned skills to a novel passage.

- Plan a special reward for the hard work students have done (for example, a drawing, a pizza party).

Once a Year

- Create repeated reading folders. Allow students to help you when appropriate.

- Conduct repeated reading training.

- Evaluate students on an unknown passage for CWPM and errors.

- Formally assess students on oral reading fluency and reading comprehension using standardized tests. The information obtained can be useful in instructional planning. The scores can also be compared to those obtained from preceding years to determine students' long-term progress.

- Invite parents into class for a lunch to celebrate students' work and to train parents to be repeated reading partners at home.

- Hand out special individual certificates to each student. Personalize the certificates in some way.

- Establish a plan for next year's repeated reading (possibly use the same procedure in content areas as well as fiction reading).

- Give a repeated reading presentation at a teachers' meeting. Show student data and describe the procedure. Other teachers may find it helpful, and the administrators should be apprised of fluency work being done in the classroom.

Related Internet Resources

Building Fluency: Do It Well and Do It Right:
http://www.ed.gov/teachers/how/tools/initiative/summerworkshop
/mccabe/index.html

This Web site provides PowerPoint presentation notes by Molly McCabe, Lynn Figurate, and Caryn Lewis on fluency building at a professional development workshop through the U.S. Department of Education's Teacher-to-Teacher Initiative. Information on fluency contains its rationale, assessment, the instructional approach of repeated readings, and other information.

National Institute for Literacy (NIFL):
http://www.nifl.gov/partnershipforreading/publications
/reading_first1fluency.html

The NIFL provides information on scientifically based fluency instruction to improve students' oral reading fluency. The described fluency instruction is a part of the publication "Put Reading First: The Research Building Blocks for Teaching Children to Read: Kindergarten Through Grade 3" by the Center for the Improvement of Early Reading Achievement (CIERA), U.S. Department of Education.

Texas Center for Reading and Language Arts:
http://www.texasreading.org/utcrla/materials/primary_fluency.asp

The Texas Center for Reading and Language Arts in the College of Education at the University of Texas at Austin developed a comprehensive professional development guide, titled "Reading Fluency: Principles for Instruction and Progress Monitoring," to help practitioners and educators become competent in (a) the knowledge of fluency and its importance to reading, (b) effective strategies to foster fluency, and (c) practical approaches to monitoring students' reading fluency. The guide provides presenters' notes, presentation slides, handouts, and a list of references related to fluency building.

PART THREE

Improving Social Competencies

CHAPTER 7

Behavior Management

Ms. Fowler

Ms. Fowler was a teacher in an inner-city general education fourth-grade class. Although she was an experienced teacher, this was her first assignment within an inner-city classroom. Ms. Fowler encountered several new difficulties that she communicated with one of her former professors, whom she hoped would help her become more successful in this teaching assignment. Some of these challenges (as discussed in this chapter) pertain to school organization, cultural differences, instructional style, and pupil management.

Ms. Fowler was surprised to learn that the school district had tremendous difficulty in getting substitute teachers into the schools, particularly the more impoverished schools, which also were the schools that tended to have highest absentee rates among regular teachers. When teachers were absent, the children from these teachers' classes were divided among the other classrooms. On any given day, Ms. Fowler might have five to eight of these additional students in her classroom. This condition increased the chaos in Ms. Fowler's classroom and made it harder for the students to learn anything there. Ms. Fowler states:

> I've tried to have hands-on enrichment type activities available. When it is just my class we are able to have more presentations and discussions, move a little more freely and work with partners or small groups. When we try to do any of this with extra students, my students start showing off and are out of control in a heartbeat. As a result of this I have made the enrichment materials off limits when we have extra students (not a popular decision). To make matters worse, the principal is planning on permanently moving three students into my room from an overcrowded, out-of-control fourth-grade class. Needless to say, these new students are not qualified for the advanced placement in my class. At this point, however, qualifications are the least of my concerns. This constant moving in and out of students, whether or not they are assigned, placed, or just visiting is extremely difficult to handle.

In addition to the administrative glitches, Ms. Fowler was baffled by the cultural differences she observed between herself, a white middle-class female, and her inner-city African American students. She was stunned, for example, to learn that when confronted with a situation of a stranger needing help at their door and they were home alone, her students uniformly stated that they would not call the police. The children explained that calling the police when home alone most likely meant that they would be taken to Children's Service. No matter how frightened they were, the children said, they had emphatic directions from their parents never to call the police. Ms. Fowler also discovered the importance of learning about her students' community and social relationships. She writes:

> Before the first day of school three moms came in to meet me, and each one named people her child could or could not work with. One mom was quite clear that I

needed to move the desks; her daughter was not to work anywhere near a certain student. I listened politely, took it under consideration, and chose to leave the groupings. I was certain that we would be able to work through their problems. I should have listened to the moms. What I didn't know is that many of the social problems are second-generation problems. The mothers are quite young and in some cases have been carrying on arguments and grudges that they had with each other before these youngsters were even born. It is as though their children have a responsibility to carry on.

Ms. Fowler struggled with her instructional style, which leaned toward the indirect and process approach: lots of discussions, group decisions, self-directed learning, and cooperative activities. Initially, she framed her directions to the students as questions, often giving students the impression that the assignment was optional or negotiable. To foster a democratic classroom and student independence, students were permitted to move about the classroom at will and to dismiss themselves for special situations such as using the lavatory. Ms. Fowler stated that she came to this school knowing that these approaches could work, but she was having considerable difficulty getting the class to perform smoothly under these conditions. Both in their previous schooling and in their homes, the students in this class were used to more direct approaches where instruction was teacher directed and directives were delivered firmly, precisely, and unequivocally.

The preceding notwithstanding, Ms. Fowler's greatest challenges were with pupil management, getting students to follow classroom rules, to respond respectfully and immediately to her directives, and to interact positively with their peers. Problem situations were especially likely to erupt during transitions, that is, when she was trying to get the students to move from one activity to another, and during small group instruction. Ms. Fowler reported that when some of the students were working in small groups with her, the other students assigned to independent work would begin talking or arguing about something. Any type of free movement, which came from using materials or project work, generally led to talk, then loud talk, and eventually to arguments. Particularly problematic was the tendency for some children, especially girls, to talk back or challenge her directions. In one case she directed a student to put away her materials, sit down, and join the class activity. The student defied her by telling her she did not want to sit down. She would put her materials away, but she would not sit down. The other students, sizing up the situation, were pondering whether or not to join this act of defiance when Ms. Fowler was able to muster enough authority to get them to think otherwise.

Helping the students to manage their anger was central to Ms. Fowler in bringing about more adaptive behaviors in her students. She felt that anger was an area of special difficulty. According to Ms. Fowler, many, although not all, of her children, seemed to express so much anger in the things they said to each other, in their exaggerated body language and gestures, and in the way they slammed chairs, desks, books, and themselves when they were annoyed about something. Over time, however, she learned to decipher when these were fairly normal behaviors and when the students had reached out-of-control anger. Angry gestures and tears characterized the latter state, probably reflecting true frustration. Because the students were so easily set off, fights were fairly commonplace. Ms. Fowler relates the following example:

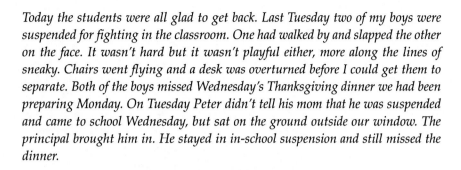

Today the students were all glad to get back. Last Tuesday two of my boys were suspended for fighting in the classroom. One had walked by and slapped the other on the face. It wasn't hard but it wasn't playful either, more along the lines of sneaky. Chairs went flying and a desk was overturned before I could get them to separate. Both of the boys missed Wednesday's Thanksgiving dinner we had been preparing Monday. On Tuesday Peter didn't tell his mom that he was suspended and came to school Wednesday, but sat on the ground outside our window. The principal brought him in. He stayed in in-school suspension and still missed the dinner.

Why Explicit Training in Behavior Management?

Next to the family, the school is the most important socializing institution for children in our society. Children spend approximately half of their waking hours throughout their developing years under the supervision of teachers and other school staff. Thus school personnel are empowered to enable children to develop the behaviors needed to become disciplined and socially competent individuals. These are behaviors that foster success in school and later life. The methods for helping all children acquire these critical behaviors are not readily obvious, and some children need and deserve specialized approaches. Behavior management strategies need to be an explicit aspect of the school curriculum.

All staff need to be trained in the strategies that are most likely to bring about desired results. They also need to understand what actions to avoid and how school staff can unwittingly cause children's behaviors to worsen. Children with special control issues, for example, are not likely to get better if they are punished excessively. Instead, if these youngsters do not receive specialized interventions, their school adjustment will steadily deteriorate. School personnel who are inclined to systematically increase the severity of punishments will find themselves entangled in a conflict cycle with no positive resolution for either the student or the school. This chapter focuses on the milder behavior problems common among the majority of students in urban schools. Individualized interventions for more severe behavior issues are addressed in Chapter Nine of this handbook.

What Is Behavior Management?

For the purposes of this handbook, the term *behavior management* may be misleading. Rather than managing student behaviors or reacting to them after they occur, our focus is on preventing problem behaviors. In addition to prevention, we want to identify and intervene early with the young child whose risk markers indicate the potential for chronic behavior problems. We also want to target students, regardless of age, when problem behaviors first begin to emerge. It is important that schools and classrooms are organized and run smoothly so that problem behaviors do not escalate and permeate the entire school. Healthy school environments can do much to help young children become socially competent and efficient learners. These are children who eventually make substantial contributions to the larger society. Therefore, we define behavior management as the process of creating well-structured, disciplined school environments effective in preventing problem behaviors and helping children acquire adaptive replacement behaviors.

Importance of Behavior Management for Urban Learners

Behavior management for urban learners is much more than applying punishing consequences for misbehavior. Although wrongdoing should never be overlooked or encouraged, our intent is to get children not only to behave but to be motivated to do the right thing. Research shows that disciplinary referrals for urban and minority students are higher than they are for other groups (Skiba, Michael, Nardo, & Peterson, 2000; Turnbull et al. 2002), but we do not have evidence that these higher levels of punitive consequences result in more adaptive behavior or improved school environments for either the referred students or their peers (Lo & Cartledge, 2004; Noguera, 2003).

The term *behavior management* connotes something that we do to the individual in order to exact control, but in actuality we want children to experience success in managing their own lives. Therefore, we need to teach them behavioral information that increases their own awareness of their various options and how to make choices in the best interest of themselves and others.

An overwhelming percentage of our urban learners are impoverished, subjecting them to conditions of excessive violence, poor role models, and a culture of poverty where ways of doing things are at odds with the culture of the school and the larger society. Under these conditions, schools become critical arenas for learning rules and behaviors essential for social and academic success. Behavior management within these settings means that school personnel are valuable role models of the desired behaviors. Children who have not learned the appropriate respectful and formal language for managing conflict, for example, should not only be taught these skills but also should hear and receive this respectful language from school authorities.

Behavior management means that we consciously work to build good relationships with urban students. Through these relationships we are able to identify and nurture the students' strengths. Urban students, who are keenly aware of their subjugated status in this society, especially need to be affirmed in school and to believe that they are valued members of the institution where they spend their days. Thus an important feature of behavior management for urban learners is to help them to set and achieve worthwhile goals. Students are encouraged to dream lofty goals, they are helped to make small steps toward their goals, and every achievement is celebrated. These and other positive actions can be extremely empowering for urban learners, helping them to move from a state of dependence, where they act almost exclusively according to external controls, to one of independence, relying largely on their own resources to result in socially appropriate behaviors and wise decisions.

Importance of Behavior Management to Teachers

Student discipline problems continue to be a dominant concern among public school teachers. According to data from the National Center for Education Statistics (2003), the number one discipline problem is bullying, followed by students' disrespectful behaviors toward teachers. Other complaints include widespread disorder in the classroom, verbal abuse of teachers, and gang activity. Needless to say, these conditions make it very difficult to teach and undoubtedly contribute to teacher attrition—where the highest rates are in urban schools. Here are just some of the advantages of effective behavior management to teachers:

- Increases in instructional time
- Increases in pupil achievement
- Improvements in classroom climate
- Higher levels of job satisfaction
- Greater tenure in the teaching profession
- Higher levels of professionalism among teachers and other educators
- More talented personnel in the profession
- More opportunities for enriching classroom activities
- Greater likelihood of building positive relationships with students
- Fewer exclusionary and punitive actions required

Creating Positive Environments for Urban Learners

For students to display disciplined and orderly behavior, we have to provide disciplined and orderly school environments. One of the first steps in structuring our classrooms is to devise and post classroom rules. See Figure 7.1 for an example of a poster of classroom rules. We recommend that these rules be generated in collaboration with the students so that they will understand the reasons for these rules and take some ownership in adhering to them. Rules should be few in number (say, between five and eight), and they should be positively stated (for example, "Get permission to speak" rather than "Don't talk out"). Rules need to be specific and observable. The rule "Respect others" has merit, but it needs to be specific so that students know when they are being respectful. "Use an 'indoor' voice when speaking to others in the classroom" is an example of respecting others. Rules must be taught as well as listed. Each rule needs to be discussed, modeled, rehearsed by each student, practiced, and reinforced. The rules need to be reviewed daily, and students need to demonstrate regularly that they know exactly what they are to do to abide by them.

Consistency

Student problem behaviors are more likely to occur when classroom rules and behavioral consequences are delivered inconsistently. A teacher who is inconsistent can expect outcomes like these:

- Students become confused about what is expected of them.
- Students become sneaky and are willing to gamble on not receiving a punishing consequence for their wrongdoing, therefore increasing the likelihood of the problem behaviors. (That is, they think, "Maybe I won't get caught this time.")

FIGURE 7.1

Poster of Class Rules

Our Classroom Rules

1. When the teacher is talking, be quiet and listen.

2. Raise your hand and wait to be called on before speaking or getting out of your seat.

3. Be polite and courteous to others. Use kind words.

4. Use an indoor voice while speaking to others in the classroom.

5. Always walk in the classroom and hallways.

- The teacher is perceived by students to be unfair and unreasonable. (For example, "Joseph is also talking, so why doesn't he have to go to time-out?")
- Classroom structure is weak, resulting in negative teaching and learning environments.

Being familiar with the established classroom rules (including consequences) and frequently reviewing them will help teachers achieve consistency. We also recommend that teachers make the application of consequences conspicuous so as to be more consistent. For example, Ms. Fowler might use a large chart posted in front of the class listing the names of all students to "document" the consequences each student received when an infraction was observed (for example, first verbal warning, second verbal warning, five-minute time-out). This chart not only provides direction as to what consequence would be delivered if a certain behavior recurs, it also gives students a visual prompt as to what will happen if they misbehave again.

Within urban schools teachers often struggle with external events that interfere with the smooth running of their classrooms. This means that urban teachers need to be super-organized and to plan well for any eventuality. The school's failure to secure substitute teachers may mean your class is frequently overrun with nonassigned students, for example, but taxing as this is, it need not totally derail your class. Such events require that we devise strategies for addressing these events and to train our students accordingly. To illustrate, Ms. Fowler's class was considered academically advanced relative to the other students in the school. In training her students, she might point out to them that they were selected to be academic and social models for the other students in the school. As such, they had the responsibility to show other students how to conduct themselves in the classroom and how to achieve academically. When other students entered their classroom, it was a special opportunity to display these behaviors. Ms. Fowler and her class would then take time to identify a list of five or six behaviors that her students were to perform when a set of nonassigned students were placed in their class. A sample list might look like this:

- When directed by the teacher, greet the students and welcome them to your class.

- Remain in your seat and continue with your work until assigned to a new location by the teacher.

- If you need the teacher's attention, put out your flag; talk-outs are absolutely forbidden at this time. (See Chapter Nine for an example of a flag.)

- Be prepared to participate in responsible peer instruction when directed by the teacher. (See Chapters Five and Six.)

- Be prepared to participate in responsible cross-age tutoring for one of the nonassigned students if directed by the teacher.

- Following these and our regular classroom rules will earn the class triple bonus points toward this week's group goal.

Implied in this sequence is the understanding that Ms. Fowler is training her students in a set of peer-based skills such as peer and cross-age tutoring that would enable them to be more independent, yet meaningfully engaged in academic activities, while she is attending to the needs of the other students. These roles also provide her students with a socially appropriate alternative to the acting-out or showing-off behavior they tended to resort to when other students entered the classroom. With this strategy, Ms. Fowler's students still could be showcased, but the outcomes would be to the advantage of all involved.

Cultural Competence

We are all products of our environments; our culture dictates our lifestyle, the language we speak, the way we perceive the world, and our behavior. Due to cultural differences, teachers of urban students typically have to make a special effort to learn the culture of their students and to understand ways to reach the students most effectively. Urban students are often astute at reading these differences; they know their verbal and nonverbal behaviors often confuse their middle-class teachers, and they are inclined to use this confusion as a means to seize classroom control. Ms. Fowler confessed that she was clueless about reading and confronting her students' behaviors. She was particularly challenged by the tendency of her students to openly defy her directives. Wynn (1992) refers to this behavior as the "showdown." He states:

Many teachers, particularly substitute teachers, don't understand the showdown and depending upon their own self-esteem, personal confidence, and whether or not they have a natural tendency to be afraid of our young men, don't respond in a way that establishes the foundation for discipline in the classroom—discipline that is established on the foundation of cultural understanding. When our young men don't feel loved or respected, when they're not motivated to learn, they exhibit anger and rebellion toward the teacher. This further alienates or frightens the teacher and no learning is achieved. (p. 19)

Although Wynn attributed this behavior largely to males, Ms. Fowler found it to be most prevalent among her female students, and in our research we found the number one complaint teachers had with urban females was insubordination or noncompliance (Lo & Cartledge, 2004). Wynn suggests that this behavior is not only a plea for attention but a request to be respected, valued, and motivated to achieve. It is important to bond with these students, letting them know that you care about them but that this behavior is unacceptable. Wynn cautions teachers against trying to control these situations through force or intimidation. Instead, teachers want to approach these students with confidence, letting them know that you are capable of caring for them, teaching them, and maintaining class control. Some educational authorities assert that relationships can be the most powerful motivator for poor students and note that individuals who have overcome poverty typically attribute the genesis of their success to some relationship—teacher, counselor, or coach (Payne, 1998). We develop relationships with students by letting them know that we care for them, by taking a personal interest in and celebrating their personal and academic successes, and by helping them acquire the academic and social skills to be successful on a daily basis. Here are some examples of specific activities for developing positive relationships with students:

- Schedule a one-on-one lunch with each of your students for informal conversation.

- Direct students to write weekly essays that tell about something special for them such as "My favorite thing in class this week."

- Encourage students to bring to school pictures of family members, friends, or pets that they would like to share with you.

- Send each student a note once a week, describing something special about that student. For example, "One thing you did this week that I really liked is . . . ."

- Set aside a five- or ten-minute period each week to work with each student either on a remedial or advanced learning activity.

To become more culturally competent, teachers might try the following activities:

- Schedule a meeting with each student's family. If possible, meet in the child's home. This should be a very positive meeting, focusing on the child's goals and expected achievements.

- Participate in some activity in the child's community such as a local fair or a playground activity.

- Go to the local library and perhaps one or more of the churches in the child's community and get some information about the history of this community.

- Invite a community leader and historian to school to discuss something about the community that might be of interest to you and the students.

- Give students a structured or semistructured interview form to interview family or community members to get information about the community. Students could conduct these interviews with tape recorders or in writing by completing the forms.

Managing Instruction

When we analyzed Ms. Fowler's day, we found that she was spending too little time in direct instruction. She relied heavily upon cooperative and small-group activities that were oriented toward discovery learning. Although these strategies can be effective with highly able learners, the students in her class had not mastered the prerequisite skills to be successful in this format. This indirect approach often resulted in objectives that were vague and unclear to both the students and the teacher. We know that students learn best when they make an active response to academic material. Methods for active student response are discussed in Chapters Three, Four, Five, and Six of this handbook. These are some of the basic principles that should be considered:

- Fast-paced presentations are probably more effective than rambling lectures.

- Students need to be prompted so that they make the correct response.

- Students need to continue responding to the skill being taught until they are responding without errors or prompting.

- Direct rather than indirect speech is most effective.

- Students will benefit from higher level strategies once they have developed the prerequisite skills.

Large- and small-group instruction has an important place in the classroom for urban students. Small groupings may be especially needed for students who evidence difficulty in mastering the basic skills in reading and math. Large-group instruction minimizes planning time and can circumvent disruptive behaviors resulting from the teacher's attention being diverted to one group while others are working independently. Regardless of the format, there is a need to provide for ample pupil response and to teach the academic-related behaviors. When participating in a group, students need to learn how to do a number of basic but surprisingly nonobvious things:

- Enter the group appropriately.
- Take turns speaking.
- Listen to others.
- Use the appropriate voice volume.
- Respect others' opinions.
- Avoid put-downs.
- Include all group members.
- Leave the group appropriately.

While the teacher is teaching small groups, children working independently need to be able to perform the following skills:

- Listen carefully to the teacher's directions.
- Request clarification, if needed, when directions are given.
- Begin work immediately.

- If help is needed, display the help flag and continue working on other assignments until the teacher is available to assist.

- Check your work on each assignment.

- Remain in your seat unless given permission to move.

- Mark the independent work chart each time the buzzer rings (see Chapter Nine).

Once we have taught a skill, we need to make sure the skill is well developed in the learner's repertoire. For most basic skills, we need to provide for over-learning. Peer-mediated strategies, such as those discussed in Chapters Five and Six, can be useful for this purpose. Independent practice activities can be employed in classroom learning centers or structured for homework or family practice. Reward systems can help keep students motivated to learn. Many students are especially encouraged when they get to chart their daily or weekly performance and note the gains they are making.

Managing Pupil Behavior

A major focus in behavior management is to help students become more responsible in their own behavior. Being responsible is not simply accepting the consequences for some wrongdoing; it is recognizing beforehand what goals one wishes to achieve and taking responsibility for achieving those goals. It also relates to helping students assume more and more responsibility for the orderliness in their classroom and larger environment. These are important understandings and behaviors that should be directly and systematically taught. Goal setting is an extremely important activity for urban youth, who are often discouraged from thinking big and setting goals beyond their immediate situation. Wynn (1992) recommends that we encourage these students to set extraordinary goals and not be dissuaded from viewing themselves as national athletes, as physicists, or even as president of the United States. He also points out that the things we say can affirm either success or failure in students.

A counselor working with one of the students in our school gives a good example of this principle, which she learned from Wynn. Reggie was a large, athletic fifth grader who was meeting with the counselor because of some behavioral difficulties that he was having. He also was not focused academically. Reggie told the counselor that his goal was to be a football player. He wanted to play for the local Big Ten university and then go on to the NFL and to play for one of their teams. Instead of pointing out the really long odds of achieving this goal and trying to get him to focus on something else, the counselor simply wrote the following:

Reggie, I see you on the field at our Big Ten university making a great defensive play, blocking a player from our major rival university and keeping him from scoring. The team is yelling and the crowd is going wild! Your name is being broadcasted on ABC Sports and ESPN.

After graduation, you play in the NFL and help our city's professional team to finally begin to win again. Later, you become one of the greatest football coaches of all time and are inducted into the Coaches Hall of Fame. You have helped many young men to become better men by starting camps to help them with their skills, and you continue these summer camps into the school year to help them also reach their academic goals. You run a campaign and are elected mayor of our city.

You are the husband of a proud wife, and all four of your children are doing well. You live in a beautiful house next door to me.

According to the counselor, Reggie beamed after reading the counselor's note. Reggie took his note home, and his mother framed it and posted it in a prominent place. Immediately after this session, Reggie's classroom teacher reported some progress in his behavior.

Once students have set their own goal, their next step is to generate all the steps needed to achieve this goal: what to do now and what to do next to keep moving in the right direction. The students might also research role models who reflect this goal. For example, Reggie might decide that his hero is "Mean" Joe Greene of the legendary "steel curtain" of the Pittsburgh Steelers. Reggie would research Greene's childhood, his schooling, his professional contracts, his earnings, and his current activities. Reggie could compare this with the lives of some more contemporary players and speculate on (or calculate) the type of contracts and experiences that will likely be available by the time he reaches the age to enter the NFL. Reggie also could study the lives of extremely talented young men who failed to realize their promise. What were some of their pitfalls? How could he avoid these? What does he have to do now to make sure he can be successful? What are some small goals that he can set and monitor now to increase his likelihood of success? To acquire this information, Reggie may have to set many interim goals related to basic reading and math skills. His teacher and counselor would work with him to see how he is moving along the continuum. This procedure can help students maintain their enthusiasm for their goal as well as the learning process.

Goal setting also can be beneficial for managing everyday, immediate social behaviors such as following the teacher's directions, staying out of fights, and completing homework assignments. Teachers would work with students to set goals in one or two critical areas. It is important that the student wants to achieve this goal and becomes involved in setting the standards. Students often set more stringent standards than teachers, and they also are more likely to pursue a goal if they set their own standards. Here are some examples of possible goals:

- Complete at least five math assignments this week.
- Work independently for thirty minutes without any talk-outs during seatwork time.
- Ride to and from school every day this week without any fights on the bus.
- Follow the teacher's directions within ten seconds after they're given.

Periodically discuss with students the gains or progress they are making toward reaching their goals. Provide reinforcement for accomplishments and corrective feedback for ways in which they might improve.

Class Routine

We can help students become more responsible for the orderliness of their environment through the routines that we set up in our classroom. Give the students routine tasks that they can easily assume. Let the students know that you expect them to help assume responsibility for a smooth-running classroom. Students can be assigned duties such as recording daily attendance or passing out supplies. Students could be assigned long-term tasks, such as making certain that all coats are picked up in the cloakroom or that the books on a particular shelf are orderly. Students need to be taught how to perform these duties. Students with poor peer relations would especially benefit from such assignments. If well trained, students can handle these assignments successfully—at once relieving the teacher of the work and giving the students the opportunity to interact with peers in a meaningful and socially appropriate way.

Teachers tend to emphasize most task-related social behaviors such as following the teacher's directions or completing assignments, but substantial attention needs to be given to peer interpersonal problems as well because they tend to be demanding and consume considerable teacher time. Fighting can be a sizable problem in urban schools. We have found fighting or some sort of physical assault to be the number one or number two reason for disciplinary referrals in our school. Boys were more likely to fight physically than girls, although girls were frequently reprimanded for verbal aggression. Exclusionary practices such as out-of-school or in-school suspension had no effect on fighting behavior. As a matter of fact, the number of exclusions systematically increased as students progressed through the school year (Lo & Cartledge, 2004).

Fighting

Urban subcultures often encourage children to fight, under the misguided notion that fighting is a survival skill. Granted, children do need to learn how to protect themselves, but the overreliance on physical prowess as the principal means for dealing with or avoiding conflict is unwise and counterproductive. Furthermore, there are more effective ways to deal with conflict, and advocating fighting as a survival skill, even outside school, is likely to rule out any serious consideration of nonaggressive alternatives. Fighting often becomes a source of status for these students and a goal in itself. Young people who subscribe exclusively to aggressive options often become victims themselves, too frequently with fatal consequences.

Since fighting is so pervasive in urban schools, schoolwide programs should be put in place to prevent, not just punish, fighting. Administrators and staff need to declare the school a "Peacemaker Zone." At the beginning of the school year, weekly assemblies are scheduled to discuss the meaning and related behaviors that make up the Peacemaker Zone, including provisions such as these:

- We respect other students by making positive statements to and about them.

- We respect other students by touching them only in kind and positive ways.

- We respect other students by apologizing and making amends if we accidentally harm them in some way.

- If another student harms us, we will take the matter to one of the school's Peacemakers. If the Peacemaker cannot help us to resolve the problem, we will take it to a teacher or the school principal.

- We are all Peacemakers by not fighting.

Each assembly is used to address one of these principles. The peacemaking behaviors are modeled and discussed. In the classrooms the teachers provide more extensive instruction, giving each student the opportunity to practice the desired responses. Student Peacemakers should receive intensive and specialized training on how to manage conflict. (For specific steps, see Johnson and Johnson, 2004.) As part of this training, Johnson and Johnson recommend teaching students (a) the nature of conflict, (b) how to choose a strategy, (c) how to negotiate to solve a problem, and (d) how to mediate conflicts involving others. In step (d), the Peacemaker would first make sure that both parties want to solve the problem. Then the individuals must follow a set of six rules (p. 71):

- Agree to solve the problem

- No name-calling

- Do not interrupt

- Be as honest as you can

- If you agree to a solution, you must abide by it (you must do what you have agreed to do)

- Anything said in mediation is confidential

Initially, a small cadre of students might be trained to serve as Peacemakers (see Figure 7.2 for an example of a Student Peacemaker badge), but we believe that for maximum effectiveness the entire staff and student body should be trained. Initial Peacemakers should be high-status students, including those with a history of peer aggression. If committed and well trained, these students can be highly effective in this capacity. Conflict resolution training involves a significant investment of time over an extended period of years, not weeks or days, but it can be extremely worthwhile. Johnson and Johnson (2004) report a 60 percent to 90 percent decline in discipline problems across a set of sixteen school studies.

It is important to communicate constantly to students the importance of Peacemaking. Begin each school day with a reminder to students of the Peacemaker behaviors and end each school day praising students for their successes as Peacemakers. Schoolwide rewards could be made contingent on a specified number of fight-free days, for example, a schoolwide ice cream half-hour social for ten or twenty fight-free days. The small cadre of students extremely resistant to this intervention may be exempted from this contingency and subjected to special individualized plans such as those discussed in Chapter Nine.

Revisiting Ms. Fowler

Ms. Fowler worked closely and cooperatively with her consultants and made considerable progress in becoming a more effective teacher of her urban students. Among other things, she learned the importance of getting her class off to a good start, ways to present herself positively and authoritatively, and strategies for addressing group and individual behavior problems. To launch a good, productive school year, Ms. Fowler and her consultants decided it would be advantageous to send separate letters to each of her students and their parents immediately before the school year began. The students' letter welcomed the students to their new class, told the students how much she

FIGURE 7.2

Student Peacemaker Badge and Label

I am a Student

Peacemaker at

Wheeler Elementary!

looked forward to having them as students, and predicted that this would be an exciting school year for them. A separate letter sent to each child's parents was similarly positive, telling the parents how much she looked forward to having their child in her class, how she hoped to work with the parents in the interest of their child's school success, and how she and the family might communicate over the coming school year. See Figures 7.3 and 7.4 for sample letters.

Ms. Fowler saw the positive effects of these letters on the first day of school. Several parents made their way to her classroom to comment favorably about the letters. The parents told her how impressed they were that a teacher would spend the time and money to write to them and their child in this manner. They also encouraged their children to listen to their teacher because she obviously cared about them.

It was also decided that Ms. Fowler needed to get off to the right start on each school day by teaching her students the appropriate classroom-entry behavior. This meant that students were to walk in an orderly manner down the hallway to their classroom, stop at the classroom door, make eye contact with Ms. Fowler, smile, and say, "Good morning, Ms. Fowler," then go directly to their desks and be seated. Once everyone was seated, Ms. Fowler permitted students individually to go to put away garments and retrieve materials needed for class. Students began practicing this sequence on the first day of class and continued to perform these behaviors each school day for the entire year. Students were not permitted to enter the classroom until they performed the requisite behaviors as specified. Ms. Fowler made certain that she always greeted her students in a cheery, upbeat manner, letting them know that she was glad to have them in her room and that this was going to be a good day. Initially, the sequence was time-consuming, but within a couple of weeks the students were performing the routine automatically. Most important was that these steps helped to eliminate much of the disruptive behavior that typically occurred during transitions. Furthermore, it helped to set a positive tone for the rest of the day.

To enhance the class orderliness for the remainder of the school day, she was helped by behavior specialists to develop a set of rules and a related strategy for reinforcing desired behaviors. In collaboration with her students, Ms. Fowler

FIGURE 7.3

Welcoming Letter to New Students in Class

Oak Street Elementary School
Middletown, Ohio 00040

Dear *Andreya:*

It is hard to believe that summer is almost over and in two weeks we will all be back in school. I am Ms. Fowler, your fourth-grade teacher. This letter is to welcome you back to school. I know this will be a good and exciting school year for you. Just think: This year you will be in the fourth grade!

I have already been in our classroom to prepare materials for the coming year. We will have a great new reading book where we will learn about children your age from all around the world. We also will be able to look at videos about these young people to see how they live compared to the way we live.

I have something very special planned for you and the other students. This year we will get to write letters to children in South Africa. They will be your pen pals. They will send us their pictures, and we will send them our pictures. We also will read good stories about South Africa. What do you know about South Africa? If you have a chance, go to your local library and ask the librarian to help you find a book about South Africa for boys and girls your age. One story that you might like is *Journey to Jo'burg,* by Beverly Naidoo.

I am looking forward to having you in my class. Enjoy the rest of your summer and I will see you in two weeks.

Sincerely,

Ms. Fowler

FIGURE 7.4

Welcoming Letter to Parents of Students

Oak Street Elementary School
Middletown, OH 00040

Dear Parents:

My name is Ms. Ellen Fowler, and I will be your child's fourth-grade teacher this coming school year. The summer is almost over, and I have been preparing for the coming year. I am sending this letter to introduce myself to you and to say that I am looking forward to having your child in my class.

This is my fifth year teaching at Oak Street Elementary School. For the past two years I have taught fourth grade; prior to that I taught fifth grade. Before coming to Oak Street Elementary, I taught third-grade students at Locust Academy for five years. I changed schools because my family and I moved to Middletown five years ago. This is my tenth year of teaching school, and I thoroughly enjoy it. I have enjoyed my years teaching at Oak Street Elementary.

I am planning some activities that I hope your child will find exciting and will motivate your child to learn. Our reading curriculum will enable the students to read about other children around the world. I have set up the opportunity for my students to have pen pals from children their age in South Africa. We hope to exchange pictures and to read other stories from each other's country. I hope you will encourage your child in reading these stories. I also hope you will help your child to go to the library to get a storybook from South Africa. One story might be *Journey to Jo'burg*, by Beverly Naidoo.

I hope you are able to come with your child on the first day of school. I would like to meet you. I also hope to have a conference with you shortly after school begins so that we can share our goals for your child for this school year and set up a plan for regular communication. I am excited about this year and know it will be a good one for all of us, especially your child.

Sincerely,

Ms. Ellen Fowler

identified a set of eight positively stated rules that instructed students to follow teacher directions immediately and described how to get the teacher's attention, do their class work, and interact with peers, as well as what they were permitted to do in the classroom. The rules were posted prominently in the classroom and reviewed regularly with the students. Also displayed in the classroom was a large laminated chart with two sets of the names of all the students in the class (like the one in Figure 7.5). The names were on a grid with seven squares following each student's name. One grid was for the morning and the other for the afternoon. Each time an infraction occurred, Ms. Fowler simply put the number of the rule broken in one of the squares beside the student's name. If all the squares were filled in by the end of the morning or afternoon, the student forfeited a simple reward the teacher provided at that time. Rewards might consist of five minutes of extra computer time, a pencil, or a positive note home. Disruptive behaviors declined by nearly half after the first ten weeks that this strategy was in place. Over time the number of squares following students' names were gradually reduced so that students had to become increasingly adaptive in their behavior. The ultimate goal was for appropriate student behaviors to be maintained and reinforced largely through praise and natural reinforcers such as academic progress and improved grades.

When dealing with individual students, particularly those who were not responding to her classwide strategy, Ms. Fowler learned to deliver precise requests and avoid power struggles (Colvin & Lazar, 1997; Rhode, Jenson, & Reavis, 1992). In delivering these requests she learned to get close to the student and speak quietly, calmly, firmly, assertively, and with authority. She learned not to use a question format (for example, "Where does that book belong?") and to be direct (for example, "Put the book in your desk"). She would use the student's name and speak to the student respectfully. She also would make eye contact and be brief. If the student did not respond immediately, she would follow up with more of the same, except she would say, "I need you to . . . ." If the student still did not respond, Ms. Fowler quietly pointed out that the student had the choice of following that direction or some negative consequence. The student was then given a few seconds to decide. Ms. Fowler developed the following hierarchy of negative consequences:

- Verbal warning from the teacher

- Required to wait three minutes in seat when class is dismissed for recess

- Lose ten minutes recess time

- Receive extra academic assignment for lost recess time

- Loss of special activity during reinforcement time

- Assigned to sit near the teacher for the day

- Call parent in presence of teacher and explain problem behavior and what the child will do to improve the behavior

- Walk to the principal's office with the teacher and explain to principal the problem behavior and what the child will do to improve

- Note sent home to parents describing problem behavior

Ms. Fowler learned not to argue with students or to let them sidetrack her by discussing nonrelevant points. It was important that she remain focused and not get caught up in power struggles. If reductive consequences had to be employed, it was repeatedly pointed out to the student that this was the student's choice: "By

FIGURE 7.5

Classroom Behavior Chart

AM	1	2	3	4	5	6	7
Tiffany							
Hennessy							
Miesha							
Ashley							
Eric							
Shantae							
Elizabeth							
Cherell							
Ricardo							
Dyron							
Andreya							
Tomeisha							
Spencer							
Natasha							
Lauren							
Timothy							
Pierre							

PM	1	2	3	4	5	6	7
Tiffany							
Hennessy							
Miesha							
Ashley							
Eric							
Shantae							
Elizabeth							
Cherell							
Ricardo							
Dyron							
Andreya							
Tomeisha							
Spencer							
Natasha							
Lauren							
Timothy							
Pierre							

not following directions, you are choosing to go to the principal's office to explain this problem." Ms. Fowler successfully used this approach with reinforcing consequences to increase the level of compliance in her students.

Effective Strategies for Teachers

Teachers need to be proactive, anticipating possible problem behaviors and putting in place various strategies that are likely to prevent problem situations from occurring. Positive interventions will be more cost-effective than reactive punitive ones. Some suggestions follow.

Once a Day

- Begin each school day with a review of desired behaviors and possible positive consequences.

- Count the number of praise statements that you deliver in a school day. Use a golf counter or some other simple recording procedure such as transposing paper clips from one pocket to another to keep track of the number of praise statements delivered to students. Try to increase the number of praise statements over the previous day's. Continue this counting for at least two weeks. See if students' adaptive behaviors increase correspondingly as your praise statements increase.

- Send a positive note home with at least one student each day: Select different students each day so that within the first three weeks of school, each student gets to take at least one note of praise home.

- At the end of the school day, review with the students their special accomplishments that day and what behaviors they might try to improve the next school day.

Once a Week

- Review with the class the number of infractions charted for that week. Set a goal of at least 10 percent fewer infractions for the coming week. Determine whether the class met the goal set for that week and reward students accordingly, if the goal is met. If the goal is not met, discuss with the class strategies to help meet the goal for the following week.

- Review with students their progress toward academic and behavioral goals. Assist students in charting their progress and in setting new goals. Provide praise and corrective feedback, as appropriate.

- Direct students to write a note to their families detailing the progress they have made on their individual behavioral goals and goals they hope to meet the coming week. Students also are to describe what they plan to do to enable them to achieve these goals.

- Send home to the students' families a positive note sharing the progress that the class has made on their class behavioral goals (like the one in Figure 7.6).

- Invite the school administrator (principal, assistant principal, counselor, or comparable personnel) to your classroom to learn of the progress your class has made on their class goals.

Once a Grading Period

- Chart and evaluate class progress for the grading period. Share observations with the school's behavior specialist and make suggestions for changes, as needed.

- Send notes to each family detailing the progress of each student on meeting behavioral goals. Specify behaviors where improvement continues to be needed. Provide suggestions as to how desired behaviors might be reinforced at home.

- Schedule conferences with families of students with more significant behavior problems. Discuss the progress the student has made and what additional skills need to be developed. Review existing home and school interventions and revise as needed. Consider ways to strengthen home-school communication, if needed.

- Celebrate with the class the progress they have made on their goals. Celebration might be in the form of a mini party, such as a popcorn party or a special forty-five–minute game recess.

- Permit students to put on a skit where they act out specific skills that they learned during that grading period, such as "How Alexander Learned to Enter the Classroom." Encourage students to be creative in

FIGURE 7.6

Good News Report

Student: *Andreya Front*   Date: *February 23, 2006*

Grade: 4

Dear *Ms. Front:*

Our class is happy to report the progress we are making in our classroom behavior. This week all the students in our class were successful in:

- Entering the classroom appropriately by greeting the teacher and going to their seats in an orderly way.

- Playing appropriately on the playground with the other students without getting in any fights.

Please join us in congratulating your child for this very good behavior. Ask your child to tell you what special things *Andreya* did this week in order to reach these goals. Encourage *Andreya* to continue with this good conduct.

Sincerely,

Ms. E. Fowler

Fourth-Grade Teacher

---

developing the dialogue and costumes for the skit. Invite other classes to your room to view the skit.

Once a Year

- Chart and evaluate the progress students made in behaviors over the course of the year. Share observations with the school's behavior specialist and make suggestions for changes, if needed, for the coming year.

- Early in the school year, perhaps during the annual open house for parents, permit students to present skits on classroom rules and how students are to observe the rules. Include suggestions on how these behaviors can be reinforced at home. Give parents a listing of the social behaviors you are trying to develop during the first grading period (List no more than two or three behaviors—for example, appropriate classroom entering behavior). Advise parents that similar lists will be sent home at the beginning of each grading period. Request that parents reinforce these behaviors at home.

- At the end of the school year, send each family a brief report on their child's progress toward academic and behavioral goals. Emphasize the progress the student made, and note possible goals or areas of focus for the coming year.

- Celebrate with students the behavioral progress made over the school year. Provide some special event (such as a mini party) and discuss the progress they made. Praise students generously for legitimate accomplishments.

- Discuss progress on goals with each student. Praise achievements, give corrective feedback as needed, and help to identify possible future goals.

Related Internet Resources

Positive Behavioral Interventions and Supports: http://www.pbis.org/

The Technical Assistance Center on Positive Behavioral Interventions and Supports (PBIS) offers fruitful information and resources on a technology of positive schoolwide behavioral interventions and support. It provides demonstrations on feasible and effective behavior supports at the levels of individual students, classrooms, families, and the entire school.

Second Step: A Violence Prevention Program: http://www.cfchildren.org/program_ss.shtml

Second Step is an award-winning program aimed at teaching social and emotional skills for violence prevention. The program includes research-based, teacher-friendly curricula, training for educators, and parent-education components.

The Tough Kid Book from Sopris West: http://www.sopriswest.com

The Tough Kid Book provides practical classroom management strategies that are not only effective but can be both cost-effective and time-saving for teachers. The book can be ordered online through the Sopris West Web site. The "Tough Kid Tool Box" and "Tough Class Discipline Kit" are recommended supplements to the book.

CHAPTER 8

Social Skills Instruction

Significa

Significa is an eight-year-old second-grade student in an urban elementary class. Significa performs near average academically, but because she has been assigned to the lowest performing second-grade class, she is one of the best students in her class. Despite being adequate academically, Significa presents several troubling behaviors. Most noticeably, she appears to be unhappy or angry most of the time, scowling and refusing to speak to her peers or teachers when approached. When she enters the classroom each morning, she does not look at her teacher even though Ms. Robin specifically greets her by saying, "Good morning, Significa." During classroom activities, she does not make eye contact or smile at her classmates if they try to talk with her. She fails to acknowledge their presence as she passes them in the classroom and she even ignores other teachers who provide specialized instruction for her. As a rule, Significa maintains a glum demeanor, making little verbal or nonverbal contact with other children or adults in her school.

Since the beginning of the school year, children in the class have begun to shun Significa, refusing to invite her to participate in various classroom or playground activities. Similarly, adults now limit pleasantries or noninstructional comments to her since they do not expect her to respond. This isolation and exclusion means that Significa will have even fewer opportunities to practice and refine her social skills. Significa does not have a performance problem—she knows how to greet and acknowledge others. On infrequent occasions in school, she has displayed these behaviors. What Significa needs is an instructional program that motivates her to respond and persist in these behaviors on a sustained basis.

Why Teach Social Skills?

Social skills are socially valued behaviors that enable us to be reinforced and affirmed by others rather than punished or rebuked. Social skills typically are taught informally through observation and prompting, beginning in the earliest years of life. Existing research indicates that social skills correlate positively with school success and that significant deficiencies result in constant peer and adult conflict (Cartledge & Milburn, 1995, 1996). This research also informs us that peer rejection is predictive of later-life mental health and adjustment problems. As a matter of fact, deficits in fundamental social skills can do even more than learning problems to undermine success in life.

Although many critical social behaviors are acquired through informal means, formal social skills instruction can benefit most children and is imperative for many children who present special needs based on disabilities or cultural differences or both. Many children, particularly those with disabilities, often misperceive lessons that are obvious to most others. Many of these misperceptions occur with nonverbal behavior. For example, physical proximity is one strategy often used by classroom teachers to get the attention of a student who is off task and to get the student back on track. An imperceptive student is likely to misread the teacher's behavior and perhaps use this as an opportunity to engage the teacher in a conversation on an unrelated matter. This is likely to lead the teacher to be more direct with the student, possibly punishing or reprimanding the inattentive behavior. Another example is the student who misperceives the good-natured teasing of a peer. Instead of reciprocating with humor, the student becomes angry and aggressive in response, causing a harmless interpersonal interaction to deteriorate into peer conflict.

Another reason for providing formal instruction is that even children who do correctly perceive the social situation often choose the wrong option or find themselves unable to perform the right one. Consider a student who is being taunted or ridiculed for hurtful reasons and accurately perceives this situation: It is still a challenge to determine the best action and how to correctly perform it. Possible options might be to counterattack, to walk away, to cry or throw a tantrum, to make an assertive statement, to ignore the affront, or to tell someone. The most adaptive options would be the second or the last three. The socially unskilled youngster is likely to select the first or third—the least effective and least socially appropriate responses. Either of these is likely to cause the aggression to escalate, entangling the child even further in a conflict cycle and punishing outcomes. Performance problems may be an additional area of difficulty. A child may choose a more adaptive response, such as making an assertive statement, but still not know how to select or deliver a statement to produce the desired effect.

It is important to note that informal social skills instruction is ongoing all the time. Unfortunately, as teachers, parents, and other important individuals in children's lives, we often teach the very behaviors we would like to extinguish in children. Authority figures who respond to children's misbehavior with caustic words or corporal punishment are often teaching children that they can control their environment and get their needs met primarily through aggressive means. Suppose a student named Richard is punished for getting into a fight with a student who called him a rude name. The principal takes Richard into his office and yells at him for fighting in school. The principal tells Richard that he is ashamed of him and that Richard is not the kind of student he wants at his school. Richard is hurt and angry at the principal's words. He feels that he would not be in trouble if the other student had not called him a name. He feels that what he needs to do is to really beat up the other student for getting him in trouble. This time, he will try to catch the student outside school. Richard has not been disciplined, only punished. He has not learned an alternative way to handle situations when people offend him; instead, he is convinced that he should respond with anger and aggression when people do things he does not like.

A fourth reason for formal instruction to be mentioned here is that social skill lessons can help to counter negative messages children get in their immediate and larger environment. Many children, particularly those in urban environments, often witness or experience aggressive or violent behavior as the principal means for achieving goals. Children who are socialized to avenge every slight through aggression often have not been taught nonaggressive means to deal with problem situations. Direct instruction that helps students think through nonaggressive options and to realize their beneficial effects can help children learn more adaptive ways to behave.

The media—television, music, movies, and books—do not always present the most wholesome models for children to emulate. In fact, some of the most popular material and selections present the most antisocial actions. Many children from urban environments disproportionately get their messages about life from these sources. Social skills instruction can be instrumental in helping these students develop a more realistic worldview and model for social interaction. Formal social skills instruction is intended to address these and other issues that interfere with appropriate social development. Children who fail to receive such instruction are likely to be subjected to a life of progressively negative outcomes.

What Is Social Skills Instruction?

Social skills instruction is a positive, proactive effort to prevent problem behaviors from occurring, to correct existing problems, or to keep them from worsening. In contrast to punishment, social skills instruction is a preventive rather than reactive strategy. By anticipating and teaching the skills that children need to develop, social skill interventions cannot only foster children's social development but also help to make schools more attractive and nurturing environments for both students and teachers.

Social skills instruction or training typically follows a social modeling paradigm of identifying and providing a rationale for the skill, modeling the skill, providing for guided practice, providing for independent practice, and programming for behavior generalization (Cartledge & Milburn, 1995, 1996; Goldstein & McGinnis, 1997). When we begin to teach social skills, we first must identify the behaviors we wish to teach and try to give students a reason for wanting to perform that behavior. Social skills are positive behaviors that need to be framed in terms of what we want children to do. Because the need typically emerges from problem situations, it is often necessary to think in terms of what behavior we want to stop as well as what we want to start. For example, thinking back to the opening case, Ms. Robin wants Significa to greet others and to interact with a positive affect, and she also wants her to stop scowling and avoiding eye contact with others.

Helping students understand the importance of learning a new social behavior is not always an easy task. Therefore, we need to *identify and provide a rationale* for the skill. We essentially want students to recognize the need for this skill and that it is to their benefit to learn it. Many times we can simply discuss the problem with students to help them to see that the ways in which they responded in the past were counterproductive. This approach is more likely to be effective with older students. With younger—elementary-age—students we recommend using media such as stories or puppets.

To illustrate, in a social skills lesson on greetings for younger children, the teacher may present a puppet play or story. Here's one we have used successfully. It involves three characters: Kelli, Polli, and Mandy. When Mandy enters the classroom, Kelli speaks to her, but Mandy has a scowl on her face, keeps her head down, and only mumbles something to Kelli. Kelli later tells Polli that Mandy never speaks to others and that she is not going to say anything to

Mandy when she sees her. The other students also stop speaking to Mandy and never ask her to play when they are on the playground. Mandy begins to feel bad and decides she will not try to talk to the other students. Later Polli tries to talk to Mandy and finds out that Mandy is sad because others will not talk to her. Polli tells Mandy that she needs to learn how to greet others in a friendly way and that maybe the students will not speak to her because Mandy is not good at greeting the other students. Mandy is puzzled, but Polli explains that when you greet someone you must do three things: (1) look the person in the eye, (2) smile at the person, and (3) say hello in a friendly voice. Mandy practices these behaviors with Polli. The next day she starts greeting the other students in a friendly way. The other students are quite surprised but very happy. They begin to ask Mandy to play with them. In teaching this skill, the teacher might provide the students with an illustrated copy of this story such as the one presented in Figure 8.1.

During and following the story, the teacher uses modeling to emphasize the exact responses that Mandy has to make in order to display the appropriate greeting skill. The teacher models the behavior several times. As the teacher models the behavior, she talks her thoughts out loud, making statements such as "I am getting ready to enter the classroom. My teacher is standing at the door. I must remember to look at her eyes, smile, and say, 'Good morning, Ms. Robin,' in a friendly voice." The students should be directed to observe the teacher's modeling and to note each time the teacher makes a correct response—that is, eye contact, a smile, and a friendly greeting.

In the next step of *guided practice*, students act out the greeting behavior. Each child is given several opportunities to perform the skill under the teacher's supervision. To help students perform all the steps correctly, the teacher might give the students a greeting skill card (see Figure 8.2), which contains the specific components of the greeting skill. This could be enlarged and posted in the classroom. As much as possible, guided practice needs to reflect real-life situations. Thus the teacher might give the students scenarios such as the following prior to each enactment.

> *Suppose I'm Mandy:*
>
> 1. *Ms. Brown, the art teacher, comes into our classroom and speaks to me. I say, . . .*
>
> 2. *I am on the playground. Alexander, a first grader, comes up to me and says, "Hi, Mandy." I say, . . .*
>
> 3. *I come into the classroom. Ms. Robin, our teacher, is alone in the classroom, sitting at her desk. I say, . . .*
>
> 4. *I take the class report to the office. The secretary, Ms. Roberts, greets me. I say, . . .*

If students fail to follow all three steps, direct them to the greeting skill card. Also, initially, encourage the students to say their thoughts out loud so they would be cognizant of what they are doing. Provide students with corrective and reinforcing feedback, being specific with statements such as "Mandy, I really like the way you smiled when you spoke to Larry" or "Mandy, when you speak to Olivia, use a stronger, more friendly voice. Let's try that again." Happy-face stickers placed on students' reinforcement cards can be used for this purpose (see Figure 8.3).

Another part of the instruction might be to help students discriminate between friendly and unfriendly faces, particularly their own. Many socially un-

FIGURE 8.1

Student Copy of Social Skill Story

Mandy Learns to Greet

Polli   Kelli

Once there were two happy friends: Kelly and Polli. They were the best friends in the world and they liked to play with each other. Many times they liked to ask other children to come and join them in their games.

Kelli   Mandy

One day Kelli saw Mandy, another student from their class.
"Hi, Mandy! How are you?" Kelli asked.
Mandy answered with a low voice.
"OK," she said, and then she turned away.
"Oh, boy! That Mandy isn't very friendly. I wouldn't like to play with her. I am going to stop talking to her," Kelli thought.

Mandy   Polli

A few hours later Polli saw Mandy.
"Hey, Mandy! What's up?" Polli asked.
"Nothing," Mandy replied.
"Is something wrong? You look sad!" Polli wondered.
"Nooo!" Mandy answered and began to walk away again.
"Hey, wait a minute! Don't you want to stay and talk?" Polli asked.
"Um, yeah! I want to talk, but nobody ever asks me to stay and talk."
"But I just did it!" Polli replied with a big smile on her face.
"Nobody invites me in their games. Nobody ever asks me to play," Mandy said sadly.
"Well, Mandy, maybe it's because you act like you don't want to stay around and play with us. Look at what just happened! I talked to you, and you didn't even greet me!" Polli said.
"What do you mean by 'greet'?" Mandy asked.

Figure 8.1 (continued)

1. Look in the eyes.

2. Smile.

3. Hello!

"Greeting someone means looking in the person's eyes, smiling, and saying hello in a friendly, happy voice. When you greet people nicely, then they are friendly with you, and you will feel so good!" Polli explained.

"Hm, I've never thought about it! I guess it's important to greet others, right?" Mandy asked.

"Aha! It's very important to look people in the eyes, smile, and say hello to them! Then you will look nice and friendly and the other students will want to have you in their games," Polli said, spelling it out.

"But I am not sure I can greet other children in the right way," Mandy said.

"Let's practice how to greet!" Polli shouted with joy.

Big Thank-You!

Mandy   Polli

Polli helped Mandy improve her greeting behavior. Now Mandy is so happy that she feels more comfortable looking people in the eyes, smiling, and saying hello to them.

Kelli   Mandy

Next morning Mandy saw Kelli again. Kelli looked at Mandy but she didn't say anything. Then immediately Mandy looked Kelli in the eyes, smiled, and said, "Hi, Kelli! How are you?" Kelli was surprised! Soon a big smile was drawn on Kelli's face and she replied, "Good morning! I am fine. Thank you!" Then Kelli asked Mandy, "Hey, Mandy, how about coming to play with Polli and me during recess?"

"Oh! I would love to come!" Mandy answered happily.

FIGURE 8.2

Greeting Skill Card

Greeting others

1. Look in the eyes.

2. Smile.

3. Say, "Hello," in a friendly voice.

FIGURE 8.3

Student Reinforcement Card

(Front)

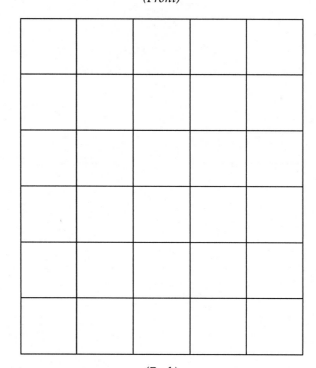

(Back)

skilled children have social perception problems and fail to read the nonverbal behaviors of others or to understand how their own expressions might be perceived. The teacher might begin with having students look at pictures and label friendly and unfriendly faces (see Figure 8.4).

This should be followed by the teacher's personally demonstrating both friendly and unfriendly expressions for students to label. While it is appropriate for the teacher or other adults to present this activity, it is important *not* to invite students to present unfriendly faces during this exercise. We do not want students to practice inappropriate skills. Finally, students should be encouraged to make friendly faces and to discuss how their face and body feels when they are smiling compared to when they are scowling. Mirrors might be used to help students to see how much more attractive they are when they are smiling. This activity might be capped with a class photo with everyone smiling. This photo might be posted on the class bulletin board.

Another consideration is the impact of personal behavior on the feelings of others as well as on the person doing the behavior. Point out to children that when we smile and use a friendly voice, we make others feel better. This, in turn, makes us feel good as well. During the enactments, the teacher might ask students how it made them feel when another student smiled while speaking to them.

For larger classes, it may take multiple sessions to give each child several opportunities to display the skill. As students gain competence, gradually remove the greeting skill card and let them continue to enact the steps under your supervision until they are doing so without prompting or corrective feedback. At this point, students are ready for *independent practice*. This is usually done through some game or *role-playing* activity. One example might be to arrange students in two parallel lines (line A and line B) facing each other. Students in line A are to first greet the students they are facing in line B, making sure that they follow all the steps taught in the social skills lesson. Students in line B are to tell whether the students in line A greeted them appropriately and what they failed to do, if anything. All the students in line A then deliver their greeting again. The procedure is then reversed with students in line B delivering the greeting. The teacher then rings a bell or gives some signal, and the first person in line B moves to the end of the B line. All the students in line B move up so that they are now facing a different student, and the sequence of greetings is repeated. This routine can be continued until each student gets the opportunity to practice greetings with four or five different students in the class.

After presenting several positive models, the teacher should present some negative models to make sure students can discriminate desirable and undesirable behaviors. For example, the teacher might respond to a greeting, correctly performing skill steps 2 and 3, but looking down, refusing to look the greeter in the eyes. At this point an activity can be devised where children are given STOP/GO or color-coded RED/GREEN preprinted response cards (like the ones introduced in Chapter Four). When the model makes the correct response, the students hold up their cards so that the GREEN or GO is displayed. The RED or STOP is shown when the model is responding incorrectly.

Once students demonstrate the ability to discriminate and perform the skill, the next step in the teaching sequence is to achieve *behavior generalization* or to get the newly taught behavior to transfer to different settings and to be maintained over time. That is, we want Significa and her peers to demonstrate ap-

FIGURE 8.4

Discrimination Training: Friendly and Unfriendly Faces

Figure 8.4 (continued)

propriate greeting behaviors not only in our social skill lessons but also throughout the day with students and adults. We also want the appropriate greetings to persist over time for weeks, months, and years to come. To get this to occur, we would have to praise the behavior profusely when it is observed under regular school conditions, for example, upon entering the classroom. The teacher might occasionally dispense little "greeting tags" (see Figure 8.5) to students who enter the classroom with greetings that make use of the taught skill. These tags could then be exchanged for special privileges such as extra computer time.

Since students do not know when these tags will be given out, they need to be prepared with their best greetings each day. If necessary, we would use more tangible rewards such as stickers or points that could be exchanged for backup reinforcers in order to encourage Significa to make the greeting. Another option would be to train students to monitor their own greeting behavior. Using a self-monitoring card like the one in Figure 8.6, the students would record their greeting behavior throughout the day. On this card, the students would mark whether they greet the teacher appropriately when entering the classroom in the morning and afternoon. Appropriate greetings for a period of four or five days could also result in special privileges. Over time, we would gradually fade reinforcement contingencies and train students to monitor their own behavior. We also would ask others (for example, parents, teachers, administrators, paraprofessionals) to prompt and reinforce this behavior.

The final step is to assess whether the social skills instruction was effective. A simple monitoring procedure similar to the card in Figure 8.6 could be used to track the progress students make in their greeting behaviors. The teacher might record how often each student made these responses prior to instruction. Once instruction began, the teacher could record these behaviors daily to assess whether they had been learned. Afterward, the teacher might assess them periodically to make

FIGURE 8.5

Greeting Tag

FIGURE 8.6

Self-Monitoring Card

Greeting Behaviors		MON	TUE	WED	THU	FRI
1. Look in the eyes.	AM					
	PM					
2. Smile.	AM					
	PM					
3. Say, "Hi" or "Hello."	AM					
	PM					
4. Use a friendly voice.	AM					
	PM					

sure that they are being maintained. If declines are observed, booster sessions might be employed in which students are reminded of the appropriate greeting behaviors. Posters close to the classroom door might be used to prompt students to use this skill upon entering the classroom each day. Most important, teachers should serve as role models for the students, brightly greeting students as they enter the classroom and prompting and reinforcing students accordingly.

To make social skills instruction most effective, we suggest several considerations and applications:

- Social skills instruction should begin early in a child's life. It would be best to start the interventions in the preschool and primary grades rather than waiting until problem behaviors have set in and possibly become intractable in the middle and secondary grades.

- Instruction needs to be provided on a regular basis, several times a week, throughout the school year, and throughout the child's formal schooling: primary through secondary school.

- Skills need to be taught to mastery, not simply presented as a part of the social skills curriculum with fond hopes that the students will acquire the skills. Teachers need to present the skills one skill at a time and continue teaching each skill until it is clear that the behavior is well established in the learner's repertoire. This is especially the case for skills that are critical to the child's overall success. Greeting, for example, is a basic social skill that should be mastered by all children. Any child who displays significant deficiencies in greeting others should receive remedial instruction until this behavior is at an acceptable level.

- Teachers need to be skilled in teaching social skills. If the child is not responding to the instruction, resource personnel and other curriculum programs might be employed to assist with this instruction. Often the activities might simply need to be revised or supplemented in order to bring about the desired changes in pupil behavior.

Social Skills Needs of Urban Learners

We are all products of our environment, and children from urban settings, particularly those from low socioeconomic backgrounds, often bring to the school ways of doing things that are in conflict with the culture of the school. U.S. schools reflect largely a European American or Western culture that emphasizes individualism and competition, and that values a Eurocentric curriculum. In contrast to the culture of the school, many children in urban settings come from collectivistic rather than individualistic subcultures (Cartledge & Milburn, 1996). These children are taught to emphasize the group rather than individual or personal achievement. Children socialized to believe that their first allegiance is to family or peers are likely to give preference to those groups over the school. Additionally, if these youngsters feel alienated from the school, they will seek other arenas, often antisocial ones, by which to validate themselves.

Schools are a primary socializing agency, and they transmit culture and social behavior on both a formal and an informal basis. Not all of the messages communicated are positive ones, and schools may inadvertently teach the very behaviors they wish to extinguish. Teachers who try to increase appropriate classroom behavior through excessive punishment for infractions, for example, may find themselves caught up in a conflict cycle with disruptive behavior escalating rather than declining. Central to this situation is the fact that children have not been taught the desired classroom behaviors or how to respond when confronted with some wrongdoing. A particularly important issue pertains to communication. These children often have language differences or are not familiar with the indirect language common among middle-class teachers. These children are more familiar with the direct language used in their homes. Therefore, the child who is used to a parent's "Sit down and don't get up till I tell you!" is inclined either to misread or not take seriously the teacher who says, "Is this where you belong?"

A related issue involves teaching urban children to use language to get their needs met and achieve their socially appropriate goals. Many of these children come from backgrounds where they are taught to be either verbally passive or verbally aggressive, whereas the larger U.S. society values verbally assertive behaviors. Children whose teachers punish them for being verbally aggressive or ignore them when they are passive fail to learn the necessary verbal skills. Children who learn appropriate ways to tell a peer that they do not like something that the peer has done or said, to give corrective feedback to a peer for some wrongdoing, or to tell a teacher when they feel they have been treated unfairly are much more socially competent than those who respond aggressively or do nothing. Children equipped with assertiveness skills are empowered to manage their affairs competently and can contribute to a much more orderly school environment. A final point to be made here is that many urban learners come from situations where their experiences and models are limited. Poor neighborhoods are often plagued with violence and conflict. The children are burdened by the stressors of poverty and often have few coping mechanisms. This means they have been taught many behaviors that have to be unlearned. Not every slight from a peer, for example, must be avenged with aggression. Furthermore, children need to learn that the ability to manage conflict peaceably is a sign of strength, not weakness. Other important beliefs are for students to value school and to believe that they are capable of being good learners and succeeding in and beyond school. Compassionate, skilled teachers can be instrumental in helping students acquire these interpersonal and academic related social skills.

Benefits of Social Skills Instruction

Social skills instruction is a positive, proactive intervention that is designed to prevent a lot of behavior problems or to keep existing problems from worsening. All children can benefit from social skills instruction, but some children with more pronounced deficits will require more intensive instruction. Here are just some of the beneficial effects of social skills instruction:

- It contributes to a more positive school climate for all students.

- It enables teachers to devote more class time to teaching academic behaviors rather than disciplining students.

- It contributes to student academic learning. Students are able to spend more time in the classroom learning academic content rather than in exclusionary settings where learning is not taking place.

- It helps students feel better about themselves. Improved social skills improve the response students receive, and students who are liked by their peers and teachers are likely to feel better about themselves.

- It empowers students, helping them to learn how to accomplish socially appropriate goals and get their needs met in appropriate ways.

- It makes teachers feel more accomplished and competent when their students are well behaved and have mastered critical social skills. Teachers feel especially accomplished if they have helped their students to master these skills.

- It offers teachers positive, affirming strategies to use in place of negative, punitive ones. Teachers who have mainly positive interactions with their students not only feel better about their students but also find teaching more rewarding.

- It helps students to lead disciplined and orderly lives.

- It improves long-term prospects for the students, as socially competent individuals tend to be highly successful in their adult lives.

Revisiting Significa

Ms. Robin knew that on very rare occasions Significa did greet others. She was not sure, however, how often Significa made these greetings or whether Significa performed all the desired responses when she did acknowledge the presence of others. To get this information and to determine whether social skills instruction would be effective, Ms. Robin decided to spend a few days observing Significa when she entered the classroom in the morning. Each day she recorded whether Significa greeted her appropriately by looking her in the eye, smiling, and saying, "Good morning, Ms. Robin," in a friendly voice. Ms. Robin used an assessment chart like the one in Figure 8.7, giving Significa a check each time the desired response occurred. After five days,

Ms. Robin noted that Significa said hi only on two occasions, and they were not with a friendly voice. She never looked at Ms. Robin or smiled when Ms. Robin greeted her. Ms Robin also did not see Significa greet any of her classmates.

Ms. Robin decided to teach Significa and the other students in the class the social skill of appropriate greeting behavior using the lesson described earlier in this chapter. Each student was given a copy of Mandy's story so that the children could follow along as the teacher read (see Figure 8.1). Ms. Robin asked the students questions about the story to make sure that they understood the problem and what Mandy needed to do to solve her problem. She helped the students identify the specific greeting responses and modeled the appropriate behaviors several times. As Ms. Robin modeled the behavior, she also would think out loud. For example, she would say:

> The school bell just rang and I am walking to my class. My teacher is standing in the doorway, waiting to greet me. I will look at her, smile, and say, "Hi, Ms. Robin," with my friendly voice.

After watching the teacher model the behaviors, the children identified and labeled each response she made. Each child then had the opportunity to practice how to greet the teacher and other children in the classroom. Ms. Robin observed each child practice the greetings so that she could give them corrective or reinforcing feedback. "That was a great smile, Significa, when you said hi to Gregory," or "Monique, let's try this again, and this time make sure you look at Erianna when you say hi to her." Each child had to make three correct greetings before Ms. Robin decided that the entire class was ready for independent practice. Significa practiced with the other students; she met the established criterion and made good progress with her greeting behavior.

For one of her independent practice activities, Ms. Robin had the children play the "Howdy Doody" game:

> In this game, all the children assemble in a circle, with one child designated as Howdy Doody. Howdy Doody walks around the outside of the circle (children are facing inward) two times and then touches one child and says, "Howdy Doody." The selected child then turns around and greets Howdy Doody according to the specified greeting skills. If the greeting is correct, that child then becomes Howdy Doody and the original Howdy Doody takes that child's place in the circle. If it is not correct, the child remains in the circle and Howdy Doody selects someone else. Children who respond correctly get only one turn and every child must perform the skill correctly before the game ends.

To make sure that the students continued greeting her and their peers appropriately each day, Ms. Robin set up a greeting container in her classroom. On certain mornings, as she stood by the door greeting the students, she would drop a marble in the can for each student who entered the class and greeted her appropriately. The students did not know which mornings she would be using the can, so they had to greet her appropriately every morning. Ms. Robin also dropped marbles in the can whenever she saw one of the students appropriately greeting another throughout the school day. When the can was full of marbles, the students received a class popcorn party. Ms. Robin made special note of Significa's greeting behavior. She continued to record Significa's greetings when she came into the classroom throughout the three weeks of instruction and practice. Significa also was taught how to monitor her greeting behavior as she entered the classroom each morning and afternoon and to complete the self-monitoring card.

FIGURE 8.7

Daily Assessment Form

Greeting Behavior	Day 1	Day 2	Day 3	Day 4	Day 5
1. Makes eye contact.					
2. Smiles.					
3. Says, "Hi."					
4. Uses a friendly voice.					
Total					

As a result of this instruction and related activities, Significa made very good progress. The graph in Figure 8.8 shows that in comparison to baseline, where she made only two of the four desired responses on two occasions, she displayed mastery during instruction and follow-up.

Despite her obvious progress, Significa occasionally had to be reminded to perform all the components of appropriate greeting. She especially had to be prompted to smile. Significa did improve, however, and other children in the class began to interact with her more regularly. Periodically throughout the year, Ms. Robin would have booster sessions about appropriate greeting behavior. Often during recess she would permit the children to practice "Howdy Doody" or other greeting games, which they really enjoyed. Ms. Robin continued using her greeting container for appropriate greetings when the students entered the class, but over the school year she found that she had to provide fewer and fewer popcorn parties. The students were not only entering with friendly, appropriate greetings, they also were generalizing these skills elsewhere, such as when they entered the lunchroom, the physical education room, and the bus. To help these behaviors transfer to these settings, Ms. Robin asked the school personnel in these settings to compliment her students when they entered and displayed greetings according to these specifications. Notes also were sent home to parents, advising them that this was a social skill being taught in school and asking them to reinforce these responses in their children. Finally, Ms. Robin pointed out appropriate greeting skills to the children when she read books to them such as *I Want to Play*, by Elizabeth Crary, or *The Grouchy Ladybug*, by Eric Carle.

Incorporating Social Skills Instruction in Your Classroom

Teachers can be effective social skills trainers for their students. All that is needed is to employ the following steps consistently and thoughtfully:

1. *Identify the skill to be learned.* This might be determined from the problem behaviors that the teacher wants to eliminate. For example, if a student fails to greet others appropriately, the skill to be learned is appropriate greeting behavior.

2. *Provide a rationale for learning the behavior.* Students need to know that they will benefit from learning this skill. A rationale might be provided

FIGURE 8.8

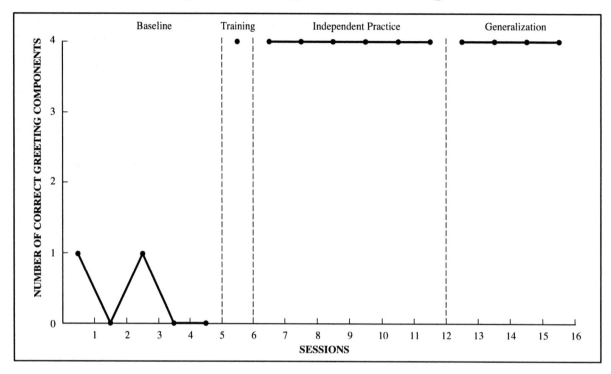

Significa's Progress in Greeting

through a simple story or a discussion that helps the students to understand how their current ways of doing things are not very effective in helping them achieve their own goals. Teachers can use questions such as these to engage the discussion:

> *What happened when Mandy didn't greet Kelli? What might have happened if Mandy greeted Kelli appropriately? Why do you think greeting a person appropriately is important?*

3. *Identify the components of the desired skill.* In presenting the social skill to the students, make sure they all understand the responses that make up that skill. Appropriate greeting, for example, might involve eye contact, smiling, a friendly voice, and a statement such as "Hi" or "Hello." It is important and useful to break down the skill into skill steps and responses for your instruction.

4. *Model the desired behavior.* Show the students how to perform the desired behavior. The teacher should model this initially, and during the modeling the teacher should think aloud, expressing what thoughts are directing the behavior. These self-statements also should address affective aspects of social skills—that is, point out that being socially appropriate makes both the learner and others feel better.

5. *Provide guided rehearsal and practice.* Each student gets the opportunity to perform the targeted skill. Students perform under the guidance and supervision of the teacher, receiving corrective feedback and reinforcement as appropriate. Guided practice should continue until students are responding without teacher prompts. When students are respond-

ing under these conditions to a specified criterion—for example, five consecutive times without prompting—they are then ready for independent practice.

6. *Allow for independent practice.* Students are given the opportunity to participate in role plays, games, and homework exercises so that they get many opportunities to perform the desired behavior and become proficient.

7. *Furnish reinforcement.* Reinforcement might take various forms, including teacher praise, special privileges, and tangible rewards. When children are first learning a skill, reinforcers should be plentiful. As children develop the skill and become fluent, the reinforcers should be thinned so that students are performing the skill naturally. Preference is given to secondary reinforcers such as praise; tangible reinforcers are used only when necessary, for example, when a child is exceptionally resistant to performing a skill.

8. *Preserve behavior generalization.* To get the behavior to be maintained and to transfer to other settings or conditions, the teacher needs to put several things in place. Others in the child's environment—teachers, parents, peers, administrators, and so forth—need to assist in reinforcing these skills in other settings. Mini lessons and props might be used to remind children to perform the desired skill. Children might be trained to perform homework assignments on these social skills and to self-monitor the behaviors.

9. *Continue to evaluate.* A simple assessment procedure at the beginning of the instruction, such as that described with Significa, could be employed to determine the effectiveness of this instruction. Tallies could be made of only one or two students showing the greatest deficits, even though the whole class received the instruction. Continue the tallies throughout the instruction and for a period during follow-up to make certain that the instruction produced the desired results.

10. *Teach a new skill.* Once it is apparent that the students have mastered the first skill taught, move on to the next skill. Depending on the social competence of your students, it may take several months to teach and master five or six skills. For this reason, teachers should select the skills where their students have the greatest need. Needless to say, some skills will take more time than others. Therefore, begin with the most important ones and teach for mastery. Greeting others appropriately, for example, is a rudimentary and critical skill that needs to be in every child's repertoire.

Most teachers will not have the time or resources to devise their own social skill curriculum and thus are advised to access some of the existing social skill curricula that provide scripted lessons for teaching social skills. Goldstein and McGinnis, for example, provide a series of curriculum programs for teaching social skills to preschool, elementary-age, and adolescent learners (Goldstein & McGinnis, 1997; McGinnis & Goldstein, 1997, 2003). Two other curriculum programs useful for this purpose include *First Step to Success: Helping Young Children Overcome Antisocial Behavior* (Walker et al., 1997) and *Second Step: A Violence Prevention Curriculum* (Committee for Children, 2002). The *First Step to Success* targets kindergarten children and provides specific strategies to eliminate antisocial behaviors such as physical aggression, tantrums, vandalism, and noncompliance. The *Second Step* curriculum provides instructional strategies for children from pre-kindergarten through middle school. The content emphasizes empathy, impulse control, and problem solving.

Effective Strategies for Teachers

Explicit instruction in desired social skills needs to take place on an ongoing basis throughout the school day, year, and grade. Following are some practical strategies that teachers might use.

Once a Day

- Post prominently in the classroom the social skill that is being taught and the specific responses that make up that skill. Use picture clues with each of the skill steps to help students remember the skill. A picture of eyes, for example, will help students to remember to make eye contact when greeting someone or speaking to them. Figure 8.2 shows an example.

- Begin each day with a brief reminder of the social skill being taught at the time. Review the steps and direct students to quickly demonstrate how the skill is performed.

- Briefly review with a few (two or three) targeted students the homework for the current social skill. For example:

   Alicia, tell us with whom you practiced your greeting skill yesterday on the school bus as you went home from school. Tell us which skills you used. Show us how you greeted Tamitha.

- Arrange for your students to practice the skill in other settings or with other persons. For example,

   Significa, would you take this class report to Ms. Alexander, the principal? Remember to use your greeting skills when you see her.

Or:

   Class, today when you go to the lunchroom, remember to use your greeting skills when you see Ms. Taylor, the lunchroom supervisor.

Once a Week

- Make a homework assignment that students should perform for the whole week. For example, students should practice their greeting skills with a variety of people: another teacher, a new student in the class, a guest in their home, the bus driver, and so forth. The students get a chance to report on these greetings on various days during the week.

- Send home a special parent note telling parents the skill that is currently being taught. Specify the components of the skill and request that parents prompt and praise their children for performing the social skill.

- Read with the students a book that has an example of the social skill being taught. Encourage students to read that book on their own later.

- Review the class chart so you can note the progress students have made in achieving the current social skill goal. For example, if the goal is to fill the greeting container to a certain mark, once a week the teacher and the students would assess their progress toward that goal.

- Reward students for the progress that they are making toward their individual goals.

- Evaluate the class on the progress being made on the current social skill. Make adjustments such as intensifying the instruction, changing the instructional activities, providing for more practice, or moving on to a new skill.

Once a Grading Period

- Review with students the social skills taught during that grading period and the progress students made toward learning those skills.

- Review with students the progress they made toward achieving their individual goals. Counsel students on setting their specific goals and what they might do to make sure they achieve their goals.

- Divide students into small groups (number of groups according to the number of skills taught that grading period). Assign each of the groups a social skill that had been taught during that period or a preceding period. Direct each group to demonstrate how to perform that skill. Permit the other students to prompt the target group appropriately if miscues occur. Use this as an opportunity to provide booster sessions for any skills that are weakening.

- Permit students to develop a simple dramatic activity that could be used to teach the social skill to another class. Arrange for students to teach their social skill to another class.

- Select a short commercial video appropriate for the children in your class. Direct students to watch the video and to look for appropriate and inappropriate examples of the social skills taught in class. For the inappropriate examples, students should suggest corrective feedback and give more appropriate responses.

- Evaluate the entire class on the progress they have made on the skills that they have been taught during that period and up to that grading period. Make adjustments such as repeating lessons on specific skills, providing booster sessions, giving more practice and homework activities, and moving on to teach new skills.

Once a Year

- During family night at school, have students present a brief skit of the social skills they are learning in school. Provide a handout for parents on the skills that you plan to teach this year and what parents can do to reinforce these skills.

- Have students prepare individual social skills notebooks that contain all the skills taught that year, how students performed on their homework assignments, and the individual goals that the students attained for these social skills.

- Evaluate the class performance for the social skills taught the entire year. Decide what adjustments might be made in coming years, such as intensifying instruction, teaching more skills, teaching fewer skills, increasing the involvement of others (parents, teachers, school personnel, peers), changing curricula, and so forth.

- Provide each child with a personal social skills certificate, listing the social skills that the child mastered during the year.

Related Internet Resources

Committee for Children: http://www.cfchildren.org

Committee for Children (CFC) is a nonprofit organization that specializes in programs and prevention curricula that focus on the topics of youth violence, bullying, child abuse, and personal safety. The Web site provides supports for teachers and resources for parents and advocates.

Cultural Diversity and Social Skills Instruction: Understanding Ethnic and Gender Differences: http://www.researchpress.com/scripts/alltitles.asp

This book provides a culturally sensitive perspective in teaching social skills. A distinction is made between behavior displayed as a result of skill deficit and behavior displayed as a result of cultural differences that need to be respected.

Second Step—A Violence Prevention Program: http://www.cfchildren.org/program_ss.shtml

Second Step is an award-winning program aimed at teaching social and emotional skills for violence prevention. The program includes research-based, teacher-friendly curricula, training for educators, and parent-education components.

CHAPTER 9

Individualized Behavior Intervention Plans

Derrick

During independent seatwork, Derrick, an urban African American third grader, constantly roamed around the classroom, made loud noises, called people rude names, yelled out the teacher's name, and engaged in other non–task-related activities. These behaviors disturbed Ms. Rodger, the classroom teacher, and the other students, who were trying to work on their assignments. Despite Ms. Rodger's efforts to deliver corrective feedback and consequences, Derrick continued to disrupt the class for thirty minutes. Ms. Rodger finally sent Derrick to in-school detention. This was the twentieth time in two months she felt she had to apply this disciplinary action as a result of Derrick's challenging behavior.

Derrick's behavior has been a source of concern among the teachers in this school since kindergarten, and the problems seem to worsen as he progresses through the grades. In Ms. Rodger's eyes, Derrick is a very smart child who knows all the rules and his student roles but elects not to follow them. Ms. Rodger feels she has exhausted her personal repertoire of pupil management strategies and has requested assistance from the Intervention Assistant Team (IAT). Academically, Derrick performs at a beginning second-grade level on a standardized reading assessment in word-letter identification, reading fluency, and passage comprehension. Unlike other students in the classroom, Derrick has made little progress in reading over the past two months, possibly resulting from his frequent exclusion from the classroom during the reading period for his misbehavior. Ms. Rodger is quite worried about Derrick's problem behavior and the impact it has on her class as well as on his own academic performance. She continues, however, to send Derrick to in-school detention when he disrupts the class.

Why Individualized Behavior Intervention Plans?

Many urban teachers, like Ms. Rodger, encounter similar situations in their classrooms. Having a "tough kid" or "troublesome child" in the classroom is often challenging and demanding for the teacher as well as other students. It can be especially frustrating if a student's frequent problem behaviors demand significant amounts of teacher time and effort and also reduce the teacher's ability to provide effective instruction to all students. As a result, teachers and school personnel continue to search for effective and efficient interventions for students with challenging behaviors.

Effective behavior intervention plans are especially important for students with a history like Derrick's, who are at risk for developing chronic challenging behaviors. For these students, more generic interventions may not be sufficient, thus requiring individualized intervention plans. Individualized interventions need to occur in the early school years because students with excessive behavior problems are the number one candidates for academic underachievement, special education, overall school failure, and unemployment, as well as for winding up in the criminal justice or adult mental health systems later in life. Well-designed plans can be effective in maintaining many students with problem behaviors within general education classrooms. These plans need to be comprehensive and backed by a team effort involving the student, the teacher and other school staff, student peers, and parents to address both the academic and social needs of the student. The primary purpose of the individualized interventions is to provide intensified, positive support so that the severity of the problem behavior is reduced and to prevent other problems from emerging. This chapter focuses on practical strategies for teachers in assessing a student's problem behavior, developing an individualized behavior intervention plan based on the assessment findings, and evaluating the effects of the intervention plan. The strategies also will be provided with a cultural perspective, which urban teachers may find useful when working with students from low-income, culturally diverse backgrounds.

What Are Individualized Behavior Intervention Plans?

Individualized behavior intervention plans are comprehensive, systematic programs designed for students with severely challenging behaviors that interfere with academic and social success. The goals of a behavior intervention plan are to assist the student in eliminating problem behaviors, developing more adaptive social skills, and increasing academic performance and overall school success. To develop an effective intervention plan, it makes sense to understand the nature of the student's problem behavior and the purposes the behavior serves. Just as we conduct assessments on students' reading performance so as to design effective reading instruction, we also need to assess a student's problem behavior before we can devise an effective behavior intervention plan. The process of understanding the causes of the problem behavior to help in developing effective interventions is called the functional assessment.

Functional assessment is a set of procedures used to obtain information regarding a student's problem behavior—what constitutes the behavior, what triggers it, and what sustains it (Sugai, Lewis-Palmer, & Hagan-Burke, 1999–2000). Subsequently and more important, the information gathered from this assessment procedure is used to design a plan to reduce the problem behavior and ideally prevent it from occurring.

Several rationales support the development of functional assessment and intervention plans. It is important to keep these rationales in mind so as to conduct the assessment appropriately and develop the most effective intervention plans.

- All behaviors are purposeful, and each of them serves a function for the student. Generally, a student displays a problem behavior either to get something or to avoid something or both. For example, Derrick may exhibit off-task behavior to get Ms. Rodger's attention or to avoid doing the assigned tasks.

- Whether a problem behavior occurs or not is closely related to the events occurring in the student's environment. Specifically, these events may make the problem behavior occur more often or less often. For example, a peer's provocation may encourage Derrick to engage in off-task behavior. Similarly, if name-calling is the only way for Derrick to get peer attention, he will be more likely to call people names whenever he wants peers to pay attention to him.

- Intervention strategies are most effective when they directly address the function (that is, the cause) and those environmental events that are related to the problem behavior.

- Problem behaviors are multifaceted, and therefore the understanding of the problem behavior should be multifaceted, involving multifactored assessments and team-based efforts. Similarly, interventions are most effective when they address multiple aspects of the problem behavior. For instance, the most effective intervention for Derrick may require behavioral changes by Derrick, his peers, and his family, as well as various members of the school staff. It may also require that interventions be implemented across various school settings, at home, and in the community.

Several steps are involved in conducting a functional assessment to develop a behavior intervention plan (Salend & Taylor, 2002; Sterling-Turner, Robinson, & Wilczynski, 2001). Following is a brief description of how to conduct a functional assessment and to develop a behavior plan. An applied example is given later in this chapter.

Step 1: Form a Multidisciplinary Team

Because a student's problem behavior can be complicated, an effective assessment and intervention process will require input and collaboration from a variety of professionals as well as nonprofessional staff and parents. The resulting multidisciplinary team may include

- The student's teachers

- Professionals with expertise in functional assessment and interventions (such as school counselor, school psychologist, or behavior specialist)

- Administrators who can provide leadership and guidance to ensure that the assessment and intervention plans are implemented

- Family or community members or both

- Other professionals who are culturally or linguistically knowledgeable about the student's background and therefore may provide meaningful recommendations for culturally responsive interventions for the student

Step 2: Identify and Describe the Problem Behavior

The second step is to gather information from multiple sources to understand the student's problem behavior. This process can be both formal and informal. For instance, teachers may do a simple classroom observation, talk with other teachers who are familiar with the student, or conduct a brief academic and social skills evaluation. To be more comprehensive and to ensure that the information obtained is accurate, it is important for teachers to use multiple methods rather than rely on one or two sources.

Useful methods for gathering initial information include

- Archived record reviews such as disciplinary records, grades or standardized test scores, attendance reports, medical records, and Individualized Education Programs (IEPs) for students with special needs

- Interviews with fellow teachers or school staff, students, parents, and others who are familiar with the student

- Self-made or commercial behavioral rating scales or checklists

- Direct observations of the student in the classroom and other settings

No matter which methods are used, the goal of this step is to answer the following set of questions:

- What is the problem behavior you want to eliminate? Is the behavior a real problem or a misunderstanding of the student's culture?

- What is the behavior you want to reinforce? Does the student have this skill at present? That is, has the student ever been observed to perform the skill?

- How would you describe the problem behavior in clear and specific terms so that all the team members (including the student) can understand what it involves? How would you define the behavior so that it can be overtly observed and measured?

- When, where, and during what activities is the student more likely (and less likely) to exhibit the problem behavior? What happened right before the problem behavior occurred (that is, what are its antecedents)?

- When the problem behavior occurs, what are the responses from people around the student, and what are the consequences for the student? Do the responses and consequences reduce the problem behavior, or do they worsen the problem behavior?

- Did the student previously receive any kind of intervention? Which part was effective and which part was ineffective?

- Why does the student behave that way? What is the student trying to communicate to you?

- Are there other events that may be either directly or indirectly related to the occurrence of the student's problem behavior?

Step 3: Analyze the Information and Develop Summary Statements

Once the information about the problem behavior is obtained, the next step is to analyze the information you gathered from Step 2 and develop a summary statement about the information. A summary statement should address the following four aspects:

- The problem behavior (for example, tantrums, off-task behavior, hitting)

- Antecedents or events that typically precede the problem behavior (for example, difficult task demands, lack of attention)

- Consequences or events that immediately follow the problem behavior and make it more likely to happen in the future (for example, avoid difficult tasks, obtain teacher attention, attract peer attention, receive certain rewards)

- Other events that possibly make the problem behavior worse (for example, frustration from a previous class, lack of sleep, no breakfast, fights on the bus, being reprimanded by parents at home)

Step 4: Verify the Accuracy of the Summary Statement

Once the summary statement is developed, it is important to ensure its accuracy. This is especially critical when the team members are not entirely confident about the information gathered during Step 2 or when there is inconsistency among the team members or among the multiple assessment methods. For example, a few classroom observations may show that Derrick frequently talked out to get attention from the teacher. However, an interview with Derrick may indicate that he did not want to be ridiculed by his classmates when requested to read a passage because he could not read well, and therefore talked out to escape from reading. A simple way to check whether the summary statement is correct is to conduct systematic observations of the identified events and the problem behavior. Because of the demands placed on classroom teachers, team members other than the classroom teacher are in a better position to conduct such observations. When conducting the observations, the team members should pay more attention to the behavior and the events identified in the summary statement and observe how one relates to another. Using the current example, the team member would be advised to pay special attention to the teacher's requesting behavior, Derrick's reading and talking-out behaviors and interactions with other students in the class, and the interactive relationships of these events.

Step 5: Develop and Evaluate the Intervention Plans

After the problem behavior is clearly identified and understood, the intervention plan can be developed, implemented, and evaluated. When developing intervention plans, the team members should consider the following goals:

1. Modify the antecedents to decrease the likelihood that problem behavior will occur. For example:

   - Provide for task preferences or interests (for example, allow preferred materials to avoid a sense of boredom; therefore reduce the chance of acting out).

   - Rearrange schedules or routines (for example, move the student's seat close to the teacher).

   - Use preliminary interventions to clarify the task (for example, brainstorming prior to a writing task to make sure the student knows what to do; teaching the sight words that the student will encounter during reading to avoid frustration).

   - Provide choice interventions (for example, offer a selection of activities and allow the student to decide what to do).

   - Provide instructional modifications (for example, provide easier tasks or shorten the length of the task).

2. Modify the consequences to weaken the problem behavior and strengthen the appropriate behavior. For example:

- Provide stronger rewards for appropriate behavior (for example, frequently praise the student for staying on task).

- Provide no reinforcement for problem behavior (for example, ignore students who exhibit disruptive behavior to get attention).

3. Teach the students socially appropriate skills through social skills instruction strategies such as modeling, behavior rehearsal, and reinforcement (see Chapter Eight). For example:

- Teach appropriate alternatives to the problem behavior (for example, teach the student how to appropriately ask for teacher attention by raising a hand).

- Teach desired skills (for example, teach the student to stay on task).

4. Rearrange or eliminate other events that may increase the problem behavior. For example:

- Develop a quiet corner for independent seatwork.

- Alternate small- and large-group activities.

- Reduce the noise level in the classroom.

- Reduce classroom traffic to avoid conflicts among students.

Once an intervention plan is developed, the team members need to continue to observe, record, and monitor the student's progress to determine whether the student's behavioral changes are satisfactory as a result of the interventions. When necessary, the interventions should be modified to better address the student's problem behavior.

Behavioral Needs of Urban Learners

The majority of the children in urban schools come from poor families. Compared to their more affluent peers, these impoverished children tend to evidence more behavioral challenges, attributed to a variety of factors including school, family, and community conditions as well as individual temperament (Gardner & Miranda, 2001). Children's social behaviors often deteriorate as these factors interact. For example, children in urban settings often present greater deficits and more learning needs than their nonurban peers. Teachers are doubly challenged to meet these needs and keep the students meaningfully engaged in high rates of academic response. Teachers who fail to meet this challenge tend to experience high rates of off-task and disruptive behaviors among their students. The most disruptive children are typically excluded from the learning environment, further increasing their frustration with learning and their tendency to violate classroom and school rules. Without a sense of school success and adequate adaptive behaviors, a student is likely to achieve self-worth in an unsupervised community through antisocial actions. These aggressive, maladaptive behaviors further interfere with the learning process, causing school officials to escalate exclusionary practices. A vicious cycle occurs. Figure 9.1 demonstrates this interaction.

It is therefore very important to understand and address the behavioral needs of urban learners from multiple perspectives. A functional assessment

FIGURE 9.1

Cycle of Poor Behavioral Outcomes

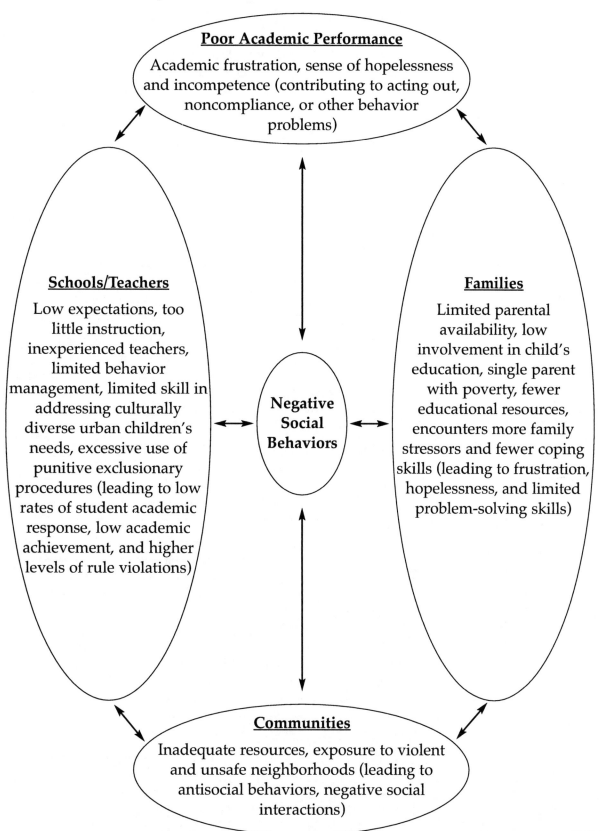

155

is particularly useful and meaningful, as it enables teachers and school personnel to understand why a child behaves in a certain way and what factors cause the behavior to occur—the student's skill deficits, inadequate instruction and lack of active academic engagement, inadequate behavior management in the classroom and other school settings, limited parental involvement, or negative community influences. A better understanding of the student's needs will then allow the teachers and school personnel to select and develop the most adequate intervention plans—that is, plans that will bring about positive academic and social outcomes for the student effectively and efficiently.

Benefits of Behavioral Assessments and Interventions

Teachers derive a number of benefits from implementing functional assessments and intervention plans for students at risk for or with challenging behavior:

- An effective behavior intervention plan based on functional assessments can successfully reduce, if not completely eliminate, the student's problem behavior, allowing teachers to spend more time on instruction. This also relieves the teachers of much pressure and tension in dealing with students' problem behavior while trying to teach.

- An appropriate implementation of a functional assessment allows teachers and school personnel to develop some understanding of the function a particular behavior serves for a student. This understanding enables teachers to address the student's problem behavior more accurately. The functional assessment findings provide directions for which behaviors to target and how one might intervene.

- A functional assessment takes much of the guesswork out of designing behavior interventions for troubling students. This is efficient because it saves valuable time that might be wasted in trying out various ineffective or less effective strategies. It also reduces the likelihood of using strategies that inadvertently reinforce the problem behavior.

- The information gathered through a functional assessment can provide important messages about student behavior, classroom dynamics, and what impact the teacher and other school staff may have on developing or nurturing the problem behavior. For example, Ms. Rodger may realize from the functional assessment process that sending Derrick to in-school detention when he disrupts the class is very rewarding for him, and that he purposely disrupts so that he can stay in the detention room (either to receive one-on-one adult attention or escape from the reading instruction altogether). This information tells Ms. Rodger that it is important to make staying in the classroom more attractive to Derrick by providing more rewarding and engaging reading instruction.

- A student whose problem behavior is reduced through the behavior intervention plan is more likely to concentrate on learning. This will lead to increased academic achievement, and increased achievement is likely to further reduce problem behavior. A more positive learning environment is therefore established for the student—and the teacher.

Revisiting Derrick

As indicated in the introductory scenario, Derrick's problem behavior has been a concern since kindergarten. All his classroom teachers have noted his behavioral difficulties. Fortunately, his behavior was kept under control with the help of effective reading interventions and a behavior intervention plan during his first-grade and second-grade years. These classroom teachers consistently provided a structured learning environment with clear and firm discipline practices for Derrick, which also contributed to his positive behavior changes during these early school years. But even though the reading instruction and the behavior intervention plan have produced improvements in academic achievement and reductions in problem behavior, Derrick's behavior deteriorated during the first grading period of his third-grade year. Contributing factors may have included his exposure to unruly and unsupervised neighborhoods over the summer, which reinforced his antisocial behavior, the unclear and inconsistent classroom management strategies of his current teacher, the inactive and limited academic instruction he has been receiving, and consequences for problem behaviors that he perceives as rewards. Based on Derrick's behavioral profile, it is clear that a comprehensive and individualized behavior plan should be developed and implemented consistently throughout his formal schooling. These early school years are especially critical, as an effective intervention plan should help prevent Derrick from developing more challenging and unmanageable behavior later in life. The ultimate goal of the behavior intervention plan is to break the vicious cycle in which each of the factors impacts the others, resulting in long-lasting problem behaviors. Following the steps described earlier, Derrick's intervention plans were developed, implemented, and evaluated.

1. *Forming a multidisciplinary team.* To start the functional assessment for Derrick, a multidisciplinary team was formed. The team includes the following members:

   Classroom teacher (Ms. Rodger), who initiated the request for such a team

   Behavior specialist, who has expertise in functional assessment and behavior interventions and who has worked with Derrick for more than a year

   School counselor, who has regular weekly contact with Derrick

   Derrick's mother, who is a single parent and works part time

   Parent liaison, who is knowledgeable and sensitive about African American culture and perspectives and who also has good rapport with Derrick's mother

   Principal, who has played an important role in supervising Ms. Rodger and making sure instruction is implemented as planned

2. *Identifying, defining, and gathering information.* The team decided to use several assessment methods to gather information regarding Derrick's problem behavior:

   Reviews of Derrick's school records, including his disciplinary reports

   Interviews with Ms. Rodger, the school counselor, Derrick, and Derrick's mother

   A published behavioral rating scale (Problem Behavior Questionnaire; Lewis, Scott, & Sugai, 1994)

Direct classroom observations, including a scatter plot recording (to identify the times of day during which Derrick experienced the most and least difficulty; see Figure 9.2) and Antecedent-Behavior-Consequence recording (to identify the antecedents and consequences related to Derrick's problem behaviors; see Figure 9.3)

The team focused on reducing Derrick's off-task behavior because it occurred most frequently and often led to more serious class disruptions. To be more precise, the team defined Derrick's off-task behavior as follows:

Delaying performance of an assigned task for more than five seconds after the request was given by the teacher

Turning or looking away from an assigned task, an activity, or task materials for more than five seconds

Engaging in a non–task-related activity (for example, touching or playing with noninstructional objects, talking to peers about non–task-related subjects during academic instruction)

Leaving an assigned area without permission, lying on or hanging out of the chair

Making any noise or inappropriate sound by pounding his hand or an object against another object

According to the multiple assessments, a number of observations were identified as important information for the intervention plan:

Derrick's off-task behavior was most frequent when Ms. Rodger was instructing the whole class or when she was not readily available for Derrick. For example, Derrick would talk out loud or continuously bang on his desk with increasing intensity until he drew her attention. His off-task behavior rarely occurred when Ms. Rodger provided one-on-one instruction or supervision.

Derrick experienced his most difficult time between 10:00 A.M. and 11:30 A.M. daily (see Figure 9.2), when he was required to do independent seatwork while Ms. Rodger was working with other students in small reading groups.

Derrick often got angry when Ms. Rodger did not call on him to answer a question or respond to the lesson. His problem behavior often escalated from that moment forward. His need for constant teacher attention was evident.

Derrick frequently engaged in name-calling to get attention from peers. His use of inappropriate language often led to peers' immediate responses (for example, responding to Derrick by calling him another rude name).

The primary consequences for Derrick's problem behavior were verbal warnings, reprimands, redirection, and detention. These consequences seemed to serve as an avenue for receiving intensive one-on-one attention from an adult at the detention center. When he demonstrated on-task behavior, he rarely was acknowledged for being appropriate in his behavior.

Ms. Rodger said that Derrick showed little ability to control his disruptive, or off-task, behavior.

Derrick said he wanted other students to like him and also wanted to have a special privilege to work with the teacher individually. He also

FIGURE 9.2

Scatter Plot Recording Form and Results for Derrick

Scatter Plot Recording Form

Student: ___Derrick___   Observer: ___Ms. Rodger___

Behavior: **Off-task behavior** (turning away from an assigned task, engaging in non–task-related activities, leaving an assigned area without permission, hanging out of seat, banging on desk or making noises, yelling out an adult's name or making non–task-related responses to an adult)

Starting date: ___11/7/05 (Mon.)___   ☐ seldom   ◺ half the time   ▨ frequent (90%)

Derrick had the most difficult time during the day.

Time	Activity	M	T	W	R	F	M	T	W	R	F
8:30–9:00	Breakfast (N/A)										
9:00–9:30	A.M. work				/						
9:30–10:00	Whole-group reading lesson			▨	▨		/				
10:00–10:30	Small-group reading lesson	▨	▨								
10:30–11:00	Small-group reading lesson	▨		/	▨						
11:00–11:30	Writing	▨		/	▨						
11:30–12:00	Math	/		/	/						
12:00–12:30	Lunch (N/A)			/							
12:30–1:00	Recess (N/A)										
1:00–1:30	Self-selected reading (SSR)										
1:30–2:00	Centers										
2:00–2:30	Centers/Social Studies		▨								
2:30–3:00	Science/Health										
3:00–3:15	Dismissal										

Comments:

When the teacher is working with one reading group during the small-group reading lesson, other students are required to do independent seatwork.

(N/A) refers to the student's not being observed because the teacher is not with the student.

FIGURE 9.3

A-B-C Observation Recording Form and Results for Derrick

A-B-C Observation Recording Form

Student: __Derrick__   Date: __11/07/05__   Setting: __Classroom (reading)__
Observer: __Behavior specialist__   Starting time: __10:00 A.M.__   Ending time: __10:40 A.M.__

Time	Antecedents (A)	Behavior (B)	Consequences (C)
10:02	Ms. R reads and class follows along	Making noises, spacing around, asking where they were at	Ms. R walked over & pointed to the paragraph
10:03	Ms. R reads and class follows along	Flipping through pages, raised hand, then slammed the book down	Ms. R came over "what's wrong"
10:05	Ms. R came over "what's wrong"	Said he wanted to read out loud	Ms. R told him that he will have his turn
10:06	Ms. R reads out loud	Tearing up paper and shooting it at garbage can	Ms. R said to him "No more"
10:08	Ms. R reads out loud	Talking to a student, playing with notebook	Ms. R walked over and stood next to him
10:10	Ms. R reads out loud	Talking to another student	Ms. R reprimanded him "You need to pay attention"
10:15	Ms. R moves away from his desk	Continues talking to the student	Ms. R reprimanded him "Stop, that's a detention"
10:20	Ms. R reads	Playing with paper	Ms. R walked over and pointed to the place he should be looking at
10:26	Independent seatwork	Completed his work quietly	Ms. R remained sitting next to him
10:33	Ms. R teaches entire class	Hanging out of his seat, raising his hand	Ms. R called on him to answer the question
10:35	Ms. R asks the class a question	Raising his hand	Ms. R called on another student
10:36	Ms. R called on another student	Slammed his hands on his desk	Ms. R told him that he has to wait and it's others' turn
10:39	Ms. R told him that he has to wait and it's others' turn	Banging on desk louder and louder	Ms. R reprimanded "That's enough. You are going to the detention room."

Antecedents: Ms. Rodger's attention was directed to the whole class or other students

Consequences: Ms. Rodger provided attention (verbal warnings, reprimands, or redirection) when Derrick exhibited off-task behaviors felt that Ms. Rodger could help him control his behavior if she would call on him faster and more frequently when he raised his hand.

Figure 9.4 provides a summary of functional assessment for Derrick, which is reflected in the preceding statements.

3. *Preparing a behavioral summary statement.* On the basis of the information they gathered, the team summarized Derrick's problem behavior:

> *When given a reading activity in which teacher attention was directed to the whole group or other students (antecedents), Derrick was most likely to engage in off-task behavior such as roaming around the room, making noises, and talking with peers (problem behavior). His off-task behavior was often followed by teacher attention in the form of verbal warnings or reprimands, and then detention when the problem behavior escalated (consequences). Derrick engaged in the off-task behavior to obtain teacher and peer attention.*

To ensure that this summary statement about Derrick's problem behavior was accurate, the team decided to do a small experiment to test their theory:

Ms. Rodger purposely arranged two situations in the classroom during her reading lessons: (situation A) whenever Derrick was off task, she reprimanded him and followed with one-on-one attention; (situation B) whenever Derrick was off task, she ignored him. Each situation was carried out across three reading lessons. The school counselor and the behavior specialist conducted direct observations during these "arranged lessons" to see in which situation Derrick was more likely to stay off task.

The school counselor and the behavior specialist also observed Derrick's behavior under regular lessons across a few days to see if Derrick's off-task behavior was more frequent when Ms. Rodger was working with other students than when she was working directly with Derrick.

The observations showed that Derrick indeed engaged higher levels of off-task behavior when Ms. Rodger was busy working with other students and when she reprimanded him for being off task. This finding indicated that the team's speculation about Derrick's problem behavior was accurate—Derrick displayed off-task behavior to get Ms. Rodger's attention. A behavior intervention plan was then put into action.

4. *Preparing intervention plans.* Using the assessment results, the team developed a behavior intervention plan for Derrick to address his needs (see Figure 9.5).

The goals set for Derrick included the following:

To reduce off-task behavior

To increase appropriate solicitation of teacher attention

To increase involvement in academic instruction

To increase positive social interactions with peers

To achieve these goals, interventions were developed as follows:

Teach Derrick appropriate on-task and attention-recruitment behaviors (for example, raise hand and wait patiently until called on) using social skills training procedures (see Chapter Eight).

Teach Derrick to self-monitor his behavior in the classroom (to help Derrick exercise his self-control in staying on task and request teacher attention appropriately; see Figure 9.6 for a sample self-monitoring

FIGURE 9.4

Functional Assessment Results for Derrick

Problem behavior: Off-task behavior

Antecedents of the behavior	Problem behavior	Consequences of the behavior	Functions of the behavior
• Unavailability of teacher attention • Whole-class reading instruction • Independent seatwork • Peers' provocation	Derrick yells out the teacher's name, bangs on his desk, lies on his chair, plays with non-instructional materials in his drawer, leaves his seat without permission, engages in conversations with peers, and initiates name-calling.	• Receives teacher attention in the forms of verbal warning and reprimands • Receives one-on-one adult attention in the form of detention • Receives peer attention	• To obtain teacher attention • To obtain peer attention

Summary statement:

When given a reading activity in which teacher attention was directed to the whole group or other students, Derrick was most likely to engage in off-task behavior. His off-task behavior is often followed by teacher attention in the forms of verbal warnings or reprimands, and then detention when the problem behavior escalates. Derrick engaged in the off-task behavior to attract teacher and peer attention.

Personal goals:

• Derrick wishes to be a good student, to have other students like him, and to have a special privilege to work with the teacher.

• Derrick feels that his teacher could help him control his behavior if she would call on him faster and more often.

Academic performance:

• Derrick likes and is good at math.

• Derrick performs one year below his grade level in reading. He enjoys reading, yet the reading instruction is too difficult for him.

Family and sociocultural issues:

• Derrick is socialized to use aggressive acts to solve conflicts.

FIGURE 9.5

Behavior Intervention Plan for Derrick

Goals	Interventions	Methods of Evaluation
1. To reduce Derrick's off-task behavior	• Teach Derrick appropriate on-task behavior. • Teach Derrick to self-monitor his behavior. • Ms. Rodger applies the behavioral consequences consistently. • Move Derrick's desk near Ms. Rodger's. • Implement group-oriented contingency system. • Implement a "passport" system (check in and check out). • Observe and record Derrick's off-task behavior daily. • Supervise Ms. Rodger's use of consequences and behavior management system. • Monitor Derrick's use of self-monitoring.	• Provide frequent teacher attention for Derrick's on-task behavior; ignore him when he is off task.
2. To increase Derrick's appropriate solicitation of teacher attention	• Teach Derrick appropriate ways of soliciting attention. • Provide frequent teacher attention for Derrick's good behaviors. • Adopt attention-soliciting sign for Derrick to use when he needs teacher attention, then wait for the teacher to come over.	• Observe and record Derrick's appropriate attention recruitment behavior daily.
3. To increase Derrick's involvement in academic instruction	• Implement effective reading instruction with high student response rates. • Train Derrick's mother to be a reading tutor, a home behavior manager, or an adult mentor.	• Conduct daily and weekly assessment on reading fluency and comprehension.
4. To increase Derrick's positive social interactions with peers	• Engage Derrick in peer-mediated repeated reading program. • Teach Derrick anger management and appropriate social interaction skills. • Train peers to ignore Derrick's inappropriate behaviors and interact with Derrick when he demonstrates appropriate behaviors. • Train Derrick to be a cross-age tutor. • Train Derrick to be a playground monitor.	• Monitor Derrick's tutoring behavior and playground leadership behavior every session. • Monitor Derrick's interactions with peers.

FIGURE 9.6

Sample Self-Monitoring Chart

"How am I doing?"			
1. Sit in seat and work quietly	1	☺	☹
	2	☺	☹
	3	☺	☹
	4	☺	☹
	5	☺	☹
2. Check my work	6	☺	☹
	7	☺	☹
	8	☺	☹
	9	☺	☹
3. "Need my teacher?"	10	☺	☹
	11	☺	☹
	12	☺	☹
	13	☺	☹
4. Raise my hand	14	☺	☹
	15	☺	☹

recording chart). Derrick was instructed to observe and record his own behavior on his recording chart during independent seatwork while Ms. Rodger was working with other students. The behavioral specialist met with Derrick at the end of the session to discuss his on-task and self-monitoring behavior.

Teach Ms. Rodger to provide positive attention and praise frequently when Derrick was on task and to ignore Derrick when he was off task.

Restructure Ms. Rodger's classroom rules and behavior management plans to ensure that the rules are clear and the behavior management plans implemented accurately, consistently, and effectively (revisit Chapter Seven for strategies).

Train peers to ignore Derrick's inappropriate behaviors and to interact with Derrick when he demonstrates appropriate behaviors.

Continue to implement effective reading instruction that provides Derrick with many opportunities for active academic engagement and responses (revisit Chapter Three for strategies). Instruction such as peer tutoring (Chapter Five) and repeated readings (Chapter Six) are especially desirable for Derrick.

Train Derrick to be a cross-age tutor in tutoring a second-grade student on high-frequency words. Reinforce Derrick for good tutor behavior.

Train Derrick to be a playground monitor, handing out "Caught Being Good" tickets (described in Chapter Ten) to students who follow the playground rules appropriately. Reinforce Derrick for good leadership behavior.

Implement an adult mentor system for Derrick to check in and check out when he tutors or monitors. All the team members can serve as adult mentors. When Derrick checks in with an adult, the mentor goes through the behavior goals and expectations with Derrick and encourages him to follow through during the day. When Derrick checks out, the adult mentor praises and reinforces his good behaviors and discusses his inappropriate behaviors. This also provides Derrick with opportunities to receive adult attention with good behaviors. Figure 9.7 shows selected pages of a "passport" that Derrick used for checking in and out.

Actively involve Derrick's mother in his behavior intervention plans. Train Derrick's mother to be a reading tutor, a home behavior manager, or an adult mentor (revisit Chapter Eleven for strategies).

5. *Evaluating progress.* All the team members should continue to evaluate the effectiveness of the intervention plans by monitoring Derrick's progress regularly. Once the intervention plan is under way, the team should meet at least once a month to report Derrick's behavioral progress. If his behavior does not change in a desired direction, the team members will need to conduct additional assessments and modify the plans as necessary. The frequency of the meetings can be reduced, if Derrick progresses positively.

Effective Strategies for Teachers

Dealing with students who exhibit challenging behaviors can be demanding for teachers. Teachers often grow frustrated because they have to spend so much time managing these students' problem behaviors that they are unable to provide instruction as they have planned. Following are several practical strategies that teachers can implement in their classrooms for students with the most challenging behaviors.

Once a Day

- Continue to adopt effective academic strategies (see Chapters Two through Six), behavior management systems (see Chapter Seven), social skills instruction (see Chapter Eight), schoolwide behavior support systems (see Chapter Ten), and parental involvement methods (see Chapter Eleven). These strategies not only are critical for preventing more severe behavioral problems but also provide the foundation for the effectiveness of an individualized behavior plan.

- When a certain student is observed to display high levels of problem behaviors, pay close attention every day to that student's behavior.

FIGURE 9.7

Sample Passport

for
Derrick

PASSPORT

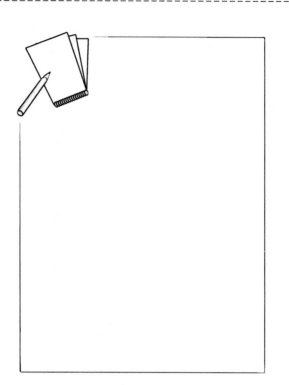

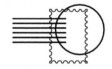

My Goals

1. To be a good student
2. To have other students like me more
3. To have a special privilege of working with teachers

Passport Rules

1. Follow teacher's directions (do what she asks you to do)
2. Ignore bad comments (don't look, don't say anything, think about passport)
3. Help other students (tutor, use nice words)
4. Obtain attention appropriately (raise hand & use flag)
5. Get GLAD (smile, say good things about self)

(Front)

Figure 9.7 (continued)

Devise a simple data collection method to record the level of the student's behavior. For example, placing a paper clip in a jar every time the student yells out is a simple and easy way to tally the number of times the student yells out. Seek assistance from other school professionals, as necessary, to conduct more extensive and systematic observations of the student's problem behavior.

- If a behavior intervention plan already exists for a certain student, daily record keeping is imperative. This record keeping will allow teachers to evaluate the student's behavioral changes more accurately.

- Look carefully into various events in the environment surrounding the student and his behaviors. These events, including your behaviors, may possibly be contributing to the student's behaviors. For example, you may be attending only to the undesirable behaviors and failing to recognize the times when the student is acting appropriately.

- Instruct students to self-monitor their behavior, as part of the behavior intervention plans.

Once a Week

- Help students develop their own weekly behavioral goals the first day of each week. Review and discuss students' progress the last day of each week to see if they have all reached their individual behavior goals. Reward students who reached their goals with certificates or other reinforcers.

- Celebrate students' progress in their behavior improvements. A small celebration party at the end of the week can be exciting and rewarding for students.

- Communicate, as much as possible, with other team members weekly to evaluate the student's behavioral progress. Adopt their suggestions, when appropriate. Compile the student's behavioral progress from other team members as permanent records.

Once a Grading Period

- Schedule a meeting of the behavior intervention team to review the effectiveness of the intervention plan and student progress. Determine whether the individualized intervention plan should be continued, modified, or terminated.

- Communicate with parents regarding the student's behavioral changes and updates of the behavior intervention plans.

- Recruit a fellow teacher or other school professional to evaluate your classroom behavior management system or academic instruction. A discussion with other teachers or staff can be useful in improving your instructional techniques. This can be done by visiting each other's classrooms and exchanging tips. Such visits are also helpful in finding out the dynamics between the troublesome students and the teacher or other students.

- Arrange an informal interview with the students. Obtain information from students regarding their perception of school, instruction, family, and goals. Take into consideration the student's point of view and incorporate it into the intervention plan, if appropriate.

- Conduct a behavior scanning to see which students may be in need of an individualized behavior intervention plan.

Once a Year

- Begin your school year by training students to display good behaviors that they are expected to follow throughout the school year. It is critical that these skills are taught clearly and thoroughly. The time spent on good skills training will pay off as students acquire the skills and use them adequately.

- Follow up with the student's behavior intervention plan over the summer, where possible. Provide parents with a simple chart listing behaviors they might focus on during the summer months as well as ways they might reward these behaviors when they occur. For students with the most challenging behavior, it is important to prevent the students from learning more problem behaviors or reverting to where they were before the intervention was implemented.

Related Readings

Chandler, L. K., & Dahlquist, C. M. (2002). *Functional assessment: Strategies to prevent and remediate challenging behavior in school settings.* Upper Saddle River, NJ: Prentice Hall.

McConnell, M. E. (2001). *Functional behavioral assessment: A systematic process for assessment and intervention in general and special education classrooms.* Denver, CO: Love.

O'Neill, R. E., Horner, R. H., Albin, R. W., Sprague, J. R., Storey, K., & Newton, J. S. (1997). *Functional assessment and program development for problem behavior: A practical handbook* (2nd ed.). Pacific Grove, CA: Brooks/Cole.

Ryan, A. L., Halsey, H. N., & Matthews, W. J. (2003). Using functional assessment to promote desirable student behavior in schools. *Teaching Exceptional Children, 35*(5), 8–15.

Scott, T. M., & Nelson, C. M. (1999). Using functional behavioral assessment to develop effective intervention plans: Practical classroom applications. *Journal of Positive Behavioral Intervention, 1,* 242–251.

Shippen, M. E., Simpson, R. G., & Crites, S. A. (2003). A practical guide to functional behavioral assessment. *Teaching Exceptional Children, 35*(5), 36–44.

Witt, J. C., Daly, E. M., & Noell, G. (2000). *Functional assessments: A step-by-step guide to solving academic and behavior problems.* Longmont, CO: Sopris West.

Related Internet Resources

Center for Effective Collaboration and Practice: http://cecp.air.org/fba/

The Center for Effective Collaboration and Practice offers detailed information on functional behavior assessment and behavior intervention plans. This is divided into four topics: (1) an IEP team's instruction in functional behavior assessment and behavior intervention plans, (2) conducting a functional behavior assessment, (3) creating positive behavior intervention plans and supports, and (4) a trainer of trainers' guide.

Multimodal Functional Behavior Assessment: http://mfba.net/

> This Web site provides downloadable forms for functional behavior assessment and behavior intervention plans. Several samples of the functional assessment and intervention plans are also provided. This Web site is also linked to a list of research literature on functional assessment.

Positive Behavior Support and Functional Assessment: from ERIC
Clearinghouse on Disabilities and Gifted Education:
http://ericec.org/digests/e580.html

> This article provides a brief description of positive behavioral support and how a school can implement such a system at three levels (schoolwide, small groups, and individual). Information on individual behavioral support, including the use of functional assessment, is included.

Positive Behavioral Interventions and Supports: http://www.pbis.org/

> The Technical Assistance Center on Positive Behavioral Interventions and Supports (PBIS) offers fruitful information and resources on a technology of schoolwide positive behavior interventions and support. It provides demonstrations on the feasible and effective behavior supports at the levels of individual students, classrooms, families, and schools.

CHAPTER 10

Schoolwide Behavior System

Stevenson Elementary

Mrs. Baldwin is a recently employed principal at Stevenson Elementary School, an urban K–5 school. After three months of observations and examinations, she had enormous concerns about excessive rule violations among students. Mrs. Baldwin suspected that physical fighting was one of the most frequent and serious misbehaviors at Stevenson. However, she was uncertain about why it occurred so often, where and when it was most likely to occur, and what students were most commonly involved. To develop a better understanding of this issue, she decided to take a closer look at the existing office disciplinary referral data. After reviewing the office referral data, Mrs. Baldwin found that fighting was indeed the leading infraction; it mostly occurred on the playground between 12:00 p.m. and 1:00 p.m. (during the afternoon recess), and 90 percent of the fights involved students at the fourth- and fifth-grade levels. Further, more than half of the student population had been involved in fights, and three-quarters of the physical fights were initiated by males. A small number of students identified as troublemakers by the classroom teachers tended to engage in fights repeatedly, and students involved in fights were often suspended for one to five days. Strikingly, Mrs. Baldwin found that many students had only a vague idea of what the school rules were and what was expected of them. Armed with this information, Mrs. Baldwin decided to initiate a schoolwide behavioral intervention program to address the frequent fighting among students and to create a more positive and successful school climate at Stevenson, where all students would experience success in learning.

Why Schoolwide Positive Behavior Interventions?

Discipline has been one of the utmost concerns for educators, parents, and students in today's American schools. School personnel are often challenged to deal with pervasive student misbehavior, and parents worry about the safety of their children as well as the quality of their education. Students with academic or behavioral difficulties, especially those from culturally and linguistically diverse backgrounds, may continue to struggle within their schooling and even feel neglected when the academic and disciplinary program does not address their needs. Creating an effective disciplinary program to have a positive and lasting effect on students' behavior is an essential yet most challenging task for school personnel. When developing a school disciplinary program, educators may find it useful to revisit the definition of the word *discipline*. According to the *American Heritage Dictionary of the English Language* (2000), the word refers both to prevention and to remediation—through training, teaching, or punishment—to produce a specific pattern of behavior. Although discipline may involve the use of punishment, many educational researchers have joined the dictionary in emphasizing the more positive and proactive aspects of this term in implementing a set of training procedures to enhance the students' academic and social success (for example, see Cartledge, Tillman, & Talbert-Johnson, 2001).

To ensure student safety and academic learning, schools often have a certain set of disciplinary procedures for dealing with students' problem behaviors. Although schools vary greatly, many teachers and school administrators tend to rely heavily on the use of exclusionary practices such as time-out, detention, in-school or out-of-school suspension, and expulsion when a problem behavior is observed. The intention is clear: to suppress the problem behavior and to send a message to every student that the behavior is inappropriate and will result in punishing consequences. However, the effects of such actions may not always have the desired outcomes.

Potential benefits of exclusionary punishment:

- It may suppress the problem behavior effectively among good—that is, relatively willing—students who find the exclusionary practices punishing and who understand the message.

- Teachers tend to find such practices very rewarding. ("That's one troubled child I don't have to deal with in my classroom.")

- It is necessary when dealing with behaviors that may endanger the students or others.

Negative impacts of exclusionary practices:

- Many students enjoy being excluded from demanding or less rewarding classroom situations and therefore may even misbehave deliberately in an effort to be removed from the classroom.

- Students are excluded from the learning environment, which further contributes to their academic difficulties or social behavior deficits.

- Very little, if any, academic instruction or teaching is provided when the student is in the exclusionary settings (outside the classroom, in the detention room, on the street).

- Students may experience anger toward the person who suspended or expelled them, which contributes to negative staff-student interactions.

- Repeated exclusions are strongly related to academic failure, negative school attitudes, negative self-image and peer relations, grade retention, and high dropout rates (Shingles & Lopez-Reyna, 2002).

- The school climate may become aversive and hostile when exclusionary practices are used instead of reinforcement.

- Students from culturally and linguistically diverse backgrounds, regardless of their socioeconomic status or the severity of their behavior—especially African American males—are more likely than their peers to experience exclusionary practices (Skiba, Michael, Nardo, & Peterson, 2000).

Effective school disciplinary practices should contain a set of empirically based strategies that focus on directly teaching students expected behaviors as well as reinforcing or acknowledging appropriate behavior on a schoolwide basis in order to address the social and behavioral needs of all students. The strategies and principles discussed in this chapter are based largely on the schoolwide positive behavior support (PBS) model developed by Rob Horner and George Sugai and their colleagues (for example, see Horner et al., 2000; Lewis & Sugai, 1999; Sugai et al., 2000). PBS is one approach that has been demonstrated to be effective in preventing student problem behaviors, facilitating student achievement, and creating a positive, successful school climate (Lewis & Sugai, 1999).

In addition to its positive impact on pupil and staff behavior, the adoption of schoolwide PBS also enables schools to meet the requirements of the Individuals with Disabilities Education Act (IDEA) Amendments of 2004 to provide appropriate services for students with disabilities. Many school administrators face conflict between the demands to discipline students with disabilities with exclusionary practices while adhering to the IDEA mandates (that is, provision of free and appropriate public education, implementation of functional behavioral assessment and behavioral intervention plans, and adoption of positive behavioral interventions and supports). PBS provides schools with tools not only to address the unique needs of students with disabilities, but also to maintain the rights of all students, with and without disabilities, to receive an appropriate education.

What Is Schoolwide Positive Behavior Support?

Schoolwide PBS enables schools to develop and implement effective practices to address schoolwide, classroom, and individual problem behaviors (Lewis & Sugai, 1999). It consists of multiple components that can respond effectively to the multiple behavioral challenges faced within our schools. The aim of a schoolwide PBS is to provide a continuum of behavioral support in bringing about positive changes in the school system (policies, routines, and structures), school physical environments, and student and adult behaviors (Sugai et al., 2000).

The professional literature identifies the following as important features of a schoolwide PBS program (Lewis & Sugai, 1999; Metzler, Biglan, Rusby, & Sprague, 2001):

- *Team-based problem solving and planning.* Because of its comprehensive and system-driven elements, the development and implementation of a schoolwide PBS requires a team-based effort. It requires team expertise and collaboration.

- *Administrator and staff commitment and support.* To be successful, a schoolwide PBS requires long-term commitment from the administrators and all staff members in the school. All members should actively and continuously participate in the implementation of the schoolwide PBS, with the school administrator as the active leader.

- *Systematic assessment of disciplinary practices and processes.* A set of systematic and ongoing assessments is necessary to evaluate the school disciplinary practices. Only in this manner can school personnel know whether the school disciplinary program is effective and what changes should be made to enhance its success.

- *Ongoing staff development.* An effective PBS program requires a behaviorally competent member to provide ongoing staff support in skill development. A behavioral consultant from outside the school system may be necessary.

- *Data-based decision making.* School data including office referrals, student attendance, and school reports should be reviewed regularly to provide ongoing monitoring of student behavior, guide decision making and planning, and determine whether the interventions are working. School personnel should not depend on feelings or guesses to make their decisions, as personal impressions can provide false or inadequate information.

- *Establishment of clear policies and agenda.* A schoolwide PBS program requires the school to establish a clear set of disciplinary policies and agenda so that everyone involved in the PBS has specific guidelines to follow. The policies and agenda should prescribe primary interventions as priorities to maximize the positive effects.

- *Adoption of evidence-based practices.* The implementation of research-validated practices (see other chapters in this handbook) including direct social skills training, proactive behavior development, effective academic instruction, individual behavioral plans, and parent training and involvement is one distinct feature of the traditional disciplinary programs. A successful schoolwide PBS approach depends heavily on the implementation of evidence-based procedures or strategies.

- *Application of functional assessment.* All behaviors are purposeful. A function-based approach should serve as the foundation for addressing students' problem behaviors. This will enable school personnel to identify the source of the problem behavior and consequently to develop appropriate interventions.

With the recognition that each student has unique academic and behavioral needs, schoolwide PBS is designed to provide different levels of support including *universal* (primary prevention), *specialized group* (secondary prevention), and *individual student* (tertiary prevention) interventions to promote the success of all students (Lewis & Sugai, 1999; Sprague, Sugai, Horner, & Walker, 1999). Therefore, schoolwide PBS is a continuum of instructional and behavioral supports provided to all students and staff. Table 10.1 lists the assumption, purpose, and recommended academic and behavioral interventions at each level. Figure 10.1 illustrates their relationships.

As described in Table 10.1, school administrators and educators must adopt strategies that are evidence driven and that address a continuum of schoolwide academic and behavioral supports across all school settings and all students. Procedures for these supports should focus on developing positive expectations for behavior, teaching and reinforcing the academic and behavioral expectations, and monitoring students' progress and the intervention effectiveness.

Like other research-based practices, schoolwide PBS also requires a system to evaluate the success of the program. Office disciplinary referrals may be a good option. Office referrals are perhaps one of the most commonly used means for managing pupil behavior. A typical sequence is that a student's

TABLE 10.1

Continuum of Schoolwide Positive Academic and Behavioral Support

	Universal Interventions	Specialized Group Interventions	Individual Student Interventions
Level of prevention	Primary	Secondary	Tertiary
Targeted students	All students	Students at risk for academic or behavioral difficulties	Students at high risk for academic or behavioral difficulties
Assumption	80–90 percent of students will arrive at school with readiness for important academic and social skills	5–10 percent of students who present significant risks for school failure may not respond to universal interventions and will therefore require more intensive and specialized interventions	1–5 percent of students with chronic, long-standing academic failure or challenging behavior are in need of highly specialized and individualized interventions to be successful
Purpose	• To ensure that students with academic and social readiness will continue to develop and sustain the use of mastered skills	• To provide at-risk students with additional academic and behavioral support	• To provide high-risk students with intensive academic and behavioral support
Purpose	• To prevent academic or behavioral difficulties from occurring	• To prevent academic and behavioral difficulties from developing into disabilities	• To prevent chronic academic and behavior disabilities from further increasing in severity
Academic strategies	• High rates of student responses	• High rates of student responses	• High rates of student responses
	• Preventive and proactive academic instruction	• Intensive academic instruction	• Intensive one-on-one instruction
		• High academic efficiency	• Assessment-based instruction
Behavioral strategies	• Schoolwide social skill training	• Group-specific social skills training (such as problem solving and anger management instruction)	• Functional assessment
	• Positive and proactive discipline	• Self-management programs	• Function-based, individualized intervention plans
	• Specific and clear behavioral expectations and routines	• Adult mentors	• Intensive social skills training

Table 10.1 (continued)

Universal Interventions	Specialized Group Interventions	Individual Student Interventions
• Behavioral reinforcement systems		• High levels of parent involvement
• Active supervision and monitoring		• Multi-agency collaboration

problem behavior is reported, the student is sent to the principal's office, a consequence is delivered, and the event is documented in writing for the school. However, these data generally are collected to meet administrative requirements rather than to determine whether the disciplinary practices are effective in improving student behavior. Since the office referral data are permanent and available in most schools, they provide school personnel with easy access to the data at any time for evaluation. In addition, the office referral data allow school administrators and teachers to identify appropriate interventions to address students' disciplinary problems more effectively. For example, the types of frequent infractions may alert teachers to focus on teaching students how to interact with others more appropriately. The identification of repeated offenders may advise teachers which populations need more intensive support.

A primary purpose for collecting and analyzing office referral data is to help school administrators evaluate the existing discipline program and design more effective interventions to increase all students' success. When students' behavior patterns continue over time, or when the misbehavior remains at high levels despite regular disciplinary action, existing procedures should be reexamined and modified. This reevaluation points to an important task for the school administrators to examine the office referral data more carefully and functionally. When analyzing the office referral data, administrators and teachers may find the indicators listed in Table 10.2 useful for determining the appropriate PBS interventions.

The stressors of low-socioeconomic-level urban environments are reflected in the schools, resulting in greater learning and behavioral challenges when compared to their nonurban counterparts. These conditions in urban schools not only demand more teacher time and effort, they also reduce the teachers' ability to provide effective instruction to the misbehaving students and their peers. The impulse to exclude misbehaving students so as to free up time for those who welcome instruction is strong. However, as mentioned earlier, exclusion typically fails to create an environment where urban learners are provided with rich learning opportunities for both academic and social development. The application of the traditional exclusionary practices in urban schools is counterproductive, most likely exacerbating problem behaviors. This is particularly destructive for those students with or at risk for learning and behavior disorders, who most frequently experience exclusionary actions. Furthermore, as the problem behavior increases, administrators—in their zeal to find a better solution—frequently fall into several traps: believing that the tougher they are the better, that fixing the most challenging students is all they need to

FIGURE 10.1

Levels and Systems of Supports of Schoolwide PBS

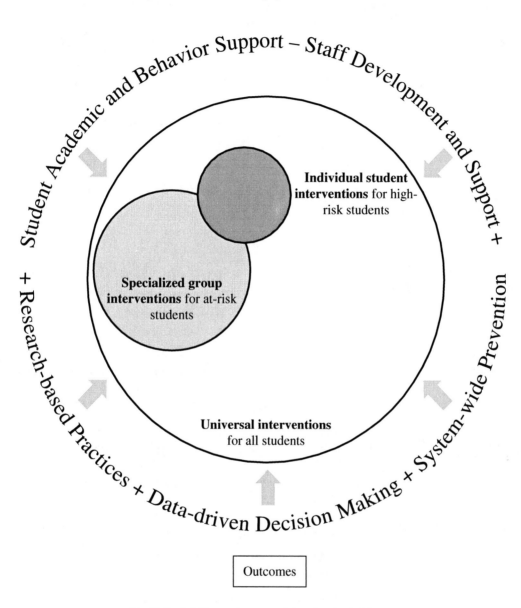

Outcomes

• Pupil Social Competence and Academic Achievement
• Positive School Climate
• School Discipline Improvements

do, that what they need is a quick fix with one powerful magic trick, that someone else has the solution, and that more of everything is better (Horner et al., 2000). Unfortunately, these beliefs are irrational and have been found to be ineffective and even detrimental. What is needed is a proactive schoolwide disciplinary system that emphasizes prevention based on effective instructional principles, incorporates empirically validated behavior-change techniques, focuses on a systems approach, and addresses ongoing professional development.

TABLE 10.2

Linking Office Referral Data to Schoolwide PBS Program

Office Referral Data	Directions for Interventions
1. Number or percentage of students receiving referrals	Program universal, schoolwide interventions if the number is high
2. Number of referrals by month	Provide booster or additional behavioral contingencies for high-referral months
3. Infraction types	Target the behaviors (alternatives to the infractions) for social skills instruction
4. Repeat offenders	Develop specialized group or individual student interventions
5. Locations or classrooms in which the infractions occur	Implement classroom- or setting-specific interventions
6. Period of time during which high referrals exist	Emphasize interventions during the targeted periods
7. Types of disciplinary actions	Reevaluate the effects of these actions if the number of referrals increases or remains unchanged over time
8. Office referrals by grade level or classroom	Target the grade levels or the classrooms with high referrals for intervention

Benefits of Schoolwide Positive Behavior Support

Teachers and schools reap a number of benefits when they begin to implement the schoolwide PBS program:

- It facilitates a positive school climate.

- It can successfully reduce students' problem behaviors and improve their academic performance.

- It enhances students' positive attitudes toward the school.

- It improves the positive interactions among students and between students and staff members.

- It provides different levels of behavior supports that allow teachers to address different student needs efficiently, from those who just need minor support to those who require more intensive, in-depth behavioral services.

- It allows teachers to focus on delivering instruction, as students' problem behaviors are reduced with the schoolwide PBS program.

- It gives teachers ongoing support and training, provided by the school administrators, the behavior support team members, and the behavioral specialists.

- It enables teachers to focus on rewarding students' desired behaviors rather than punishing their inappropriate behaviors.

- It allows all the staff members and students to have the same understanding with regard to the disciplinary issues.

- It enables teachers to meet the requirements mandated by the law when working with students with disabilities.

- It allows school administrators and teachers to meet their accountabilities with regard to student safety and academic achievement.

Revisiting Stevenson Elementary

Concerning the high levels of office referrals at Stevenson and high frequencies of student behavior problems occurring every day, Mrs. Baldwin saw a need for a schoolwide PBS program. She first held a staff meeting and identified several members to serve on the PBS team. In addition to Mrs. Baldwin, the team members included the assistant principal, the school counselor, a special education teacher with training on effective behavioral practices, two representative general education teachers (one at the primary grade level and the other at the intermediate grade level), and the parent liaison, who had expertise in prompting parent involvement and working with culturally and linguistically diverse students. A behaviorally competent and culturally sensitive professor from a nearby university, Dr. Parker, served as a consultant. Once the team members were identified, Mrs. Baldwin got down to the real business. The team first met to brainstorm ideas about the nature and components of the schoolwide PBS program, brought ideas to the staff meetings, and exchanged the ideas with other teachers concerning what was needed and what should be done.

The work fell into eight major areas:

- Develop PBS policies and agendas.

- Reconstruct and teach behavioral expectations.

- Establish specific behavioral supports.

- Improve academic performance.

- Restructure physical environments.

- Provide in-service training.

- Develop assessment methods and evaluate data regularly.

- Enhance parent and student involvement.

PBS Policies and Agendas

CONCERN

The disciplinary program implemented at Stevenson has focused on the use of office disciplinary referrals to deal with students' problem behaviors. Mrs. Baldwin had not observed any reduction of students' rule violations. In fact, most students continued to display inappropriate behaviors despite the teachers' delivery of exclusionary procedures.

INTERVENTION

To provide a clear blueprint for the PBS program, the team members first developed specific policies and agendas in writings for the PBS program. The PBS blueprint included the following:

- Goals, objectives, and purposes of the schoolwide PBS program

- A list of the PBS team members and their respective responsibilities

- Timelines for the implementation of the schoolwide PBS

- A list of the positive behavioral expectations and their definitions in each school setting

- Identification of specific PBS interventions, the responsible adults, procedures, time frames, assessment methods, and expected outcomes

- Procedures for responding to students' challenging behavior likely to endanger themselves or others

After the schoolwide PBS policies and agendas were developed, copies were distributed to all other school personnel for review and discussion of their clarity and feasibility.

Behavioral Expectations

CONCERN

Most of the existing school rules were unclear and negative ("No tattling"; "No fighting"), communicating to students only what they should not do rather than what they were expected to do instead.

INTERVENTION

All the teachers were asked to think about one or two behaviors that they perceived as the most important skills for their students to perform throughout the day. After discussion, four behavioral expectations were identified:

- Be honest—if you did it, admit it.

- Be helpful—offer help when others kindly ask.

- Be respectful—listen to your teachers; keep hands and feet to yourself.

- Be kind—say nice things about others.

Recognizing the importance of direct skills training, Mrs. Baldwin and the PBS team members involved the entire school in a full day of training involving these behavioral expectations. Prior to the student training, all the staff members received in-service training on the definitions of the behavioral expectations and how to deliver the skill instruction effectively. On the day of the training, all students participated in a thirty-minute orientation session on the behavioral expectations and what they would be engaging in for the rest of the day. Then, each class was assigned and rotated through each of the six school settings (classroom, hallway, restroom, cafeteria, playground, bus) to receive direct skill instruction on the setting-specific behavioral expectations. All the teachers and staff were to deliver the instruction through definition of the skills, modeling, role-playing, student practice, and feedback.

Posters of the behavioral goals were also developed and displayed in all school settings to remind students of their expected responsibility.

Specific Behavioral Supports

CONCERN 1

A majority of students at Stevenson engaged in infractions. The office referral data showed chronic high levels of office referrals from all parts of the school.

INTERVENTION

To provide universal behavior supports for all students at Stevenson, the PBS team members developed procedures to prevent the problem behaviors and encourage appropriate behaviors.

- *Flying flags.* The "flying flags" program is a group contingency procedure implemented throughout the school day. Each classroom was given a flag representing the whole class. Students decorated the flag with their names, indicating ownership and responsibility. At the beginning of each morning and each afternoon period, the classroom teacher hung their class flag outside the classroom door. When a student was observed to exhibit problem behavior, the classroom teacher would take down the flag indicating that the class was disqualified from receiving a reward for that period. Mrs. Baldwin visited the classes randomly each day, and students were rewarded with school supplies such as pencils, erasers, or stickers when the class flag was still displayed. Students had no idea when Mrs. Baldwin would stop by their class, and therefore they would need to be good all the time to keep the flag out and receive the rewards.

- *Behavior charting.* A behavior chart was posted on the bulletin board in the hallway showing each classroom's behavioral progress in earning the flying flag. When the class achieved the predetermined criterion, additional rewards were provided to all students in that class. A sample of the behavioral chart is shown in Figure 10.2.

- *"Caught being good" ticket.* Students received a "caught being good" ticket (see Figure 10.3) whenever they were observed to perform an appropriate behavior. The tickets were collected on Fridays for a school-wide prize drawing. Students whose tickets were drawn received small rewards from Mrs. Baldwin.

CONCERN 2

The majority of fighting involved fourth- and fifth-grade students.

INTERVENTION

The PBS team targeted all fourth and fifth graders (specialized group) for additional social skills instruction on alternatives to fighting. The school counselor delivered the social skills instruction four times a week, twenty minutes each session. Students engaged in discussions and role plays on ways to interact with peers more appropriately when encountering conflict situations. Each student was to bring in a real-life situation to the group for discussion and role-playing.

CONCERN 3

The majority of physical fighting involved male students.

INTERVENTION

- The PBS team members agreed that one reason their urban males engaged in high levels of misbehavior was the lack of good male role models and positive relationships with the adults in the school building. The majority of students at Stevenson were African American, and the PBS

FIGURE 10.2

Schoolwide Behavior Chart

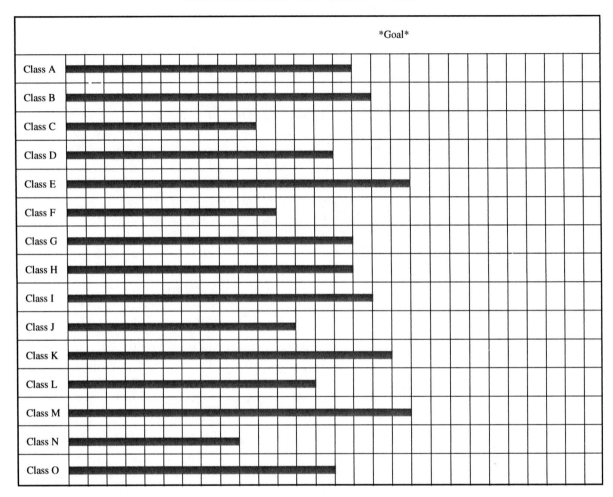

team understood the importance of male role models and positive adult relationships for this student population. Interventions for male students involved the following: With the assistance of Dr. Parker, the PBS team invited several African American male college students to speak with all students at Stevenson. The college students were selected to represent a success with a variety of majors and interests (for example, sport, science, law, medicine, education). Assemblies were held for the college students to speak with Stevenson students about their work at college, their success stories, and how they worked hard to get to the college.

• These college student speakers also agreed to volunteer working with the male student group on a weekly basis. The college students worked in pairs in collaboration with the parent liaison to deliver specialized social skills instruction (for example, be respectful, be kind) to the male students once a week. The instruction focused on real-life scenarios that students are more likely to encounter.

• Mrs. Baldwin and other staff members also took time to talk with students on a daily basis. The conversations could be short and simply involved asking students how they were doing. The purpose was to help

FIGURE 10.3

"Caught Being Good" Ticket

I was caught being good

Name: _____

For: _____

Date: _____

students establish positive relationships with adults in the school building so that the students would feel they had someone they could connect with and who also cared for them.

CONCERN 4
A small group of students were repeat offenders (called "frequent flyers" by the weary staff). These students were also the troublemakers identified by their classroom teachers.

INTERVENTION
The PBS team targeted these repeat offenders for individual student interventions. The team members conducted functional assessments and developed individualized intervention plans (see Chapter Nine) accordingly to address the individual students' problem behaviors.

Academic Performance

CONCERN
The PBS team believes that low academic performance strongly correlates with the high levels of misbehavior. A high percentage of students at Stevenson

were below grade level in reading and math. Many students were frustrated as a result of their academic inability and therefore often displayed inappropriate behaviors as a way to express their frustration.

INTERVENTION

Interventions were developed and implemented to improve student academic achievement. These interventions were as follows:

- Several teachers at Stevenson worked closely with the university graduate assistants who were under the supervision of Professor Parker in implementing effective academic instruction such as explicit phonemic awareness instruction, classwide peer tutoring, repeated readings, and response cards instruction (see Chapters Two, Four, Five, and Six). The teachers were trained and coached to deliver the academic instruction to their students.

- In collaboration with the YMCA, an after-school tutoring program was also carried out to provide additional academic support for students at Stevenson.

- A group of college students majoring in elementary education or special education continued to provide one-to-one tutoring to pupils identified as the lowest performing students. In the past, the one-hour tutoring sessions occurred twice a week. To improve students' academic performance, the tutoring sessions were increased to three times a week.

Physical Environments

CONCERN

Mrs. Baldwin found that many fighting or other violent behaviors occurred on the playground during recess. Some of the reasons for the high rates of fighting included unclear playground rules, limited adult monitoring, and few available activities for students.

INTERVENTION

To reduce and prevent the incidence of fighting on the playground, the PBS team introduced the following changes:

- Specify playground behavioral expectations with positive and clear language.

- Directly teach students playground-specific behavioral expectations. All of the students received many opportunities to practice meeting these expectations.

- Prior to entering the playground, the classroom teacher reviews the rules and reminds students about the playground expectations.

- Increase the number of teachers present on the playground from two to six. Each of the playground monitoring teachers was to heavily reinforce students' positive playground behaviors by providing verbal praise and the "caught being good" tickets.

- The PBS team selected and trained a group of ten students to be playground peer mentors. The students were taught and instructed to deliver positive statements ("Nice game you played"; "Great job with helping your teammate on catching that ball") along with "caught being good" tickets when they observed a student peer playing appropriately. The peer mentors were praised for their good monitoring behavior as well. Students earned the privilege to be peer mentors, which was a position of high status in the school. Peer mentors changed every two weeks.

- The PBS team invited the physical education teacher to develop and provide additional activities: jogging, yoga, and dance. Students could enroll in the activities if they were interested. Mrs. Baldwin also purchased more playground equipment such as monkey bars, jump ropes, swings, and basketballs. The idea was to provide students with more opportunities to engage in a variety of appropriate, interesting activities on the playground.

- The PBS team developed and implemented a group contingency system on the playground. The entire school could have a pizza party on Friday if the number of rule violations on the playground was lower that week than the previous week.

In-Service Training

CONCERN

During her supervision and evaluation of the teachers' skills in delivering instruction, Mrs. Baldwin had the following observations:

- Most teachers focused on the students' inappropriate behaviors and often ignored the students' desired behaviors. In many cases, this focus rewarded students' displays of misbehavior.

- Several classrooms had much downtime during which students received no instruction. In these classrooms, students were clearly unengaged in the instruction.

- In some classrooms, very little direct teaching was observed at all. Students were mostly given large quantities of worksheets to complete independently.

- A few teachers failed to develop clear and specific lesson plans for their students.

- Stevenson had no effective classroom management plan for its classrooms.

INTERVENTION

Mrs. Baldwin believed that skilled teachers are extremely important for students' success. All the teachers as well as other staff members should receive in-service training on schoolwide positive behavior support, effective academic instruction, social skills instruction, and effective behavior management strategies. After consulting with Professor Parker, Mrs. Baldwin arranged a full-day in-service once every two months for all the personnel at Stevenson. Professor Parker and a few national consultants provided the in-service training on effective and applied strategies in improving students' social and academic behaviors. University graduate assistants working with Professor Parker were also available weekly to provide additional support and consultation.

Assessment Methods and Regular Evaluation

CONCERN

Even though the office referral data already existed, the previous administrator at Stevenson had not used the data for intervention purposes. The office referral data were collected and filed only for individual student records.

INTERVENTION

Mrs. Baldwin believed that data could provide useful information about the school system as well as the behaviors of students and teachers. She requested that the data be collected regularly and be evaluated more carefully than in the past.

- Mrs. Baldwin requested the instructional specialists to adopt reading assessment methods to evaluate students' progress at least once every month. The evaluation results were then shared with the classroom teachers for instructional planning and intervention.

- Each of the classroom teachers was instructed to develop simple data collection procedures for students' academic performance and social behavior. Some examples of the suggested procedures for data collection included a simple tally of the number of correct words read per minute for reading fluency, the number of sight words spelled correctly on the spelling test, and the number of talk-outs during math instruction. See Figure 10.4 for a sample behavior form.

- Mrs. Baldwin and the assistant principal examined the office referral data once every week to see whether the students' rule violations declined as a result of the schoolwide PBS program. They also developed a simple bar graph to show the number of student infractions on a weekly basis. The chart was posted on the bulletin board in the hallway to show students' behavioral progress.

Parent and Student Involvement

CONCERN

Parent involvement has been a major and persistent challenge at Stevenson. Teachers acknowledged that they tended to contact parents mainly for student problems; rarely or never were contacts made to convey good news. In addition, the PBS team believed that students' feedback can provide valuable information about Stevenson's overall climate and therefore should be involved in the PBS development as well.

INTERVENTION

Interventions for parent involvement included the following steps:

- Parents were informed about the PBS program at Stevenson. The purposes and lists of intervention plans were explained clearly and provided in parent letters in simple and clear language.

- Parents were invited to monthly parent luncheons, quarterly teacher-parent conferences, and yearly open-house events.

- Parents received phone calls at least every two weeks from Mrs. Baldwin, the assistant principal, the parent liaison, or other staff members. The contacts were positive in nature, primarily lauding parents' efforts in helping with their child's education, noting the improvements in the child's academic or social behaviors, and discussing any upcoming events.

- A series of parent workshops and clubs were provided. All the parents were invited to attend either to receive educational information or to share their experience in helping with their child's education process.

FIGURE 10.4

Behavior Tally Form

Date: 05/10/2006   Class period: Reading (large group)   Time: 10:00–11:00

Frequency of behavior															Total
Talk-outs															
~~1~~	~~2~~	~~3~~	~~4~~	~~5~~	~~6~~	~~7~~	~~8~~	~~9~~	~~10~~	~~11~~	~~12~~	~~13~~	~~14~~	~~15~~	38
~~16~~	~~17~~	~~18~~	~~19~~	~~20~~	~~21~~	~~22~~	~~23~~	~~24~~	~~25~~	~~26~~	~~27~~	~~28~~	~~29~~	~~30~~	
~~31~~	~~32~~	~~33~~	~~34~~	~~35~~	~~36~~	~~37~~	~~38~~	39	40	41	42	43	44	45	
Out of seat															
~~1~~	~~2~~	~~3~~	~~4~~	~~5~~	~~6~~	~~7~~	~~8~~	~~9~~	~~10~~	~~11~~	~~12~~	~~13~~	~~14~~	~~15~~	15
16	17	18	19	20	21	22	23	24	25	26	27	28	29	30	
31	32	33	34	35	36	37	38	39	40	41	42	43	44	45	
Talk back															
~~1~~	~~2~~	3	4	5	6	7	8	9	10	11	12	13	14	15	2
16	17	18	19	20	21	22	23	24	25	26	27	28	29	30	
31	32	33	34	35	36	37	38	39	40	41	42	43	44	45	

Other observations:

- Most of the talk-outs were observed with Johnny and Pete.
- Steve talked back and refused to follow what I asked him to do.

The workshops blended in with lunch or dinner gatherings. Transportation was also provided, where necessary.

- Teachers made home visits at least twice a year.

To involve students in the PBS program, the PBS team members developed a simple survey for students to complete anonymously, asking questions such as "What is something you like about Stevenson?" "What is something you do not like about Stevenson?" "If you were to change one thing about the school, what would it be?" The PBS team members believed that students' responses would be valuable in helping to improve the school climate and the disciplinary program. More important, active student involvement would help students be more responsible for their own behavior and to be proud of being at Stevenson.

After four months of the schoolwide PBS program, students at Stevenson were observed to exhibit fewer problem behaviors. Mrs. Baldwin and teachers were pleased with the progress students were making. In addition, students also said they were excited about the rewards. The PBS program at Stevenson continued successfully.

Incorporating Schoolwide Positive Behavior Supports in Your School

To set up a schoolwide PBS program, five steps should be followed:

1. *Establish a PBS team.* The role of the team members is to develop, guide, monitor, and evaluate the PBS program. The team should include an administrator, behavioral support specialist, teacher representatives, and parents. The administrator should assume the leadership commitment during the process. All members should be committed to active participation as well.

2. *Develop an assessment system.* The assessment system (for example, office referral data) should initially be used to evaluate your school's current discipline program and determine what changes should be addressed. This assessment system is also critical of the schoolwide PBS program you adopt because it allows you to monitor the effectiveness of the program.

3. *Communicate with staff the need for support and commitment.* For a schoolwide PBS to work, active participation from all staff members at school is required. This schoolwide effort will also ensure that everyone in the school is working toward common goals.

4. *Develop an implementation plan.* The plan should be based on your assessment data. The Stevenson example shows how interventions can be derived from office referral data. The team should ensure that the plan is comprehensive, system-wide, and addresses all three levels of intervention; that is, universal, specialized group, and individual student levels (see Table 10.1).

5. *Monitor and evaluate the program.* A schoolwide PBS program cannot be judged effective or ineffective unless an evaluation system is in place. The evaluation of the program should be regular and frequent if it is to provide the best means of changing the behaviors of students and staff, the

school system, and the physical environments. Frequent monitoring and evaluation also allow the team to make modifications before the problems become too overwhelming to fix.

Effective Strategies for Teachers

Teachers can greatly improve the effects of positive schoolwide behavior support to reduce student problem behavior and provide a positive school climate by following the strategies listed here.

Once a Day

- Remind students of the behavior expected of them once they enter the classroom. Provide booster training when necessary.

- Review the specific-setting rules before the students enter that setting (for example, cafeteria, playground, restroom).

- Frequently praise and acknowledge students' appropriate behavior (using "caught being good" tickets). Provide positive instructional consequences for inappropriate behavior through teaching alternatives, practice, and reinforcement.

- Provide daily reports on students' behavioral strengths and weaknesses. Discuss behavior with students and talk about ways they can improve their behavior the following day.

- Incorporate teaching of behavioral expectations in the curricula throughout the school day. Allow students to practice the expected behavior whenever possible.

- Implement an effective behavior management system throughout the school day to encourage desired behaviors and discourage undesired behaviors.

- Develop a simple tally system to record students' behavioral progress (Figure 10.4). Note the specific problem behaviors that are most frequent and most problematic. Target those behaviors for intervention and teacher alternative replacement behaviors.

- Be firm and consistent, not punitive, with behavioral expectations and consequences throughout the school day for all the students.

- Remind yourself to deliver frequent praise on students' appropriate behavior throughout the school day. Devices such as MotivAider (a commercial vibrating system available online from a variety of sources) may be helpful in providing frequent prompts on a fixed interval. Your goal may be to deliver praise to the entire class at least once every five minutes and to an individual student at least once every fifteen minutes.

- Deliver effective instruction to engage students in high rates of academic response.

Once a Week

- Evaluate the office referral data to identify any behavioral patterns among your students, and use that information for subsequent instruction.

- Evaluate your classroom management system. Does the classroom management system result in reductions of student problem behaviors? If not, why not? What changes need to be made?

- Celebrate student progress on their behavioral improvements as a class. Encourage students to achieve their weekly behavioral goals.

- Use office referral data and daily observations to identify students with frequent infractions and develop behavioral interventions for them.

- Schedule a weekly forty-minute lesson for social skills instruction. Specific lessons may involve dealing with conflict, problem solving, winning and losing, and so forth. Consult one of the existing social skills curricula for skills and strategies that meet the needs of your students. See Chapter Eight for suggestions.

Once a Grading Period

- Celebrate student progress on their behavioral improvements as a whole school. Encourage students to continue to achieve their behavioral goals.

- Allow students to speak of how they can actively involve themselves in the schoolwide behavior support plan. For example, select certain students to be cafeteria or playground monitors, or involve older students in presenting social skills training to younger students.

- Schedule part of one day to review and retrain the behavioral expectations with all students, as appropriate. This may be most necessary after holiday breaks, at which time students may forget some of the expectations.

Once a Year

- Form a schoolwide positive behavior support team to clearly outline the school disciplinary plans. Discuss and communicate the plan with all staff members in the school to make sure they understand their roles and commitments. Closely monitor the students' progress and the effects of the school disciplinary practice throughout the year.

- Clearly identify the behavioral expectations to students with many examples and counterexamples. Directly and explicitly teach each of the specific expectations to all students on the first day of the school year. Allow students to engage in practices of these expectations.

- Post the school rules and behavioral expectations in all locations (including classrooms, hallways, cafeteria, gym, playground, restrooms, and bus stops). Keep the list posted throughout the school year.

- Develop an office referral record-keeping system, if you don't already have one, to record students' infractions and the school disciplinary practices.

- Develop a simple data analysis system such as tallies or averages to summarize the information recorded in the office referrals.

- Carefully examine the safety of the physical environment of the school, including lighting, seating, furniture, playground equipment, and so forth.

- Clear out potentially problematic school locations (for example, restrooms, hidden corners) to create trouble-free settings and to prevent problems from occurring.

- Decorate all school locations to create a welcome, attractive learning environment.

- Hold a school assembly to reward students' behavioral improvements.

Related Readings

Lo, Y., & Cartledge, G. (2001–2002, Winter). Using office referral data to improve school discipline. *Streamlined Seminar, 20*(2), 1–3.

Sugai, G., & Horner, R. H. (2002). Introduction to the special series on positive behavior support in schools. *Journal of Emotional and Behavioral Disorders, 10,* 130–135.

Related Internet Resources

New Hampshire Center for Effective Behavioral Interventions and Supports (NH CEBIS): http://www.seresc.k12.nh.us/cebis/presentations.htm

This Web site offers a number of informative presentations and resources on schoolwide positive behavior support.

Pennsylvania Training and Technical Assistance Network (PaTTAN): http://www. pattan.k12.pa.us/svs/behavior/Default.htm

This Web site provides many useful resources on procedural frameworks and training plans for schoolwide positive behavior support, samples of behavior intervention plans, and information on practical classroom management plans.

Positive Behavioral Interventions and Supports: http://www.pbis.org/

The Technical Assistance Center on Positive Behavioral Interventions and Supports (PBIS) offers fruitful information and resources on a technology of schoolwide positive behavioral interventions and support. It provides demonstrations on feasible and effective behavior supports at the levels of individual students, classrooms, families, and whole schools.

The School-Wide Information System: http://www.swis.org/index.php

The School-Wide Information System (SWIS) is a Web-based system that can assist schools in developing appropriate school disciplinary interventions using office referral data. School administrators or staff members may find this system useful in managing their discipline data and using it for decision making about their school disciplinary program.

PART FOUR

Parent Involvement

CHAPTER 11

Working with Urban Parents

Ryan and His Family

Ryan, a twelve-year-old African American male, attends fifth grade in a Midwestern urban school. Ryan was retained in kindergarten. At the middle of the fifth grade, Ryan's reading scores on the Woodcock Johnson Reading Mastery assessment showed Ryan reading at the 2.9 grade equivalent level for letter word identification and at the 2.8 grade equivalent level in passage comprehension. Ryan's teacher, Mrs. Lowell, describes him as a hardworking student whose greatest area of academic need is in expressive written language. She stated that she was unable to understand what he was trying to say in his written assignments. In response to Ryan's reading difficulty, Mrs. Lowell had advised his mother to read out loud with Ryan at home and to let Ryan read to her. She also sent some books home for this purpose, but states that the books were never returned. Mrs. Lowell says she does not think that Ryan has a learning disability; however, she referred him for testing to eliminate such a possibility.

Ryan's mother, Ms. Jefferson, expressed concern about her son's progress in school, and feels his major difficulties are with reading and comprehension. Ms. Jefferson reported approaching her son's teachers at school over the past few years regarding his reading skills, and they each advised her to read aloud to him at home—a suggestion that was not helpful, as he continues to have difficulty with reading and comprehension. Ms. Jefferson stated that she is not a teacher and does not know how to teach her son. She also indicated that she was frustrated and has given up hope that the schools will listen to her plea for help.

What Is Parent Involvement?

The preceding scenario highlights the miscommunication common between parents and teachers and the frustration apparent for both parties. How might they communicate more effectively to achieve the mutually desired goal of academic success? Parents are children's first teachers, and much learning takes place in the home in the early childhood years. Parents play a critical role in the educational life of their children, helping to equip them with the language and readiness skills that will serve them well in school. Children from low socioeconomic backgrounds come to school with relatively ineffective language and reading readiness skills compared to their more affluent peers. Many low-income families lack access to books and other reading materials; the parents may have significant educational deficits in their own backgrounds, and thus they have little or no understanding of how to instill critical cognitive or academic skills in their children. This means these children will start school behind their more privileged peers and will probably remain behind if educators do not provide effective interventions. If the services they receive are inadequate, these

Shobana Musti-Rao and Gwendolyn Cartledge contributed this chapter.

youngsters will permanently be stuck in a catch-up mode. At least two important approaches are indicated: intensive remediation in the schools, and parent involvement in the schooling of their children. Both these avenues of action are germane to the academic achievement of underperforming urban learners. In this chapter, we elaborate on the role of parents in the education of their children, the benefits of a parent-school collaborative relationship, and how teachers can work more effectively with parents in urban schools.

The term *parent involvement* means different things to different people. In a broad sense, parent involvement includes home-based activities that relate to children's education in school. It can also include school-based activities where the parents actively participate in the events that take place during the school day. These different perceptions can be seen in the varied definitions of parent involvement. Some experts, for example, analyze parent involvement according to two categories of activities, as shown in Figure 11.1.

On the other hand, Epstein (2001) describes parent involvement in terms of six major levels of parent participation, as shown in Table 11.1.

When working with parents, teachers may find it useful to evaluate the types of activities parents are involved in and also note the level of each parent's involvement in the child's education. Some parents are engaged at the highest levels, while others meet only very basic parenting obligations. Understanding parent and student needs will help teachers set realistic goals to gradually increase parent involvement and decrease the frustrations that sometimes arise when working with different parents. For example, Mrs. Lowell, Ryan's teacher, may find that Ryan's mother is currently involved at Epstein's Level 2, but would like for Ryan's mother to have greater involvement (for example, at Level 4, home-based tutoring) so that she might work effectively with Ryan at home. Parental volunteering in the classroom or school may be desired and appreciated by Mrs. Lowell, but that is much less important than the home-based learning activities.

Parents in Urban and Low-Performing Schools

Many teachers in urban and low-performing schools complain that the parents are underinvolved in the education of their children and unresponsive to the teachers' efforts. They criticize poor urban parents for their failure to develop readiness skills in their children, for their limited involvement in home-based instruction or school activities, and for their inaccessibility. Furthermore, the teachers are frustrated by the lack of academic and behavioral success of many of these students and often attribute this failure to the parents. Parents, on the other hand, particularly minority parents, counter with their criticisms of the schools. These parents contend that the schools talk to them only about their children's behavior problems, that the schools fail to treat them or their children with the respect they desire, that their children are disproportionately identified for special education but less likely to be singled out for academic and creative talents, and that their children are overly referred for disciplinary actions. These respective parent-teacher positions set the occasion for conflict cycles that limit constructive communication and further undermine the students' educational progress.

FIGURE 11.1

Parent Involvement: A Two-Part View

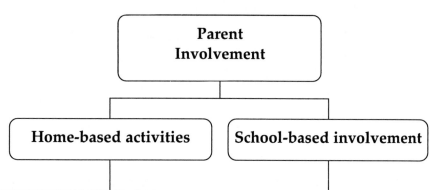

TABLE 11.1

Six Levels of Parent Involvement

Level 6	Community collaboration: Involves parents' collaborating with the community to strengthen school programs
Level 5	Decision making: Involves families in decision making, governance, and advocacy
Level 4	Teaching and learning: Involves parents' assisting their own children at home with learning activities or classwork, with teachers' guidance and support
Level 3	Volunteering: Involves parents' volunteering at the school level, assisting teachers in classrooms or providing support for their children in extracurricular activities such as sports and other events
Level 2	Information provision: Involves the schools' basic obligation to communicate with families, providing information about school programs and children's progress
Level 1	Parenting: Includes the basic parenting and child-rearing approaches that prepare children for school

When working with parents in urban and low-performing schools, teachers may encounter many angry people—people whose anger centers largely on a perception of poor quality of education for their children. Here are some specific reasons (McEwan, 1998):

- Their children are failing to read, write, or do math at basic levels.

- Schools automatically defend the system or back their teachers without listening to or trying to understand the parents' perspective.

- Teachers know the urgency of a situation, yet choose to ignore the parents' phone call or fail to provide necessary feedback.

- Teachers become judgmental about the role of the parent and engage in name-calling.

- Teachers communicate with parents in technical language rather than use lay terms to describe their child's progress in school.

- Parents feel they are being deceived by teachers.

The role of the school is to empower parents to become active and contributing partners in their child's schooling. Therefore, to foster productive interactions, school personnel need to take the initiative to understand the parents' perspectives and conduct family outreach activities that will enable families to be aligned with educators in the schooling process. Schools would be well advised to embrace the following understandings regarding parents:

- Parents count.

- Most parents do not know how much they count or appreciate the significance of their child's learning and behavior difficulties.

- Most parents care about their children.

- Most parents are doing the best they know how at this time.

- Realistic expectations of parents are critical—a parent who cannot read, for example, is not going to teach a child how to read.

- Most low-income parents do not have the resources or expertise to be effective teachers of their children; they can, however, become allies with the school and encourage their children to become more efficient learners.

- Most low-income parents see the schools as the principal (if not exclusive) purveyor of the education of their children: If we want parents to provide home-based instruction, we need to teach them the strategies they are to use.

- Research shows that urban minority parents value schools that are honest, supportive, present a nonblaming attitude, and include parents in the decision making.

How Teachers Benefit by Working with Parents

Why is parent involvement important? Teachers reap several benefits from working with parents and involving them in their children's education:

- A two-way communication system between parents and teachers not only provides teachers and parents with a clear understanding of what is expected or possible in any program, but also allows them to be on the same page regarding the child's educational progress and to work toward mutually set goals. This collaboration helps in reducing frustrations both teachers and parents may encounter.

- Home-based learning, made possible with parent-teacher collaboration, will save the time teachers spend on drills in class and will help struggling learners catch up with their classmates.

- Learning at home provides for enrichment activities that may not be possible during the school day. Children also have greater retention of skills when parents work with them during the summer.

- A collaborative relationship based on information sharing is empowering to parents and contributes to enhanced feelings of self-worth. Parents who feel good about themselves are more likely to be engaged with teachers regarding the schooling of their children.

- Children who are aware of the collaborative relationship know that parents and teachers care about their education. They are more likely to do their best academically and exhibit good behavior in class.

- Teachers who are persistent in reaching out to parents meet with enough success to realize that their efforts are effective and appreciated. Teachers whose efforts pay off are also likely to have an elevated sense of self and to persist in these endeavors.

- Information provided by parents can be beneficial to the teacher in planning activities and setting goals for the children. Ms. Jefferson, for example, tells her son's teacher, Mrs. Lowell, that Ryan enjoys studying with his sister, and that his sister has taught him many of his reading sight words. Mrs. Lowell then decides that she might structure some peer tutoring activities in her classroom and also send some activities home for Ryan to practice with his sister.

- The family activity that correlates most with pupil achievement is the communication of the value of education and high academic expectations to the children. Positive home-school involvement increases the likelihood that this will occur.

Collaboration Between Parents and Schools

Collaboration is a reciprocal process. Parents share information with schools and vice versa. Communication needs to be clear, consistent, and positive, and parents need to believe that they play an important role in their children's learning. This belief is particularly important for low-income urban parents, who tend to be less skilled in ways to promote the cognitive and academic development of their children and are less likely to see such efforts as basic to their parenting responsibilities. Teachers, on the other hand, may interpret these limitations as parental indifference and make even fewer attempts to engage the parents.

An obvious remedy is for the schools to initiate programs and conditions that will lead to positive and productive home-school interactions. A good working relationship is bound to generate positive results and is well worth the time and effort that is initially invested.

Revisiting Ryan and His Family

As stated in the scenario at the beginning of this chapter, Ryan's learning problems were first noted in kindergarten, where he was retained for one year. Ideally, Ryan should have received intensive intervention at this point to ward off later, more severe learning difficulties. Ryan's fifth-grade remedial teacher noted that Ryan had few word-attack skills, suggesting that Ryan probably would have benefited from instruction in kindergarten and first grade in phonological awareness along with the regular grade-level reading curriculum.

What Might Have Been

At the kindergarten level, home-school collaboration and interventions for Ryan might have followed the format given in the sequence that follows. It is important to point out that this plan complements the intensive instructional program Ryan receives in school; it is not intended to be used in lieu of a sound school program.

NEEDS ASSESSMENT

1. Ryan would be evaluated at the beginning of kindergarten to assess his readiness skills. Particular attention would be given to phonemic awareness, since competence in this area is most predictive of later reading performance.

INTERVENTION PLAN

2. Ryan is identified as having significant deficiencies in phonemic awareness skills, and a remedial program is prescribed for Ryan and other students who evidence comparable deficiencies.

FAMILY CONFERENCE

3. Ryan's family is contacted about this intervention program. A conference is scheduled.

4. During the conference, the intervention specialist and classroom teacher detail for the parents the exact skills that would be taught and how they would be taught.

FAMILY TRAINING AND INTERVENTION

5. The intervention specialist prepares materials for the parents and demonstrates how they could help Ryan practice these skills at home. The trainer gives the parents the opportunity to practice this review with Ryan while the trainer observes and provides feedback.

6. The parents receive a maximum of five sounds to practice with Ryan per evening.

7. It is expected that Ryan would practice each set of sounds, words, and sentences for approximately one week, then exchange them for the next set or skill.

8. Home-based learning materials are to be practiced for no more than ten minutes per evening. The parents receive a reporting form (Figure 11.2) to report to the trainer weekly whether or not they practiced the targeted sounds with Ryan and whether he demonstrated mastery of all the skills specified in that assignment.

9. The intervention specialist sends home weekly correspondence (Figure 11.3) documenting Ryan's progress in the phonemic awareness curriculum.

FIGURE 11.2

Daily Home Reporting Form

Date: _____

I, _____, used the tutoring procedure checklist with _____.
    (parent's name)   *(child's name)*

Tonight we practiced instructional set #_____.

____ My child correctly identified all the items in this set.

____ My child did not correctly identify all the items in this set. The items that he/she needs to study again are _____.

We will keep the set home and practice the items again tomorrow night.

Comments/Questions:

_____

_____

_____

_____

_____

_____

_____

FIGURE 11.3

School Weekly Reporting Sheet

Student's name: _____ Date: _____

Your child practiced the (sounds/sight words/sentences/number facts) in set # _____ in class today. Your child did/did not pass the 10-second test for this set.

Your child has successfully completed sets # _____ for the sounds/sight words/sentences/number facts.

Your child still needs to learn set # _____ for the sounds/sight words/number facts. This set will be sent home next week for additional practice.

Comments/Questions:

_____

_____

_____

_____

_____

_____

EVALUATION

10. The teachers meet with Ryan's parents every three or four weeks to discuss Ryan's progress toward meeting the phonemic awareness and reading readiness curriculum of kindergarten.

11. If Ryan's parents are unable to attend the meetings, the reports are sent along with the weekly change in home-based practice materials.

12. If Ryan fails to make expected progress after six to nine weeks of intensified instruction, other specialists are consulted for more in-depth assessments and instruction.

What Now?

Since Ryan did not receive any special interventions in his earlier schooling, by the time he reached fifth grade, his mother's anxiety had reached a fever pitch. She repeatedly commented that if her son did not learn to read soon, his "self-esteem would be on the floor." Like every other urban mother of an African American male, Ms. Jefferson feared that if her son did not learn to read and acquire marketable skills, he would be marginalized, most likely succumbing to a street lifestyle and the lure of the underground economy. At this point she was very critical of the schools, declaring that they had done nothing to help her son, that the suggestions they gave her to read to her son did not help, and she was now transferring her son in the hope that another school system could be more successful. Although valuable opportunities had been lost in the primary grades, it still was not unrealistic to provide remediation and to consult with his family at the fifth-grade level. Based on our experience, we would propose the following as an effective way to assist Ryan and his family to reach the set goals.

NEEDS ASSESSMENT

1. Ryan was assessed to be reading at the second-grade level.

INTERVENTION PLAN

2. The intervention specialist determined that Ryan would benefit from remediation through repeated reading strategies (see Chapter Six).

3. The goal was for Ryan to read 160 correct words per minute.

4. Instruction began for Ryan at the second-grade level.

5. Ryan received instruction for twenty minutes each day from the intervention specialist.

FAMILY INTERVENTION

6. The intervention specialist met with Ryan's mother to describe the remedial procedure and to demonstrate how it was implemented.

7. Ryan's mother practiced the procedure with Ryan under the supervision of the intervention specialist. Due to Ms. Jefferson's work schedule, Ryan's teenage sister also learned how to practice the repeated readings with Ryan so that she could help him in his mother's absence. She tutored Ryan for ten minutes each day, five days a week.

8. Ryan's mother or sister returned the recording form, indicating each time they practiced the readings at home.

9. Each time Ryan reached the aim of 160 correct words per minute, he was moved to another book.

EVALUATION

10. Ryan demonstrated that he especially liked to read books by and about African American males, such as those by Walter Dean Myers.

11. Ryan's mother and his teachers met every three or four weeks to discuss Ryan's progress with this intervention program. Standardized assessments showed that he was making steady progress. With specialized intervention, four months later scores on the Woodcock Johnson Reading Mastery showed Ryan reading at the 3.3 grade level equivalent for letter word identification and at the 4.4 grade level equivalent in passage comprehension.

12. The teachers and family collaborated on rewards for Ryan's reading progress, such as high-interest books.

Effective Strategies for Teachers

Many parents who express considerable interest in promoting their children's academic success by helping them at home lack a systematic method for doing so. They do not have specific strategies and thus rely on the teacher, considered to be the expert, to provide the appropriate services and guidance for their children. Straightforward and honest two-way communication will facilitate collaborative interactions between parents and teachers. Teachers have the power to facilitate a congruent home and school learning environment by providing parents with easy-to-do, low-tech interventions suitable for use at home. Teachers can employ certain strategies that will enable them to build and maintain satisfactory school-home connections. Following are three sets of strategies for this purpose. The first set is designed to build positive home-school interactions, organized as in earlier chapters according to daily, weekly, periodic, and yearly activities. The second set focuses on specific steps teachers might take to help families conduct home-based learning activities for their children. The third set addresses strategies teachers can use to work with parents who do not speak English.

Strategies to Build Positive Relationships with Families

Once a Day

- Hold classroom discussions about students' activities with their families. Topics might include family-fun activities that the students engage in, visits with extended family, or descriptions of family members. This information will be quite valuable in building the teacher's knowledge of the family members and be useful in rapport building with those individuals.

- Make daily entries in a home and school journal. Include information about the student's day; remember to include the student's successes!

- Create a daily drawing in which one student's name is drawn to designate the leader of the group discussion the next morning (see the first bullet point) and perhaps even bring in pictures or objects that represent his or her family. Figure 11.4 is a student's log containing a picture of the family and her written family activity.

- Obtain information about the children's cultural background, the traditions and rituals that the children may be accustomed to, through informal and formal meetings with parents.

Once a Week

- Urge parents to reply to the student's log (Figure 11.4) at least once a week, to maintain continuous dialogue with the home.

- Some parents may prefer weekly phone calls or e-mail exchanges instead of written dialogue. Whatever the mode of communication is, keep it regular and always start with a positive statement about the student!

- Consider setting up a rotating volunteer schedule with some parents. Each week a parent could offer to help in the classroom. Keep in mind that parents are more likely to participate in an existing program within the classroom, so it might increase participation to introduce this system to the parent as a regular activity in the classroom, rather than as a tentative program.

- When appropriate, invite and encourage parents to come to your class and share their interests, career, or expertise as a valuable part of your curriculum. For example, a parent who works as a restaurant server may come to your health class to "show and tell" how to set up a dining table appropriately.

Once a Grading Period

- Meet with every student's parent face-to-face. Personal meetings are a great way to really get to know people. Many parents will prefer this medium to phone or e-mail correspondence. Be willing and prepared to meet before or after school and in more convenient settings for the family.

- Arrive at the meeting with student information and work that illustrates the student's progress. Portfolios may work for this purpose, but also be prepared to discuss the results of the most recent testing. Some parents may be interested in their child's progress toward state-mandated goals.

- Provide a calendar (Figure 11.5) for monthly or the entire year's events. Make sure parents are aware of the community and school activities coming up. Another great way to build rapport with parents is to share your interests and to attend events in the community.

Once a Year

- Awards ceremonies at school are a great opportunity to get parents into the school and classroom. Open house is not the only way to get parents into your class!

- Establish a classroom awards ceremony with a potluck lunch or dinner for parents. Consider making the awards fun by creating funny superlatives that affirm each child's uniqueness to you and your class. For example, a particularly chatty student might get a bright, decorative certificate that reads, "Star of Stage and Screen" or "Talk Show Host" (see Figures 11.6 and 11.7 for samples). Make sure each child gets some type of positive recognition.

FIGURE 11.4

Student's Log

October 7, 2005

This week my grandma came to visit us. My grandma lives in Baltimore, Maryland. She will stay with us for a week. I like it when my grandma visits. She is a good cook. Grandma makes the best smothered chicken and gingerbread. Grandma's gingerbread is so good because she makes it with molasses. It is very sweet and rich. She knows I love these foods so she always makes them for me. We had smothered chicken and gingerbread last night. I do not know what she will cook tonight, but I know it will be good.

Another thing I like about Grandma is that she is a good singer. I love to hear Grandma sing. She is the best singer in the whole world. Every time she goes to church with us, they ask her to sing a solo. Grandma wakes us up every morning with her singing. It is very nice.

Kaila

- In addition to the awards for students, you may also present parents with awards (such as "Great Volunteer" or "Parent of the Year") to show your appreciation of their efforts.

Strategies to Train Parents to Provide Home-Based Instruction

1. Set short-term goals:

   - In consulting with parents, set realistic short-term goals for the child. Set a date that is three or four weeks away to review the program and evaluate whether the child has met the goals.

2. Provide parent training sessions:

   - Parents need specific strategies to use with their children at home. Schedule sessions when groups of interested parents are able to meet for training. The group can be as small as just one parent or as large as four or five parents.

   - The initial training can include establishing the content areas that the parents will work with at home, deciding on an optimal "exchange of information" system (for example, the teacher and parent can send a folder and other materials to each other without having to meet personally every day), and explicitly teaching the parent to implement a specific strategy such as repeated reading or home-based tutoring.

   - Provide parents with all the materials for the home-based instruction and explain explicitly and clearly how to use the materials. This will increase parents' motivation to start and follow through the instruction at home.

   - Give parents written (in addition to oral), simplified step-by-step directions for the home-based instruction (see the example in Figure 11.8).

3. Maintain a log:

   - Give the parents a notebook or a folder that they can use to document daily learning activities at home. Develop a simple system that allows you to review the contents of the log at least once a week. The

FIGURE 11.5

Sample Event Calendar for Parents

Ms. Jones's Fifth Grade Special Events in 2005–2006 School Year		
Welcome back!	August	September
	26: Meet the Teacher Night 29: Open Day*	5: Labor Day (No School) 9: Family Night 12 & 16: Open Day* 14: Professional Development Day (No School)
October	November	December
10 & 17: Open Day* 14: Capital Day (No school) 17: Share My Culture Day 28: Halloween Party	9: Professional Development Day (No School) 18: Parent Conferences (No School) 24 & 25: No School 14 & 21: Open Day*	5 & 12: Open Day* 14: Parent Association Quarterly Meeting 16: Holiday Celebrations 19 to 30: Winter Break
January	February	March
9 & 23: Open Day* 16: Dr. Martin Luther King Day (No School) 25: Professional Day (No School)	6 & 13: Open Day* 10: Parent Conferences (No School)	6 & 21: Open Day* 10: Grandma's Recipe
April	May	
10 & 17: Open Day* 14: Storytelling Night 26: Professional Development Day (No School)	12 & 19: Performance Review Day 29: Memorial Day (No School)	Have a great summer!
* I will be available on the specified days from 8:00–9:00 a.m. and 4:00–6:00 p.m. Look forward to more information on special events at the beginning of each month!		

FIGURE 11.6

Student Certification: Star of Stage and Screen

She makes
you laugh.
She makes
you cry.

She's our very own
Star of
Stage and Screen

Tonya Smith

FIGURE 11.7

Student Certification: Talk Show Host

For most talkative . . .

By the power vested in Ms. Jones's 5th-grade class . . . we hereby introduce

Ryan Brown
as our own
Talk Show Host

FIGURE 11.8

Parent Instructions for Practicing High-Frequency Sight Words at Home

As a parent you can make a difference in your child's reading skills. You can make reading fun.

Practicing sight words at home might be the start. It is simple, fast, economical, and fun. All you need are index cards, a black marker, and plain paper and crayons.

Preparation

- Start by obtaining a list of the sight words that your child is learning at school from the teacher.

- Have plain, approximately 3" × 5" index cards to use as flash cards.

- Print each word in black ink in large, bold lowercase letters on the front side of the card.

- On a piece of plain paper, prepare a progress row chart resembling a path made up of about 50 boxes.

Practice

- Schedule a daily time (approximately ten minutes) to practice a number of sight words with your child after school.

- Although the teacher might teach five new sight words each week, your child might be able to practice more words each week (try ten words per week).

- Sit in a comfortable place facing your child. Hold each card so your child can see it easily.

- Ask your child to read the word. If he or she does not read the word in approximately three seconds, say, "Try it." If he or she still cannot read it, say, "Say the word," and let him or her repeat it after you, then praise the child for saying the word. (That is, you tell the child to speak the word that is hard to read.)

- If your child reads the word incorrectly, you say, "Try again." If he or she reads it correctly the second time, praise the child. If he or she reads it incorrectly for the second time, you say, "Say the word," and let him or her repeat it after you, then praise the child for saying the word.

- Keep going over the set of words for approximately five or six minutes. Then test your child on them following the same procedure, only this time do not tell the child what words are incorrect. Just continue with the next word.

- Mark the back of each card with a check mark each time the word is read correctly, and with an X each time the word is read incorrectly. Keep doing this every day. When your child has three consecutive check marks on a certain card, it means that he or she has mastered the word.

- Using crayon and the progress chart you prepared, let your child chart the number of correct words each day, so he or she can see the progress. It helps to have the child use a different color each practice session or every day to see if he or she learns more words every day.

- Finally, make sure to set up a reward system. After your child charts a certain number of words (you decide on that according to your child's abilities), reinforce the lesson by providing something simple that he or she likes.

log should be used to show both what the child has been doing at home and what progress the child is making. This information can be used to make program adjustments or modifications.

4. Be flexible in scheduling meetings:

   • Parents' work schedules may often conflict with the school schedule. Be flexible with meeting times. Sometimes meeting in the evening may be more convenient for the parent.

   • If for some reason the parent is unable to attend a scheduled meeting, try to reschedule a meeting at the earliest possible date. A telephone interview to review program goals can also be effective.

Strategies for Dealing with Parents Who Do Not Speak English

1. Involve translators; translators must have the family's confidence and be held to a high ethical code, including confidentiality. School districts usually maintain bilingual translators in languages that have a significant population in their area. Avoid using children as translators for their parents.

2. Ask other parents who speak the same language to assist in communicating with the family.

3. Provide information, written and oral, in ways that enable the parents to understand.

4. Make school reports simple. If you are sending written reports, write them in the family's native language whenever you can. Translators can help with the development of forms and letters in the parents' native language.

5. Do not assume that you have communicated effectively; verify it by having the parents communicate to you what they heard.

6. Develop a survival vocabulary in the native languages of your families for use with parents and school personnel (Thomas, Correa, & Morsink, 2000). Include basic special education terminology, greetings, action words, calendar words, and so forth.

7. Read about other cultures, particularly those that the students in your class represent.

8. Welcome the parents to your classroom and encourage them to share their culture and experiences with your whole class.

9. Send welcome notes to new arrivals' families in their language and invite them to visit the school (see Figures 11.9 and 11.10 for letters sent to a new student in both English and Spanish).

10. Make home visits by appointment with the family member.

11. Arrange for an opportunity for new immigrant parents to meet with other parents and talk with them, especially parents who speak their language.

12. Provide written handouts in the family's language that explain their legal rights and the educational services they can access.

FIGURE 11.9

Student Letter (English Version)

Dear Lori,

The first day of the new school year is coming closer. The room is cleaned and ready. I have been to school a little each day over the last two weeks trying to have everything in place. The only thing missing now is YOU! I am anxious to hear about your summer and to see how much you have grown and changed over the last three months. We will have lots of time that first day back for all of us to talk and share our adventures.

We have a new physical education teacher and a new librarian. There may be a few other changes in the building, but those two people are the only ones I have met as of now.

We were lucky to have a mild summer. There were few days when the temperature even reached 90 degrees, and I hope we will continue to have mild temperatures when you return to school.

I am looking forward to seeing you all walk in here as mature and responsible 5th graders! Imagine that, your last year in elementary school. This should be an exciting year with lots of challenges and interesting experiences.

I'll see you on Thursday, August 31st.

Sincerely,

Mrs. F

FIGURE 11.10

Student Letter (Spanish Version)

Apreciada Lori,

El primer día del Nuevo año escolar se acerca. El salon esta limpio y listo. He estado en la escuela un poco cada día por las últimas dos semanas tratanto de tener todo en su lugar. ¡Lo único que falta ahora eres TÚ! Tengo ancias de escuchar acerca de tu verano y ver cuando haz crecido y cambiado en los últimos tres meses. Tendremos mucho tiempo en ese primer día de regreso para todos nosotros hablar y compartir nuestras aventuras.

Tenemos un Nuevo maestro de educación física y un Nuevo bibliotecario. Puede que hallan otros pequeños cambios en el edificio, pero esas dos personas son las únicas que yo he conocido hasta ahora.

Tuvimos suerte de tener un verano templado. Hubieron muy pocos días cuando la temperature si quiera llegó a los 90 grados y espero que continuemos teniendo temperatures templadas cuando regresemos a la escuela.

¡Estoy anticipando el verles entrar aquí como estudiantes maduros y responsables del 5to (quinto) grado! Imagínense esto, su ultimo año en la escuela elemental. Este debe ser un año exitante con muchos cambios y experiencias interesantes.

Les veo el jueves, 31 de agosto.

Sinceramente,

Sra. F

13. Use formal and informal school meetings and home visits to explain family rights and the services available.

Related Readings

Gestwicki, C. (2000). *Home, school, and community relations: A guide to working with families.* Albany, NY: Delmar.

Hart, B., & Risley, T. R. (1995). *Meaningful differences in the everyday experience of young American children.* Baltimore: Brookes.

Hart, B., & Risley, T. R. (1999). *The social world of children learning to talk.* Baltimore: Brookes.

Johnston, H. J., & Borman, K. M. (1992). *Effective schooling for economically disadvantaged students: School-based strategies for diverse student populations.* Norwood, NJ: Ablex.

Martin, E. J., & Hagan-Burke, S. (2002). Establishing a home-school connection: Strengthening the partnership between families and schools. *Preventing School Failure, 46*(2), 62–65.

McDermott, P. C. (2001). *New teachers communicating effectively with low-income urban parents.* (ERIC Document Reproduction Service No. ED 454207)

Miller, A. D., Barbetta, P. M., & Heron, T. E. (1994). START tutoring: Designing, training, implementing, adapting, and evaluating tutoring programs for school and home settings. In R. Gardner III, D. M. Sainato, J. O. Cooper, T. E. Heron, W. L. Heward, J. Eshleman, & T. A. Grossi (Eds.), *Behavior analysis in education: Focus on measurably superior instruction* (pp. 265–282). Pacific Grove, CA: Brooks/Cole.

Turnbull, A. P., & Turnbull, H. R, III. (2001). *Families, professionals, and exceptionality: Collaborating for empowerment* (4th ed.). Upper Saddle River, NJ: Prentice Hall.

Williams, V., & Cartledge, G. (1997, September/October). Passing notes to parents. *Teaching Exceptional Children, 30,* 30–34.

Related Internet Resources

Beach Center on Families and Disability: http://www.beachcenter.org

Conducts research and training to enhance families' empowerment, and disseminates information to families, individuals with disabilities, educators, and the general public. This Web site provides technical assistance to a national network of parent-to-parent support programs.

Family Network on Disabilities of Florida, Inc.: http://fndfl.org

A statewide alliance of individuals with disabilities, special needs, or at risk and their families. Its mission is to provide family-driven support, education, information, and advocacy.

Institute for Global Communications: http://www.igc.apc.org

This Web site contains an interactive database and networking services that facilitate public access to literature, research, Internet resources, and reform strategies to promote the effective education of immigrant students.

National Association for the Education of African American Children with Learning Disabilities: http://www.aacld.org.

The overall focus of this organization is to empower minority parents to become advocates for their children with special needs.

National Council on Disability (NCD): http://www.ncd.gov

> This Web site's purpose is to promote policies, programs, practices, and procedures that guarantee equal opportunity for all individuals with disabilities and those from diverse cultural backgrounds. Parents and teachers can have access to the Disabilities Act and other civil rights laws. NCD brochures are offered online in several languages.

Office of Bilingual Education and Minority Languages Affairs (OBEMLA): http://www.dssc.org/frc/TAGuide/obemla.htm

> OBEMLA's mission is to include various elements of school reform in programs designed to assist the language minority agenda. These include emphases on high academic standards, improvement of school accountability, professional development, the promotion of family literacy, the encouragement of early reading, and the establishment of partnerships between parents and the community.

Online Dictionary: http://www.yourdictionary.com

> This Web site offers online access to dictionaries in many languages.

Regional Resource and Federal Centers (RRFC) Network: http://www.dssc.org/frc/rrfc.htm

> These centers are specially funded to assist state education agencies in the systemic improvement of education programs, practices, and policies that affect children and youth with disabilities. The RRFCs help states and U.S. jurisdictions find integrated solutions for systemic reform, offering consultation, information services, technical assistance, training, and product development.

The Technical Assistance Alliance for Parent Centers (the Alliance): http://www.taalliance.org/description.htm

> This Web site is funded by the U.S. Department of Education, Office of Special Education Programs. It focuses on providing technical assistance for establishing, developing, and coordinating parent training and information projects under the Individuals with Disabilities Education Act. The Alliance offers a variety of resources designed to launch parent training and information centers into the twenty-first century.

References

Algozzine, B., & Kay, P. (Eds.). (2002). *Preventing problem behaviors.* Thousand Oaks, CA: Corwin Press.

Al-Hassan, S. (2003). *Reciprocal peer tutoring effect on high frequency sight word learning, retention, and generalization of first- and second-grade urban elementary school students.* Unpublished doctoral dissertation, The Ohio State University, Columbus.

American Heritage Dictionaries. (2000). *The American Heritage Dictionary of the English Language* (4th ed.). Boston: Houghton Mifflin.

Arreaga-Mayer, C., & Greenwood, C. R. (1986). Environmental variables affecting the school achievement of culturally and linguistically different learners: An instructional perspective. *NABE: The Journal for the National Association for Bilingual Education, 10*(2), 113–135.

Association for Effective Schools (1996). *What is effective schools research?* Retrieved March 12, 2005, from http://www.mes.org/esr.html

Behrmann, M. M. (1995). *Beginning reading and phonological awareness for students with learning disabilities* (ERIC Digest E540). Reston, VA: Council for Exceptional Children. Retrieved December 16, 2003, from http://www.kidsource.com/kidsource/content2/disability.phonological.html

Bell, L. I. (2002, December/2003, January). Strategies that close the gap. *Educational Leadership, 60*(4), pp. 32–34.

Campbell, F. A., Pungello, E. P., Miller-Johnson, S., Burchinal, M., & Ramey, C. T. (2001). The development of cognitive and academic abilities: Growth curves from an early childhood educational experiment. *Developmental Psychology, 37,* 231–242.

Cartledge, G., & Kleefeld, J. (1991). *Take part: Introducing social skills to children.* Circle Pines, MN: American Guidance Service.

Cartledge, G., & Kleefeld, J. (1994). *Working together: Building children's social skills through folk literature.* Circle Pines, MN: American Guidance Service.

Cartledge, G., & Milburn, J. F. (1995). *Teaching social skills to children and youth: Innovative approaches* (3rd ed.). Boston: Allyn & Bacon.

Cartledge, G., & Milburn, J. F. (1996). *Cultural diversity and social skills instruction: Understanding ethnic and gender differences.* Champaign, IL: Research Press.

Cartledge, G., Tillman, L. C., & Talbert-Johnson, C. (2001). Professional ethics within the context of student discipline and diversity. *Teacher Education and Special Education, 24,* 25–37.

Chard, D. J., Simmons, D. C., & Kameenui, E. J. (1998). Word recognition: Research bases. In D. C. Simmons & E. J. Kameenui (Eds.), *What reading research tells us about children with diverse learning needs* (pp. 141–168). Mahwah, NJ: Erlbaum.

Colvin, G., & Lazar, M. (1997). *The effective elementary classroom: Managing for success.* Longmont, CO: Sopris West.

Committee for Children. (2002). *Second step: A violence prevention curriculum.* Seattle, WA: Author.

Cooke, N. L., Heron, T. E., & Heward, W. L. (1983). *Peer tutoring: Implementing classwide programs in the primary grades.* Columbus, OH: Special Press.

Coyne, M. D., Kameenui, E. J., & Simmons, D. C. (2001). Prevention and intervention in beginning reading: Two complex systems. *Learning Disabilities Research & Practice, 16*(2), 62–73.

Crary, E. (1982). *I want to play.* Seattle: Parenting Press.

Davis, J. E. (2003). Early schooling and academic achievement of African American males. *Urban Education, 38,* 515–537.

Dewey, J. (1916). *Democracy and education: An introduction to the philosophy of education.* New York: Free Press.

Engelmann, S. (1999). The benefits of direct instruction: Affirmative action for at-risk students. *Association for Supervision and Curriculum Development, 57*(1), 77–79.

Epstein, J. (2001). *School, family, and community partnerships: Preparing educators and improving schools.* Boulder, CO: Westview Press.

Gardner, R., III, Heward, W. L., & Grossi, T. A. (1994). Effects of response cards on student participation and academic achievement: A systematic replication with inner-city students during whole class science instruction. *Journal of Applied Behavior Analysis, 27,* 63–71.

Gardner, R., III, & Miranda, A. H. (2001). Improving outcomes for urban African American students. *Journal of Negro Education, 70,* 255–263.

Goldstein, A. P., & McGinnis, E. (1997). *Skillstreaming the adolescent: New strategies and perspectives for teaching prosocial skills.* Champaign, IL: Research Press.

Good, R. H., & Kaminski, R. A. (Eds.). (2002). *Dynamic indicators of basic early literacy skills* (6th ed.). Eugene, OR: Institute for Development of Educational Achievement. Retrieved March 12, 2005, from http://dibels.uoregon.edu/

Good, R. H., Simmons, D. C., & Smith, S. B. (1998). Effective academic intervention in the United States: Evaluating and enhancing the acquisition of early reading skills. *Educational and Child Psychology, 15*(1), 56–70.

Greenwood, C. R. (1991). Classwide peer tutoring: Longitudinal effects on the reading, language, and mathematics achievement of at-risk students. *Reading, Writing and Learning Disabilities, 7,* 105–123.

Greenwood, C. R., Delquadri, J., & Bulgren, J. (1993). Current challenges to behavioral technology in the reform of schooling: Large-scale, high-quality implementation and sustained use of effective educational practices. *Education and Treatment of Children, 16,* 401–440.

Grigg, W. S., Daane, M. C., Jin, Y., & Campbell, J. R. (2003). *The nation's report card: Reading 2002* (NCES 2003–521). Washington, DC: National Center for Educational Statistics, Institute of Education Sciences, U.S. Department of Education. Retrieved March 12, 2002, from http://nces.ed.gov/nationsreportcard/pdf/main2002/2003521a.pdf

Grossen, B. (1991). The fundamental skills of higher order thinking. *Journal of Learning Disabilities, 24,* 343–353.

Gunter, P. L., Reffel, J. M., Barnett, C. A., Lee, J. M., & Patrick, J. (2004). Academic response rates in elementary-school classrooms. *Education and Treatment of Children, 27,* 105–113.

Hale, J. (2004, November). How schools shortchange African American children. *Educational Leadership, 62*(3), 34–38.

Hall, R. V., Delquadri, J., Greenwood, C. R., & Thurston, L. (1982). The importance of opportunity to respond in children's academic success. In E. B. Edgar, N. G. Haring, J. R. Jenkins, & C. G. Pious (Eds.), *Mentally handicapped children: Education and training* (pp. 107–140). Baltimore: University Park Press.

Hallett, J. (2004, December 12). DeWine lays it on the line: Ohio is in sorry shape; listening, legislators? *Columbus Dispatch,* p. C5.

Hart, B., & Risley, T. R. (1995). *Meaningful differences in the everyday experience of young American children.* Baltimore: Brookes.

Hart, B., & Risley, T. R. (1999). *The social world of children learning to talk.* Baltimore: Brookes.

Hettleman, K. R. (2003). *The invisible dyslexics: How public school systems in Baltimore and elsewhere discriminate against poor children in the diagnosis and treatment of early reading difficulties.* Baltimore: Abell Foundation.

Heward, W. L. (1994). Three "low-tech" strategies for increasing the frequency of active student response during group instruction. In R. Gardner III, D. M. Sainato, J. O. Cooper, T. E. Heron, W. L. Heward, J. Eshleman, & T. A. Grossi (Eds.), *Behavior analysis in education: Focus on measurably superior instruction* (pp. 283–320). Pacific Grove, CA: Brooks/Cole.

Heward, W. L. (2000). *Exceptional children: An introduction to special education* (6th ed.). Upper Saddle River, NJ: Prentice Hall.

Heward, W. L. (2003). *Strategies for effective group instruction.* Unpublished course materials for EDU PAES 831. Columbus: The Ohio State University.

Heward, W. L., Gardner, R., III, Cavanaugh, R. A., Courson, F. H., Grossi, T. A., & Barbetta, P. M. (1996). Everyone participates in this class: Using response cards to increase active student response. *TEACHING Exceptional Children, 28*(2), 4–10.

Hoover-Dempsey, K., & Sandler, H. (1997). Why do parents become involved in their children's education? *Review of Educational Research, 67,* 3–42.

Horner, R. H., Sugai, G., & Horner, H. F. (2000). A schoolwide approach to student discipline. *School Administrator, 57*(2), 20–23.

Institute for Development of Educational Achievement (IDEA). (2002). *The big ideas in beginning reading.* Retrieved March 12, 2005, from http://reading.uoregon.edu/big_ideas/trial_bi_index.php

Johnson, D. W., & Johnson, R. T. (2004). Implementing the "Teaching Students to Be Peacemakers Program." *Theory into Practice, 43,* 68–79.

Kourea, L. (2004). *The effects of total class peer tutoring on sight-word acquisition, maintenance, reading fluency and comprehension for students at risk for reading failure.* Unpublished master's thesis, The Ohio State University.

Kozol, J. (1990). *Savage inequalities: Children in America's schools.* New York: Crown.

LaBerge, D., & Samuels, S. J. (1974). Toward a theory of automatic information processing in reading. *Cognitive Psychology, 6,* 293–323.

Lambert, M. C., Cartledge, G., Lo, Y., & Heward, W. L. (in press). Effects of response cards on disruptive behavior and academic responding during math lessons. *Journal of Positive Behavior Interventions.*

Lewis, T. J., Scott, T. M., & Sugai, G. (1994). The Problem Behavior Questionnaire: A teacher-based instrument to develop functional hypotheses of problem behavior in general education classrooms. *Diagnostique, 19,* 103–115.

Lewis, T. J., & Sugai, G. (1999). Effective behavior support: A systems approach to proactive schoolwide management. *Focus on Exceptional Children, 31,* 1–24.

Lo, Y., & Cartledge, G. (2004). *Office disciplinary referrals in an elementary school: Special issues for an urban population.* Manuscript submitted for publication.

Losen, D. J., & Orfield, G. (Eds.). (2002). *Racial inequity in special education.* Cambridge, MA: Harvard University Press.

Lyon, R. (2003, November/December). What principals need to know about reading. *Principal,* pp. 14–18.

Mathes, P. G., & Torgesen, J. K. (1998). All children can learn to read: Critical care for the prevention of reading failure. *Peabody Journal of Education, 73*(3 & 4), 317–340.

McEwan, E. K. (1998). *Angry parent, failing schools: What's wrong with the public schools and what you can do about it.* Wheaton, IL: Shaw.

McGinnis, E., & Goldstein, A. P. (1997). *Skillstreaming the elementary school child: New strategies and perspectives for teaching prosocial skills.* Champaign, IL: Research Press.

McGinnis, E., & Goldstein, A. P. (2003). *Skillstreaming in early childhood: New strategies and perspectives for teaching prosocial skills.* Champaign, IL: Research Press.

Metzler, C. W., Biglan, A., Rusby, J. C., & Sprague, J. R. (2001). Evaluation of a comprehensive behavior management program to improve school-wide positive behavior support. *Education and Treatment of Children, 24,* 448–479.

Miller, A. D., Barbetta, P. M., & Heron, T. E. (1994). START tutoring: Designing, training, implementing, adapting, and evaluating tutoring programs for school and home settings. In R. Gardner III, D. M. Sainato, J. O. Cooper, T. E. Heron, W. L. Heward, J. Eshelman, & T. A. Grossi (Eds.), *Behavior analysis in education: Focus on measurably superior instruction* (pp. 265–282). Pacific Grove, CA: Brooks/Cole.

National Center for Education Statistics (2003). *Indicators of school crime and safety, 2003.* Institute of Education Sciences, U.S. Department of Education. Retrieved March 15, 2005, from http//nces.ed.gov/pubs2004/crime03/index.asp

National Institute of Child Health and Human Development. (2000a). *Report of the National Reading Panel. Teaching children to read: An evidence-based assessment of the scientific research literature on reading and its implications for reading instruction* (NIH Publication No. 00–4769). Washington, DC: U.S. Government Printing Office.

National Institute of Child Health and Human Development. (2000b). *Report of the National Reading Panel. Teaching children to read: An evidence-based assessment of the scientific research literature on reading and its implications for reading instruction: Reports of the subgroups* (NIH Publication No. 00–4754). Washington, DC: U.S. Government Printing Office.

Noguera, P. A. (2003). School, prisons, and social implications of punishment: Rethinking disciplinary practices. *Theory into Practice, 42,* 341–350.

O'Shea, L. J., & O'Shea, D. J. (1988). Using repeated reading. *TEACHING Exceptional Children, 20*(2), 26–29.

Payne, R. K. (1998). *A framework for understanding poverty.* Highlands, TX: RFT Publishing.

Ravitch, D. (1998, August). *A new era in urban education?* Retrieved March 15, 2005, from http://www.brookings.edu/comm/policybriefs/pb35.htm

Resnick, L. B. (1999, June 16). Making America smarter. *Education Week Century Series, 18*(40), 38–40. Retrieved March 12, 2005, from http://www.instituteforlearning.org/media/docs/Making AmericaSmarter.pdf

Rhode, G., Jenson, W. R., & Reavis, H. K. (1992). *The tough kid book: Practical classroom management strategies.* Longmont, CO: Sopris West.

Robinson, P. D. (2004). *The effects of peer-mediated repeated readings on the reading fluency and comprehension of urban elementary students.* Unpublished undergraduate honors thesis, The Ohio State University, Columbus.

Salend, S. J., & Taylor, L. S. (2002). Cultural perspectives: Missing pieces in the functional assessment process. *Intervention in School and Clinic, 38,* 104–112.

Samuels, S. J. (1979). The method of repeated reading. *Reading Teacher, 32,* 403–408.

Shingles, B., & Lopez-Reyna, N. (2002). Cultural sensitivity in the implementation of discipline policies and practices. In L. M. Bullock & R. A. Gable (Eds.), *CASE/CCBD Mini-library series: Safe, drug-free, and effective schools.* Arlington, VA: Council for Children with Behavioral Disorders.

Sindelar, P. T., Espin, C. A., Smith, M. A., & Harriman, N. E. (1990). A comparison of more and less effective special education teachers in elementary-level programs. *Teacher Education and Special Education, 13,* 9–16.

Skiba, R. J., Michael, R. S., Nardo, A. C., & Peterson, R. (2000, June). *The color of discipline: Sources of racial and gender disproportionality in school punishment* (Policy Research Report SRS1). Bloomington: Indiana University, Indiana Education Policy Center. Retrieved March 12, 2005, from http://www.indiana.edu/~safeschl/cod.pdf

Smith, R. A. (2004, November). A call for universal preschool. *Educational Leadership, 62*(3), 38–39.

Smith, S. B., Simmons, D. C., & Kameenui, E. J. (1998). Phonological awareness: Instructional and curricular basics and implications. In D. C. Simmons & E. J. Kameenui (Eds.), *What reading research tells us about children with diverse learning needs* (pp. 61–128). Mahwah, NJ: Erlbaum.

Sprague, J. R., Sugai, G., Horner, R., & Walker, H. M. (1999). *Using office discipline referral data to evaluate school-wide discipline and violence prevention interventions* (OSSC Bulletin Vol. 42, No. 2). Eugene: University of Oregon, College of Education.

Stallings, J. (1980). Allocated academic time revisited, or beyond time on task. *Educational Researcher, 9,* 11–16.

Stallings, J., & Freiberg, H. J. (1991). Observation for the improvement of teaching. In H. C. Waxman & H. J. Walberg (Eds.), *Effective teaching: Current research* (pp. 106–131). Berkeley, CA: McCutchan.

Staubitz, J., Cartledge, G., Yurick, A., & Lo, Y. (2004). *Repeated reading for students with emotional or behavioral disorders: Peer- and trainer-mediated instruction.* Manuscript submitted for publication.

Sterling-Turner, H. E., Robinson, S. L., & Wilczynski, S. M. (2001). Functional assessment of distracting and disruptive behaviors in the school setting. *School Psychology Review, 30,* 211–226.

Sugai, G., Horner, R. H., Dunlap, G., Hieneman, M., Lewis, T. J., Nelson, C. M., Scott, T., Liaupsin, C., Sailor, W., Turnbull, A. P., Turnbull, H., R., III., Wickham, D., Ruef, M., & Wilcox, B. (2000). Applying positive behavioral support and functional behavioral assessment in schools. *Journal of Positive Behavior Interventions, 2,* 131–143.

Sugai, G., Lewis-Palmer, T., & Hagan-Burke, S. (1999–2000). Overview of the functional behavioral assessment process. *Exceptionality, 8,* 149–160.

Thomas, C. C., Correa, V. I., & Morsink, C. V. (2000). *Interactive teaming* (3rd ed.). Upper Saddle River, NJ: Prentice Hall.

Torgesen, J. K. (2002). The prevention of reading difficulties. *Journal of School Psychology, 40*(1), 7–26.

Turnbull, A. P., Edmonson, H., Griggs, P., Wickham, D., Sailor, W., Freeman, R., Guess, D., Lassen, S., McCart, A., Park, J., Riffel, L., Turnbull, R., & Warren, J. (2002). A blueprint for schoolwide positive behavior support: Implementation of three components. *Exceptional Children, 68,* 377–402.

U.S. Census Bureau (2004). *U.S. Interim projections by age, sex, race, and Hispanic origin.* Retrieved March 18, 2004, from http://www.census.gov/ipc/www/usinterimproj/

Utley, C. A., Reddy, S. S., Delquadri, J. C., Greenwood, C. R., Mortweet, S. L., & Bowman, V. (2001). Classwide peer tutoring: An effective teaching procedure for facilitating the acquisition of health education and safety facts with students with developmental disabilities. *Education and Treatment of Children, 24*(1), 1–27.

Walker, H. M., Stiller, B., Golly, A., Kavanagh, K., Severson, H. H., & Feil, E. (1997). *First step to success: Helping young children overcome antisocial behavior.* Longmont, CO: Sopris West.

Williams, B., & Newcombe, E. (1994). Building on the strengths of urban learners. *Educational Leadership, 51,* 75–78.

Wynn, M. (1992). *Empowering African-American males to succeed: A ten-step approach for parents and teachers.* Marietta, GA: Rising Sun.

Yurick, A.L., Robinson, P.D., Cartledge, G., Lo, Y., & Evans, T.L. (in press). Using peer-mediated repeated readings as a fluency-building activity for urban learners. *Education and Treatment of Children.*

Authors and Contributors

Authors

Gwendolyn Cartledge, Ph.D., is a professor at The Ohio State University, School of Physical Activity and Educational Services, special education programs. She teaches courses that focus on the academic and social development of children with mild disabilities, emphasizing students with serious emotional disturbances. Her professional background includes teaching students in general and special education programs, supervising special education programs, and teacher preparation. Her professional research and writings have centered on the development of social and academic skills in children with and without disabilities, with a more recent focus on learners from culturally diverse backgrounds. She currently is investigating issues related to disproportionality for learners with disabilities from culturally diverse backgrounds. She is the author and co-author of several books, curriculum programs, and other publications.

Ya-yu Lo, Ph.D., is an assistant professor in the Department of Special Education and Child Development at the University of North Carolina at Charlotte. She completed her doctoral studies at The Ohio State University in 2003. To complete a post-doctorate in 2004, she directed an urban model school project focused on reducing disciplinary and special education referrals. Her research interests include behavioral disorders, positive behavioral support, and effective instruction. She has published several articles in these areas.

Contributors

Suha Al-Hassan, Ph.D., is an assistant professor of Queen Rania Faculty for Childhood, vice dean at The Hashemite University, Zarga, Jordan. Her professional interests include early identification and intervention for children with learning and behavior disorders, and effective instruction.

Michael "Chuck" Lambert, Ph.D., is an assistant professor of special education at Western Washington University in Bellingham. His interests include students with disruptive behaviors, the effects of academic interventions on social behavior, applied behavior analysis, and urban youth.

Shobana Musti-Rao, M.Ed., is an assistant professor in special education at the University of Cincinnati, Ohio. Her research interests include academic and behavioral strategies for urban students with behavior disorders, early reading intervention for students at risk of failure, and family and school partnerships in urban schools.

Amanda Yurick, M.Ed., is a third-year doctoral student in special education at The Ohio State University, Columbus. Her professional interests include behavior disorders, urban gifted education, and effective instruction.